WE HAVE SINNED

Sin and Confession in Judaism

Ashamnu and *Al Chet*

Other Jewish Lights Books by Rabbi Lawrence A. Hoffman, PhD

My People's Prayer Book: Traditional Prayers, Modern Commentaries, Vols. 1–10

My People's Passover Haggadah: Traditional Texts, Modern Commentaries, Vols. 1 & 2
(coedited with David Arnow, PhD)

The Art of Public Prayer, 2nd Ed.: *Not for Clergy Only*
(A book from SkyLight Paths, Jewish Lights' sister imprint)

Rethinking Synagogues: A New Vocabulary for Congregational Life

Israel—A Spiritual Travel Guide: A Companion for the Modern Jewish Pilgrim

The Way Into Jewish Prayer

What You Will See Inside a Synagogue
(coauthored with Dr. Ron Wolfson)

Also in the Prayers of Awe Series

Who by Fire, Who by Water—Un'taneh Tokef

All These Vows—Kol Nidre

PRAYERS OF AWE

WE HAVE SINNED

Sin and Confession in Judaism

Ashamnu and *Al Chet*

Edited by
Rabbi Lawrence A. Hoffman, PhD

JEWISH LIGHTS Publishing
Nashville, Tennessee

We Have Sinned:
Sin and Confession in Judaism—Ashamnu *and* Al Chet

Grateful acknowledgment is given for permission to use the following: p. 61, "My heart has died within me," public domain; p. 64, "We closed our ears to the cry of the poor and wretched," © by Rabbi Mordechai (Moti) Rotem; p. 67, "For the sin we have committed through violence," used by permission of Binyamin Yogev (Buja); p. 71, "For the sin which we have sinned against You…", used by permission of Rabbis for Human Rights; p. 72, "For the sin we have committed against you through degrading human image, theirs and ours," used by permission of Yesh Gvul (www.yeshgvul.org); "For the sin we have committed against you through stuttering tongues," used by permission of Reuven (Ruvik) Rosenthal; p. 78, "What can we say to you…", used by permission of Rivkah Lubitch.

Library of Congress Cataloging-in-Publication Data
We have sinned : sin and confession in Judaism : Ashamnu and Al chet / edited by Lawrence A. Hoffman. — 2012 hardcover ed.
p. cm. -- (Prayers of awe)
Includes the text of the Vidui in Hebrew and English.
Includes bibliographical references and index.
ISBN 978-1-58023-612-6 (hardcover)
ISBN 978-1-68336-478-8 (paperback)
1. Confession of sins (Jewish prayer) 2. Confession (Liturgy)—Judaism—Texts. 3. Yom Kippur—Liturgy—Texts. 4. Judaism—Liturgy—Texts. 5. Sin—Judaism. 6. Confession (Prayer)—Judaism. 7. Repentance—Judaism. I. Hoffman, Lawrence A., 1942– II. Confession of sins (Jewish prayer). English & Hebrew.
BM670.C64H64 2012
296.3'2—dc23

2012025292

Manufactured in the United States of America
Front Cover: Jeff Miller
Cover Mechanical Design: Grace Cavalier

Published by Jewish Lights Publishing
An imprint of Turner Publishing Company
4507 Charlotte Avenue, Suite 100
Nashville, TN 37209
Tel: (615) 255-2665
www.jewishlights.com

Contents

Acknowledgments

As with previous volumes in this series, I begin by acknowledging the many worshipers for whom the High Holy Days are central to their Jewish consciousness. To these worshipers in general, I add the many colleagues, artists, composers, poets, philosophers, theologians, and critics who lend more technical voices to the conversation. Many of them are included here. To them—to all the contributors whose commentaries find their way into this volume—I am grateful.

I continue to be blessed with support from my extraordinary publisher, Stuart M. Matlins, founder of Jewish Lights, and from Emily Wichland, vice president of Editorial and Production there. It was Stuart who first approached me with the idea for the Prayers of Awe series, as suggested to him by Dan Adler in response to a High Holy Day program developed by Rob Eshman, editor in chief of the *Jewish Journal of Greater Los Angeles*, and David Suissa. Their program sprang from an idea first conceived by Rabbi Elazar Muskin of Young Israel of Century City. Emily continues to amaze me in all she does: her abundant wisdom, skill, patience, and perseverance are precisely what an author most desires. For her copyediting and proofreading, my thanks go again to Debra Corman. I happily include as well all the others at Jewish Lights, especially Tim Holtz, director of Production, who designed the cover for this book and typeset the English text.

Special mention should be made of Rabbi Dalia Marx, PhD, whose contribution here includes references to the work of many contemporary authors and poets in Israel, all of whom demonstrate the remarkable power of *Al Chet* as a cultural icon in Judaism. Rabbi Marx cites the work of Rabbi Moti Rotem; Aryeh Uri; Buja Yogev, whose work was made available through Mekhon Shitim, the archive and educational center of the kibbutz movement, located on Kibbutz Bet Hashitah; Rabbi Arik Asherman; Michael Brizon; Ruvik Rosenthal; an anonymous composer of the confession for "drivers, bikers, and pedestrians"; Rivka Lubitch; and a composition from *Irgun Lim'ni'at Hitbol'lut B'eretz Hakodesh* and Moshe Meir. Dr. Joel M. Hoffman worked assiduously to translate the traditional confessional liturgy. In addition, he rendered this very difficult material into English, thereby giving English-speaking readers their first opportunity to see the enormous creativity that the work represents. We should be enormously grateful to all the authors mentioned and to Dr. Hoffman for devoting time and expertise to this project.

Part I

Sin and Confession in Judaism

From the Bible to Today

The Liturgy of Confession

What It Is and Why We Say It

Rabbi Lawrence A. Hoffman, PhD

Confronting our shortcomings may be central to the religious temperament. One wonders, in fact, why atheistic attacks on religion do not credit religion at least for this, since all the great religions, it would seem, have at least some mechanism by which adherents are urged to take moral inventory of their faults. Judaism certainly does, and it calls those faults "sins," thereby indicating that they are more than just issues of defective calculation or wrongheaded planning. They run counter to the will of God; they are not the way human beings are supposed to live. People have problems with the word "sin" these days—a problem that

---

Rabbi Lawrence A. Hoffman, PhD, has served for more than three decades as professor of liturgy at Hebrew Union College–Jewish Institute of Religion in New York. He is a world-renowned liturgist and holder of the Stephen and Barbara Friedman Chair in Liturgy, Worship and Ritual. He has written and edited many books, including *My People's Prayer Book: Traditional Prayers, Modern Commentaries,* winner of the National Jewish Book Award; and *Who by Fire, Who by Water—Un'taneh Tokef* and *All These Vows—Kol Nidre,* the first two volumes in the Prayers of Awe series; and he is coeditor of *My People's Passover Haggadah: Traditional Texts, Modern Commentaries,* a finalist for the National Jewish Book Award. He is a developer of Synagogue 3000, a transdenominational project designed to envision and implement the ideal synagogue of the spirit for the twenty-first century.

is addressed in this book's next chapter (see Hoffman, pp. 13–31). But for purposes of this overview, we can use the traditional term, noting simply that Judaism has resolutely insisted on the reality of God, the ubiquity of sin, and the necessity for human beings to atone for sin by one means or another.

The primary means in biblical days was personal sacrifice (see Brettler, pp. 32–38). With the rise of Rabbinic Judaism, however, prayer replaced sacrifice, and the "offerings of our lips" (as the Rabbis put it) took the place of grains and animals that had once been offered on an actual altar. One form of verbal sacrifice was confession, the Hebrew term for which is *vidui*.

We think of confession as an annual exercise for Yom Kippur, but the Rabbis did not limit it to that occasion. Without necessarily believing that human beings are innately evil (in the sense of suffering from original sin), they did believe that sin is elemental—it is sufficiently part of our nature for us to confess it regularly. Our first comprehensive Jewish prayer book, *Seder Rav Amram* (from about 860 CE) draws upon the Talmud to make room for a confession every single day. As its author, Rav Amram, puts it, "If a person wants to say a confession after completing the daily *Amidah*, it is permissible to do so."

But Amram goes farther. He includes a sample of what one might say, drawn largely from Talmudic example, starting with a request for the Temple to be rebuilt and sacrifice to be reinstituted. The topic is fitting at this point in the service, since worshipers would just have completed the *Amidah*, which they believed to have been instituted only for the interim historical era during which the sacrificial system was unavailable. They would have ended their daily *Amidah* with the thought that someday, ultimate redemption would bring a return to sacrifice. Quite noteworthy, however, is the rationale given for God's restoration of the Temple: "Do it for your sake [God], not for our sake."

This phrase recurs frequently in Jewish liturgy, where we regularly ask God to reward us for God's own sake rather than for ours. What could that mean, if not that we consider ourselves unworthy of having God act on our behalf? We shall see (in the very next essay) that biblical Jews did not think so little of themselves; but Rabbinic Jews did, and this low sense of self, this assumption of inveterate human sinfulness, became part of the Rabbinic tradition that was passed down through history to give us Yom Kippur as we know it.

Amram, therefore, follows his request for a return to Temple times with another staple from the Talmud, a private prayer that is attributed to a fourth-century Babylonian sage, Rava (see appendix A):

> My God, before I was created I was worth nothing, and now that I am created I am as if not created. While alive, I am dust—all the more so when I die. I stand before you like a vessel filled with shame and contempt. May it be your will, Adonai my God and God of my ancestors, that I do not sin, and as for the sins that I have already committed, erase them in your great mercy, but not by punishment.

This is not the only confession that Amram recommends on a daily basis. After concluding his discussion of the daily *Amidah*, he turns to the section of the service that we call *Tachanun*, "Supplications" (see *My People's Prayer Book*, Vol. 6, *Tachanun and Concluding Prayers* [Woodstock, VT: Jewish Lights, 2002]). Compared to the *Amidah*, *Tachanun* is relatively unknown to most Jews. Reform (and to some extent Reconstructionist) Jews have eliminated it altogether; Conservative and Orthodox Jews, whose prayer books still have it, are likely to rush through it. It is a medieval addition to the liturgy, a reflection of the sense of sinfulness that Rabbinic theology had imparted through the years. For Mondays and Thursdays, Amram recommends a variety of prayers, including one that we now associate purely with Yom Kippur, *Ashamnu* ... ("We have been guilty ...").

Ashamnu is not altogether unknown as a daily staple even today. Sephardi Jews still say it then. Ashkenazi Jews, however, assign it only as a High Holy Day staple, where it serves as the shorter of two confessions. Technically, it is known as *Vidui Zuta*, Aramaic for "Short Confession." It is supplemented by the better known litany of sin, *Al Chet* ("For the sin ..."), called, technically, *Vidui Rabbah*, "Long Confession." These terms go back to the early days of the European Middle Ages—they are found in literature emanating from the school of Rashi in the eleventh and twelfth centuries.

Neither of these two standard confessions is Talmudic. What we get in the Talmud is a variety of personal prayers, most of them in the first person singular, and attributed to specific sages who were known to have favored them. Some are part of a discussion on what the various

Rabbis used to say every day following their *Amidah*—we just looked at Amram's use of the daily prayer by Rava, "My God, before I was created" (see appendix A). Others are found as part of a discussion on Yom Kippur (see appendix B)—but there too, the prayers are personalized, not yet established as confessional language for everyone to employ. The Rabbis back then were quite convinced that confession should be mandatory, but no single version had yet earned universal approval.

The standardization of liturgical wording as something to be said universally occurs only after the Talmud's conclusion, in what we call the geonic age, a period that corresponded with the move of the Muslim caliphate to Baghdad, a relatively new city in the heart of what Jews called Babylonia. With money and power flowing freely to the new Muslim capital, rabbis there were emboldened to assert their authority over Jews worldwide—not unlike what the caliph was doing among Muslims. Their leading authority became known as a *gaon* (plural *geonim*). These *geonim* issued responsa that interpreted the Babylonian Talmud in such a way as to inform Jews everywhere of their various responsibilities. One such responsum, as we have seen, was an authoritative prayer book by Rav Amram, himself a *gaon*. Amram's work is the first to contain our two standard confessions, *Ashamnu* and *Al Chet*; they are bracketed by introductory and concluding prayers such as we use now. A second *gaon*, Saadiah, promulgated his own prayer book about 920. For some reason he omits *Ashamnu*, but he is the exception to the rule. Starting with Amram, the two confessions remain standard fare worldwide.

Stylistically, they are acrostics, apportioning separate words (in *Ashamnu*) or entire sentences (in *Al Chet*) to each letter of the Hebrew alphabet. But *Al Chet* was developed in different ways by different communities. Broadly speaking, there are two Sephardi traditions: those Jews who moved east across the Mediterranean and settled in the Ottoman Empire; and those who moved north into the Netherlands and, from there, into England and across the Atlantic to North and South America. By and large, Sephardi Jews of the northern branch say hardly any lines of *Al Chet* at all—they make do with six lines that establish the basic categories of sin and ignore the practice of insisting on an acrostic. The southern branch uses a single acrostic: one line per letter. Ashkenazi Jews double that, allotting two lines per letter.

These confessions are recited by the individual worshiper immediately after concluding the silent *Amidah*; they are repeated during the prayer leader's repetition of the *Amidah*'s fourth benediction. Here, too, custom has varied somewhat. Amram called for *Ashamnu* also by the individual during the fourth benediction of the silent recitation. Some communities concluded the petition by saying, "Blessed are You, the saving God" (*Barukh atah Adonai, ha'el hasalchan*). Neither custom has persisted; neither is now the norm.

A normal day of prayer comprises three services: *Ma'ariv*, *Shacharit*, and *Minchah* (the prior evening [with which the next day properly begins], morning, and afternoon). On Shabbat and festivals, we add a fourth service called *Musaf* ("Additional"). And on Yom Kippur, we feature yet a final service, *N'ilah* ("closing" of the gates), giving us five services in all. Many Jews think of there being several other services still: a memorial service (*Yizkor*), for example, the shofar service (for Rosh Hashanah), and the *Seder Avodah* (the service memorializing the Yom Kippur worship that existed during Temple days). But this terminological extension of the word "service" is technically incorrect. Properly speaking, "service" is the word we use for those prayer-book units that include an *Amidah*. *Musaf*, for example, is a service because it has its own *Amidah*. The same is true of *N'ilah*. Traditionally, the other so-called services are folded into *Shacharit* or *Musaf*. Non-Orthodox prayer books, particularly, have separated them out for purposes of making the prayers more meaningful. But as far as the confessions go, we need only take into consideration the five services properly speaking, each one of which features them.

N'ilah ("closing" of the gates) has its own character, which bears upon the confessions it contains. The idea of *N'ilah* goes back to the ancient Temple and the significance of closing its gates every night. In Temple times, therefore, to the extent that there was any synagogue service at all, *N'ilah* was more common than it is today; it was a practice assigned to all fast days, not just Yom Kippur, the idea being that we should provide every opportunity for repentance, even extending the opportunity to repent until the final moment of sunset. But after the Temple fell, *N'ilah* was reserved just for Yom Kippur, where, to this day, it constitutes a magnificent conclusion to the entire twenty-four-hour fast. In feeling tone, the various services progress from *Ma'ariv* (as Yom Kippur begins) to *N'ilah* (the next night) by going from a heavy concentration on our sinfulness to the conviction that we are about to be cleansed from sin and permitted to start anew. In keeping with the uplifting sense of renewal that sets in by the end of Yom Kippur, *N'ilah* drops the lengthy *Al Chet*.

Ashamnu is still there, but instead of *Al Chet* we have a remarkable prayer titled *Atah noten yad* ("You extend your hand ..."), an affirmation that God reaches out to sinners, pulling them out of their distress.

Sin and wrongdoing carry with them the inevitable consequence of punishment, after all. The daily prayer of confession that we saw above ended with the plea, "Insofar as I have sinned, erase it in your great mercy, but not by punishment." That God had the power to reward and to punish was taken for granted by the Rabbis. A sure sign of heresy was taken to be the charge that the universe was "without justice or judge"; the well-known Rabbi Elisha ben Abuya was excommunicated in the second century for saying just that. God, then, is the judge before whom we stand on the High Holy Days—but not a "hanging judge," a judge intent solely on punishing offenders, a judge for whom the letter of the law is all that matters. We are, after all, sinners just because we are human. The Rabbis pictured God, therefore, as a God of justice but also a God of mercy. It was said, in fact, that God would overlook a person's first sin of the year, as if to say that no one can be expected to attain perfection. Now, at the end of Yom Kippur, just as the gates close and the *N'ilah* service turns to the final confession of the day, we are told that God does not want our death as sinners; God wants us, rather, to live.

The significance of this point of view should not be minimized. It is all too easy for modern men and women to dispense with language discussing the nature of God by saying either that they do not believe in God at all or that the God in whom they do believe is more akin to an impersonal force than to a human being, so that discussion of God reaching out to bring us in or preferring pardon over punishment makes little sense. I too agree that God cannot be fruitfully imagined as human in nature; Maimonides disabused us of that notion almost one thousand years ago. But God cannot altogether be likened to anything else either. Even if God were said to be an impersonal force, it would hardly be appropriate to say that God was simply like gravity or electromagnetism. "God as a force" is no less metaphoric then "God as a person." Language cannot come to terms with God other than through metaphor, so we borrow those metaphors that work best, the metaphors that say something about the way the universe works, the ways human beings are constructed, the relationships and values that matter most, and the way things ought to be for human beings who are granted life and want to know how the life they are granted may have purpose and destiny.

Saying that God wants us to live, not die, and that repentance has the power to erase sin and guilt establishes a society rooted in compassion, care, and hope rather than punishment, vengeance, and despair. It provides models for human beings, who, to use another metaphor, are made in God's image and expected to act as God does. It establishes the conviction, internally, in each and every one of us, that we matter as individual human beings, because no matter how we may have erred, we have the power and the right to reestablish ourselves anew as the good and worthwhile creatures we know ourselves to be when we are at our best.

Unfortunately, we are not always at our best. We frequently fall short of the ideal. The liturgy has struggled, therefore, with the extent to which we should confess our wrong against the degree to which we should emphasize our basic goodness. This issue of human nature, the balance between innate goodness on one hand and proclivity to evil on the other, is what we call religious anthropology and is the subject of the next essay in this book (see Hoffman, pp. 13–31). Suffice it to say here, in the context of our discussion on the liturgy itself, that the wording of our prayers has varied over time, depending upon which of the two poles of human nature we wish to emphasize.

The best example is the introduction to *Ashamnu* (see p. 96), which reads:

> We are not so arrogant and insolent as to say before You,
> Adonai our God and our ancestors' God, we are righteous
> and have not sinned. But we and our ancestors have sinned.

The most obvious problem with the prayer as it stands is the last sentence, which begins with "But." Why "But"? If "we are not so arrogant and insolent as to say ... we have not sinned," then why conclude, "*But* we have sinned"? That second sentence should be a continuation of the first, not a disjunctive modification of it. The prayer should read, "We are not so arrogant and insolent as to say ... we have not sinned. We have sinned."

The mystery is solved by realizing that the Hebrew for "but" (*aval*) can mean "truly" (see Kaunfer, pp. 181–185). But the matter goes deeper still. The original version in *Seder Rav Amram* reads:

> We *are* so arrogant and insolent that we say before You,
> Adonai our God and our ancestors' God, we are righteous
> and have not sinned. Truly, we have sinned.

Originally, then, the prayer admitted the negative side of human personality: not only do we sin, but we are even so arrogant and insolent as to maintain that we do not. Over the course of time, such a gross admission of human weakness came, apparently, to be seen as overly pessimistic. So the wording was changed to say just the reverse: yes, we sin, but we are *not* so arrogant and insolent as to say that we don't.

In addition, the prayer as we have it admits that "we and our ancestors have sinned," whereas Amram says only, "We have sinned." Here, too, it may be that the original sharp contrast between our righteous ancestors and ourselves became just too much for people to handle. So they changed it to say that actually, our ancestors sinned just as we do—the apparent conclusion being that they were pardoned, and so, too, will we. On the other side of things, however, is a subtle change in the Hebrew. Hebrew sentences with a pronominal object (e.g., I, you, we, he/she, they) are normally written without the subject. The verbal conjugation is enough to tell the reader what the subject is. Hence the sentence "We have sinned" would normally be written, simply, *Chatanu*—the verb alone. Indeed, that is what the Talmud originally had and what Amram has. When we want to emphasize the subject, however, we add the pronoun (in this case, *anachnu*, "we"), as if to say not just "We have sinned," but "It is *we* who have sinned." And that is what we now have in our prayer books: not just *Chatanu*, but *Anachnu chatanu*. That change has even found its way into printed editions of the Talmud; manuscript copyists inserted it during the Middle Ages under the assumption that the version they had without it was mistaken. So even as tradition deemphasized the troubling notion that we, more than our ancestors, sin, it reemphasized our own sinfulness by adding the pronominal subject of the sentence, thereby redoubling the emphasis on ourselves.

We can see from all of this the extent to which our ancestors struggled with the true meaning of confession. They did not treat the liturgy as pro forma ritual that one hurries through by rote. Indeed, they knew quite well that according to Jewish tradition, even though the liturgy for confession is necessarily public, it is the individual's personal coming to terms with God and with self that matters. A word, then, about this personal coming to terms with God, an insistence on personal confession that is easily lost against the backdrop of the synagogue service and its repetitive public proclamations of guilt.

The very same legal authorities who determined the liturgical rules and regulations could not have been clearer about the priority of personal and private confession. The *Tur*, for example, the basis for the *Shulchan Arukh* and, therefore, the gold standard of sorts when it comes to codes of Jewish law, begins its discussion of confession by saying:

> On the eve of Yom Kippur, we should set our hearts on making reconciliation with all those whom we have harmed, since Yom Kippur atones for sins between human beings and God but not for sins between one human being and another—unless the wrongdoer reconciles with the person wronged. Even if the hurt we have done was only through words, we must still seek reconciliation. We must go to any person we have harmed, and if they are not willing to be appeased the first time, we must go again a second and third time.... If the person we have harmed has died in the meanwhile, we should bring ten other people with us to that person's grave and say over it, "I have sinned against the God of Israel and against this person [who then is named].[1]

Sixteenth-century commentator Joel Sirkes adds the stipulation that at the moment of seeking pardon we must stipulate precisely the sin that we have committed, since that is what we do vis-à-vis God when we say our liturgical *Al Chet*, "and all the more so is that appropriate with human beings."[2] According to Maimonides, the "essence of true repentance" (*ikaro shel vidui*) lies not in the multiplication of words in our prayers, but in simple declaration, "God, I have sinned, transgressed, and gone astray before You in doing such and such. But I am sorry, and embarrassed by what I have done. I will never do it again." The task of repentance does not end there, however. "Complete repentance [*t'shuvah*]," he continues, "occurs only when one has the opportunity to repeat a sin but then separates oneself from it, avoiding it on account of repentance [that is, moral scruple], rather than simply out of fear or inability to do it."[3]

Nonetheless, Maimonides also holds that "whoever goes on at some length in making confession is considered praiseworthy."[4] Our liturgical confessions, then, are an exercise in such praiseworthy activity, not the essence of the thing but a ritual extension of that essence in the presence of community. We are, after all, communal beings. The nature of our community matters. We can be a community that learns to hurt and to hate or to love and to pardon. It is communal ritual that establishes which one it will be. Judaism, over time, has established a year that begins with self-evaluation, repentance, and pardon. Our lengthy confessions say a good deal about ourselves but even more about the kind of community we want to be a part of.

From Penitence to Nobility

Modes of Jewish Piety

Rabbi Lawrence A. Hoffman, PhD

Does anyone still believe in sin? The word seems not just old-fashioned, but positively antiquarian. Yet it is at the very center of classical Judaism—more central than most of us care to admit. The issue is religious anthropology: the assumptions we make about human nature. Left to their own devices, are people fundamentally good or bad? Trustworthy or devious? Heroes or villains? A wealth of psychological experiments addresses this question, but when all is said and done, interpretations of the experiments differ enough to make us doubt whether anything can clinch the argument one way or the other. It eventually comes down to a matter of faith.

Are we evil from birth, inheritors of original sin (as classical Christianity teaches)—even "totally depraved" (as Reformation genius John Calvin later put it)? Do we, at least, below our civilized exterior, harbor tendencies toward mayhem and murder (as Freud would have us believe)? What, exactly, Judaism teaches about the subject is not so easy to answer, since unlike Christianity, Judaism has resisted the Hellenistic tendency toward philosophical absolutism; it rarely lays down any fundamental precept of belief "exactly." While Jews are held liable for specific halakhic demands of behavior, Judaism does not so easily prescribe parallel loyalty to some beliefs over others, and Jewish texts do not codify just what those beliefs would be even if we were to be held absolutely responsible for holding them.

It is easier to say what Jews do not believe, the outside limits beyond which claims about human nature begin sounding distinctly un-Jewish—first and foremost, in our Western world where Christianity has long dominated, the doctrine of original sin. Whatever "original sin" is, we don't believe it. But what is it? And having dispensed with it, what else is left? Just how sinful are we?

Human Sin: Original or Elemental?

There are three ways to talk about human sin: *practical*, *psychological*, and *metaphysical*. Most obvious (and the easiest to understand) is the *practical* way of looking at it—a simple and straightforward observation of the mistakes, errors, and collateral damage that we leave behind as part of the normal human way of operating in the world. The word "sin," from this perspective, is just the application of religious terminology to the negative side effects of ordinary human behavior.

But the word "sin" seems to go much deeper than that. People make mistakes, go wrong, commit errors, and so on—but they are not, on that account, "mistakers," "wrongers," and "errorers" the way people who sin are "sinners." This extension of the term implies ownership of the sin by the sinner, as if the sin were part of the sinner's very being. In large part, people object to the word "sin" precisely because of this ensuing moralistic judgment on their character—they do not want to be thought of as "sinners."

The *psychological* explanation is a modern way to understand this matter of ownership without the moralistic judgment that comes from religion. It is true that sin does not just occur here and there by happenstance; it derives from human nature because human beings are prone to doing wrong. As a science, psychology avoids the religious word "sin." But one can imagine a sort of religious psychology as the religious conviction that we are psychologically prone to evil, that the evil we do is what our religious tradition has called sin; and that insofar as we do such evil, we are sinners. Back in 1899, when psychology was still in its infancy, Kaufmann Kohler, the rabbi of Temple Emanu-El in New York, expressed the idea eloquently by defining sin as "the power of evil dwelling in no other being but man." It is part of human (and only human) nature. "The angel, as we conceive him, who cannot do wrong, and the animal which cannot be good in a moral sense, are both free from sin. Sin is the power that *induces* man to do wrong but does not *compel* him to do so, and man's God-like nature consists in his mastery over sin."[1] Most liberal followers of modern-day religion would have no trouble with all of this, as a way to harmonize science and religion.

But religious conversation about sin can go deeper. It can be *metaphysical*, in which case it makes statements about human nature that science cannot see or quantify. The mistakes we make say something about what we are at our very core of being. Christianity, especially, has developed a body of literature discussing this metaphysical aspect of human behavior, and when we refer to that body of literature, we call the doctrine "original sin."[2]

It goes back all the way to the actual founder of Christianity, Paul (first century), who wrote that "sin entered the world through one man [Adam], and death entered through sin." Moreover, just as sin entered the world through Adam, and death through sin, so too did "death spread to all men because all men sinned" (Romans 5:12). In other worlds, Adam created the primeval sin, but Adam's offspring to the end of time inherit sinfulness from Adam. This is the metaphysical part of the story: a claim about inheriting the propensity to sin from our primeval father whose original sinful act was passed along in the human genome (so to speak) so that one cannot be human without at the same time being a sinner.

The classic account comes from Augustine, a bishop in North Africa from 396 to 430. The Bible describes circumcision as a sign of the covenant. Why, Augustine wonders, does the Bible say of a boy who is not circumcised that he will be cut off from his people? It's not the boy's fault that his parents did not circumcise him. Why hold the child responsible for his parents' sin? The answer, Augustine says, is that sin can be inherited. Likewise, Adam's primeval sin is handed down as an everlasting human inheritance. We are born with sin already inside us, the sin we inherited from Adam.

Augustine's doctrine was accepted widely by Roman Catholicism and then repeated, sometimes in harsher measure still, by the Protestant churches of the Reformation, whence it was brought to the Americas and taught as a matter of course for most of American history. It is this deeper metaphysical doctrine of human sinfulness that Judaism never accepted. But it did not, on that account, deny the lesser doctrine of psychological sin. That we are all sinners was as Jewish a doctrine as it was Christian.

Jews and Christians differed on what to do about it: Jews said that even though we sin we can also do good, so that we can effect reparation from sin by our good deeds; Christians held that we are so severely sinners by nature that we can never do enough good to save ourselves. Salvation comes only through the grace of God, "grace" being a technical term for the love that God offers us, even though, sinners that we are, we do not merit it. But ignore the metaphysics and you get a Christian doctrine of human sin that Jews too have generally held. It is not, after all, so difficult to argue human sinfulness, given the course of human history.

We can deny the metaphysical doctrine of original sin, therefore, but still believe that we are inherently sinful as a matter of psychology. That was the Rabbis' position. They did not think of sin as an "original" blemish inherited from Adam, but they might have called it "elemental," in the sense of its being a necessary element in human character.

They got this belief from the Bible, where sin is usually spoken of as a burden that weighs us down with guilt.[3] God pardons us by *lifting* the sin (*nosei avon*) from our shoulders. The sacrificial cult provides a set of offerings that remove the guilt—actual "sin offerings," for example, but also an annual Yom Kippur scapegoat who, quite literally, carries off our sins and leaves us free of them. Aaron, the priest, is commanded to "lay both his hands on the live goat and confess over it all the iniquities and transgressions of the Israelites, whatever their sins, *putting them on the head of the goat*," which is then dispatched to die in the wilderness. "Thus the goat shall carry on it all their iniquities to an inaccessible region" (Leviticus 16:21–22). Sin is also likened to a stain that must be wiped clean. "Though your sins are as scarlet," the prophet Isaiah says (1:18), "they will be as white as snow. Though they are red like crimson, they will be like wool."

By the Rabbinic era, however, a different metaphor had developed. Sin was now likened to a debt. The more sins we commit, the deeper we go into debt. The Hebrew word "punishment" (*puranut*) even comes from the root *para*, "to pay off or collect a debt." It becomes important to build up a bank account of good deeds, something we do through "acts of loving-kindness" (*g'milut chasadim*); should we fail to have sufficient moral credit on hand, we may draw on the merit of the fathers, the bank account of worthy deeds that Abraham, Isaac, and Jacob bequeathed to us—a doctrine called *z'khut avot*, "the merit of the fathers." Our own good deeds, and the merit we draw down from those who came before us, are weighed and measured in heaven, set upon a balancing scale to see whether they outweigh our sins. Our final court appearance occurs the day we die, but we pass before God annually at the High Holy Day season, as a dress rehearsal for the ultimate judgment day.

As elemental as sinfulness is, however, our natural default position, the one for which we were created, is to stand alongside God in goodness.

In theory, at least, righteousness is possible. We dare not say of ourselves that we are "righteous" (*tzaddikim*)—that would be an arrogant and, therefore, unrighteous thing to do—but we know others who are righteous, and we celebrate them in our most important prayer, the *Amidah*, which provides a blessing titled "the Righteous." The Talmud, too, applauds the righteous—and not just righteous Jews, but the righteous of all nations, who are guaranteed a share in the world to come. We can, at least, strive for righteousness, a journey that begins with repentance, *t'shuvah*, the "return" to our default position of standing alongside God as creatures formed in God's own likeness.

Such striving after righteousness seems impossible from the classical Christian position as outlined by Paul and then by Augustine, for whom the default position is sinfulness inherited from Adam's Fall. Christians need two revelations, two covenants (or "testaments," as they are known): the first (Torah), to lay down the laws by which we shall live, and the second (Jesus), to relieve us of our sins when we inevitably go astray while trying to live that way. Jews suffice with a single revelation, which is both challenge and solution: a challenge, because the laws of Torah are indeed problematic—who can keep them without fail? But a solution too, because the same Torah provides a means of return to the state of being for which we were intended, a journey back to God, who waits patiently for us, wanting only our return.

One might say, then, that we are not entirely bad—we have inclinations toward both good and evil (a *yetzer hatov* and a *yetzer hara*). They struggle within us. But on Yom Kippur, at least—and regularly throughout Talmudic literature as well—emphasis is laid upon the evil inclination that wins all too often. Sin may decidedly not be *original*, then, in Judaism; but equally decidedly, it is *elemental*.

This Rabbinic position was something of a revolutionary departure from what pre-Rabbinic Jews would have held. Yes, the Bible believed in sin; and yes, the Rabbis emphasize our human sinfulness. But the matter is far more nuanced than that.

The Torah was compiled in the fifth century BCE; about 167 BCE, the Pharisees come into being—a group whom the Rabbis see as their ideological predecessors; the first authorities to bear the title "Rabbi" make their appearance only after the destruction of the Temple in 70 CE; and we get no Rabbinic writings until the end of the second century. That gives us over half a millennium of time between the Torah's canonization and the time when Rabbinic Judaism bursts full blown upon the scene. Did the farmers and priests of the early Pharisaic period and before believe—as the Rabbis ultimately did—that we are all tainted by elemental sin for which we must repent at least once a year?

From Covenantal to Penitential Piety

Of the early Rabbinic writings, none is more important than the Mishnah, the first magisterial work of Rabbinic law, promulgated about 200 CE. It is there that we first find lengthy expositions of Rosh Hashanah and Yom Kippur as a period of the new year. Biblically, the year arrived with Nisan, the month of Passover, when the Jewish People had come into being. The new moon of Nisan was to be "the first of months to you" (Exodus 12:2). Rosh Hashanah was just a "sacred occasion commemorated with loud blasts" a time to "observe complete rest" on the first day of the seventh month (Leviticus 23:23–24); Yom Kippur followed independently, ten days later, as a time of "self-denial … on which expiation is made on your behalf before Adonai your God" (Leviticus 23:26–28). The Mishnah retained the biblical new year of Nisan but "promoted" Rosh Hashanah into becoming its own separate new year, with a judgmental quality that links it with the mood of Yom Kippur.

These two new years, Passover and Rosh Hashanah, are six months apart, as if the Jewish year were an ellipse in time with two equally vital centers. Passover, the formative time of Israel's founding, is particularistic: the time when Jews gather as an extended family through time and space to relate their tale and recommit themselves to the faith and hopes that are uniquely Israel's. "Our father [Abraham] was a wandering Aramean." "God freed us from slavery ... split the Red Sea ... brought us to Sinai ... gave us the Torah. *Dayyenu* ['It would have been enough']." "Next year in Jerusalem."

Rosh Hashanah is universalistic—the occasion when "all who come into the world are made to pass before You [God]," for all humanity ("all who come into the world") are judged then for our sins. The venerable Rosh Hashanah hymn for Reform Jews "All the world shall come to serve Thee" is actually a translation of an ancient synagogue staple called *V'ye'etayu* ("And they shall come"). Equally old, and equally universal, is the beginning and end of the *Alenu*, "God spread out the heavens and established the earth…. On that day God shall be one and God's name shall be one." Since about 1400, the *Alenu* has been a daily concluding prayer as well, but it was composed specifically to introduce the Rosh Hashanah blowing of the shofar, in a liturgical unit known as *Malkhuyot*, God's "Kingship," the celebration of God's universal rule over all.

So the Rabbis celebrate the particularity of Israel, but also universal humanity: "all who come into the world" to begin with, and "all who will come to serve Thee [God]" at the end of time. As universal human beings, Jews too partake of human nature, are therefore sinners, must pass before God on Rosh Hashanah to account for their sins, and must fast on Yom Kippur to attain atonement. Jews still observe Passover, but no longer as a new year. That designation has been reserved in the popular mentality for Rosh Hashanah alone. The entire period from the first of Elul (the month before Rosh Hashanah) to the conclusion of Yom Kippur became penitential in nature, with the time between Rosh Hashanah and Yom Kippur being known as "the ten days of repentance." Synagogue goers add poetry called *s'lichot*, "poems for pardon," to their daily prayers. We can call this final triumph of Rabbinic anthropology "penitential piety."

But this is the snapshot of the situation only after many centuries, at the end of the penitential road, so to speak. There is reason to suspect that it took several centuries to unfold. Indeed, the Mishnah itself provides an earlier snapshot, not the end but the beginning of the road, that demonstrates a quite different image of human nature.

Its background is Deuteronomy 26, where farmers are commanded to take a tithe to the Temple in Jerusalem. As the farmer hands over his produce to the priest, he is to recite a formula indicating the meaning of his act:

> I have cleared out the consecrated portion from the house; and I have given it to the Levite, the stranger, the fatherless, and the widow, just as You commanded me. I have neither transgressed nor neglected any of your commandments.... I have obeyed Adonai my God. I have done just as You commanded me. Look down from your holy abode, from heaven, and bless your people Israel and the soil You have given us, a land flowing with milk and honey, as You swore to our fathers. (Deuteronomy 26:13–15)

Deuteronomy was written in the seventh century BCE. We may assume that farmers were performing this cultic ritual for at least several centuries prior to the Temple's destruction in 70 CE. By 200, the time of the Mishnah's compilation, the Temple had been gone for well over a century, and with it, the ritual of the tithe.

But as it happens, the Mishnah reports the ritual as it had once occurred, along with an interpretive gloss on what the biblical words of Deuteronomy were taken to mean. It is a tradition handed down to the Mishnah's compiler, the mind-set of farmers in an earlier time—not all the way back to Deuteronomy, but some time before the Temple fell, long enough after the Torah's canonization to reflect the Pharisaic era, but long enough before the Mishnah's compilation to reflect the situation prior to the full onset of penitential piety.

Here is part of what the farmer is said by the Mishnah to have had in mind:

> "Look down from your holy abode, from heaven": This means, "We did what You required of us; now You do what You promised us."
>
> "And bless your people Israel": This means, "with sons and daughters."
>
> "And the soil You have given us": This means, "with dew and rain and offspring of cattle."
>
> "A land flowing with milk and honey, as You swore to our fathers": This means, "give the fruit a sweet taste." (Mishnah Ma'aser Sheni 5:12)

What makes this positively fascinating is the verb used for the recitation of the farmer's formula. It is *l'hitvadot*, "to confess." The nominal form is *vidui*, "confession." But what kind of confession is it when the so-called confessor says, in effect, "I did everything right, God, just the way You wanted. Now You owe me. I gave You what You want; give me what I want: prosperity, children, and happiness." This is not a *con*fession, so much as it is a *pro*fession. It is nothing short of "getting right with God," to use an idiom we more commonly associate with stereotypical evangelical churches, but with this difference: For these churches, "getting right with God" means truly confessing the sins that depraved human beings are necessarily guilty of. For pre-Rabbinic farmers, it meant running through an honest inventory of the extent to which one had properly kept God's commandments. The farmer of the Mishnah had done quite well and didn't hesitate in saying so. Others might have done more poorly. In any case, what one said to God at such a time was a *vidui*, not just admission of demerit, however, but a bold avowal of merit as well—a very different form of piety than what ultimately prevails.

The farmer's prayer and its marginal commentary reflect the older biblical notion of covenant. Deuteronomy tells us exactly what that was in the biblical section immediately following, known as "the blessings and the curses" (Deuteronomy 27 and 28). If Israel obeys God's will, blessing upon blessing will be its lot; if not, blessing will change to curse, and the most dire consequences will flow. Traditionally, when the weekly portion rolls around to the blessings and curses, the curses are read through rapidly and under one's breath, so frightening are they.

The covenant is reflected yet again in a Deuteronomy passage that is now part of the daily synagogue service. Most Jews think the traditional *Sh'ma* (recited morning and night) is a single line, "Hear, O Israel, Adonai is our God, Adonai alone." Actually, it is a string of three biblical paragraphs, the central one of which is Deuteronomy 11:13–21, known as *V'hayah im shamo'a*, "If you carefully heed...." The essence of the blessings and curses is provided here in unmistakable shorthand. "If you carefully heed my commandments ... I shall grant your land's rain in its season ... that you might gather your grain, wine, and oil.... [But] take care lest your mind tempt you to rebel by worshiping other gods ... for then the fire and fury of Adonai will turn against you." Deuteronomy is famous for this "tit for tat" theology. We keep God's commandments and we are rewarded; we ignore them and we are punished. But it is up to us, and there is no reason to believe we are more likely to do one rather than another. Compared to the Rabbis' penitential piety, Deuteronomy's covenantal piety provides a more balanced view of human nature. The Rabbis build upon it; they too believe in a covenant between Israel and God, but they become far more jaundiced in imagining Israel can ever live up to its side of the bargain.

They also universalize the idea of covenant and generalize it to other peoples, who, they say, have their own covenants with God. Noah, who preceded Abraham, is the Rabbinic model for humankind in general, so the covenant God makes with others is called Noahide. They provide various versions of it, but generally, it contains the essential humane elements that go into any valid society: a ban on murder, theft, and cruelty to animals; and the guarantee of a fair judicial code and judges (without which Rabbis couldn't imagine any society lasting long). On Rosh Hashanah (and heading into Yom Kippur), "all who come into the world" are judged for what they have done; not just Israel. But other peoples are, as it were, outside the jurisdiction of the Rabbis, whose proper concern is to demand that Jews admit their sins—for sins they will most certainly have. The day when farmers, shopkeepers, ordinary men and women, or even the Rabbis themselves might have imagined doing it all right is long gone. The Jewish mind-set has moved to the point where sin and sinfulness dominate their religious imagination.

This changeover is true not just for Rabbis; it is mirrored in other literature of the time as well. The Dead Sea Scrolls, for instance, are saturated with concerns over sin and impurity. First-century historian Josephus reports on Essenes who had abandoned Jerusalem and city life altogether to set up an alternative society that would remain pure from urban immoralities. Apocalyptic expectations abound in any number of books that never made it into our biblical canon, but which speak of the end of time being near at hand. Their theme is the ubiquity of sin, which is about to force God's hand. Repent, they say; the end of days is near.

This is the milieu that gives us Jesus of Nazareth. His disciples ask him how to pray, and he replies, "Our father who art in heaven, hallowed be thy name. Thy kingdom come, thy will be done on earth as it is heaven" (Matthew 6:9–10). So far so good: a very Jewish, even Rabbinic, prayer, which scholars have long seen as an alternative version of what Jews call the *Kaddish*. The *Kaddish* too prays for the coming of the kingdom, for example: *v'yamlikh malkhuteih*, "May God's kingdom come."

But Jesus adds his own peculiar twist, a set of petitions—all of them on the pervasiveness of sin and the immediacy of the afterlife promised only to those who repent of their evil and turn to virtue. "Give us this day our daily bread and forgive us our debts, as we also have forgiven our debtors, and deliver us from evil. Lead us not into temptation but deliver us from evil" (Matthew 6:11–13).

The only oddity here is the term "daily bread," *epiousion* in Greek. The word is used nowhere else, so it is hard to know what it means. But the church fathers (the equivalent of the Rabbis, for the Christian tradition) who interpret the term say clearly and overwhelmingly that it refers metaphorically to the coming of the Kingdom: not the bread we put in our bodies, but the bread of eternal life. The word "debts" is exactly the Rabbinic metaphor for sin that we noted above.

The Lord's Prayer, as it is ever after known, could not be clearer. We are all sinners, and the end of the world is at hand. If we wish to be rewarded with eternal life, we must repent of our sins and ask God to forgive these trespasses or debts. But suppose the day of judgment comes tomorrow. We must still get through the night without sin, so "lead us not into temptation" and "deliver us from evil," that we may retain our purity for the unexpected moment when all will be revealed.

It is now just a short step to Paul, who knows for a fact that Jesus came to redeem us from sin, that we are justified not by our good works—we are too sinful for that—but by faith in Jesus Christ, who was sent here as the son of God to save us. Drawing on Jewish imagery that he had learned as a child, Paul tells his audience that Jesus is the final sacrifice, the lamb of God, a paschal lamb, in fact, whose blood was shed on our behalf.

The Rabbis will not go that far. They do, however, give us the prayer that is our High Holy Day staple, the essence of which is attributed to Rabbi Akiva (second century CE), *Avinu Malkenu*, "Our father our king," which concludes with words that Paul would have approved: "Our father our king, be gracious [*choneinu*] and answer us [*aneinu*] for we have no works [*ein banu ma'asim*]." This usual translation misses the theological point, however. Akiva, no less than Paul, is saying not just "be gracious" but "show us grace," the love that saves us even though we don't deserve it; we are in God's debt for our many sins, and tragically, "we have no good works to save us." By "answer," he means answer our prayer for deliverance even though we cannot plead in any way that we merit it.

This is not the official Jewish doctrine—not usually. But it does show up in Elul and the following period of repentance. Jewish theology, we should recall, is not systematized. Throughout the year, we plead the intrinsic value of good deeds to save us. They are the *mitzvot* on which the covenant at Sinai was formed. That covenant endures. We are not Paul who thought it had come to an end and been replaced by a second covenant, a covenant of faith in the saving figure of Christ. But on Rosh Hashanah and Yom Kippur, we hedge our bets. What if we do not have any good works to show for ourselves? What if we are more saturated by sin than we would have thought possible? What if God writes our deeds in the ledger book of life and death and shows us in the red, indelibly in debt for our misdeeds? Then what? Then God shows us mercy, grace, kindness; God pardons us anyway, "for God's own sake, in love" (*l'ma'an sh'mo b'ahavah*).

Official Judaism never abandons its trust in covenantal theology. God does reward and punish according to our works. But it overlays this older biblical view with penitential piety, the Rabbinic suspicion that we are not as good as the Bible thought we might become. It is penitential piety, not covenantal piety, that dominates Jewish thought and practice ever after. That is why Rosh Hashanah and Yom Kippur become the High (!) Holy Days, instead of Sukkot, which had been "The Holiday" par excellence (*hechag*) in the biblical period. Sukkot (as the Rabbis remember accurately) is *z'man simchateinu* ("the time of our joy"). The Mishnah recalls the Temple days when "anyone who hasn't seen the joy of Sukkot hasn't seen real joy at all." But unencumbered joy is an inappropriate centerpiece for a point of view newly dominated by a negative anthropology, the centrality of sin, and penitential piety. Sukkot fades into eclipse relative to Rosh Hashanah and Yom Kippur. In the new anthropology that judges human nature as sinful, we need High Holy Days of pardon, not of happiness.

That point of view gave us our traditional High Holy Day liturgy with its redundant message of sin and of utter dependence on the grace of God. It lasted some eighteen hundred years but came crashing down when Jews entered modernity, discovered the Enlightenment, and celebrated Emancipation.

Modernity and the Piety of Human Potential

We still live and breathe the atmosphere of the Enlightenment, the triumphant message of the human capacity for good: "Life, liberty, and the pursuit of happiness," as Jefferson promised us; "Liberty, equality, fraternity," in the battle cry of the French Revolution. For Jews, that message was delivered by Napoleon, who set about emancipating them from ghettoes. No longer the pariah of Europe, Jews would henceforth be free members of the Republic, just like everyone else.

The message was premature. With Napoleon's defeat, the old-guard traditionalists of the various European countries tried to roll progress back to the way things had been prior to the revolution; and in any event, Napoleon never got as far as Eastern Europe, so his message of Jewish Emancipation never got there in the first place.

But the modern genie was out of the medieval bottle and refused to be stuffed back in. Wherever societies claimed the banner of modernity, one of their first actions was to reconsider the status of Jews and make them citizens. Wherever Jews wanted to be free, they heralded modernity and Napoleon who had brought it. Behind Napoleon's doctrine of Jewish Emancipation was the intellectual revolution that we call the Enlightenment. Jews therefore practically worshiped the Enlightenment.

This new Enlightenment god for moderns had been spawned by the age of reason. It was implicit in the thought of Descartes, Newton, Spinoza, Leibnitz, and Kant, all of whom agreed on the primacy of reason as a cognitive capacity that makes all human beings equal. The Jewish apostle of reason par excellence had been Moses Mendelssohn (eighteenth century), who, among other things, argued the case for separation of church and state well before it became a matter of law in the United States. These two influences, the fresh air of reason and political equality for all members of modern nation-states, paved the way for a century when all things seemed possible.

It wasn't just Jews who felt that way. Europeans in general welcomed the changeover from the Dark Ages to the Enlightenment, its metaphorical opposite, as an era of limitless possibility. The Industrial Revolution is justly known for its harsh working conditions, child labor, and dismal urban slums. But equally worth noting is its remarkable inventiveness that made life immeasurably richer and that never seemed to end: electric lights (1809), steam locomotives and photography (1814), matches (1819), typewriters (1829), the McCormick reaper and Faraday's electric dynamo (1831), the telegraph (1837), Goodyear rubber tires and the bicycle (1839), grain elevators (1842), safety pins (1849), the Singer sewing machine (1851), pasteurization (1856), Pullman sleeping cars (1857), the internal combustion engine (1858), the Otis elevator (1861), dynamite and tin cans (1866), Tungsten steel and traffic lights (1868), telephones and carpet sweepers (1876), fountain pens and cash registers (1884), radar and contact lenses (1887), drinking straws (1888), escalators (1891), diesel engines (1898).

For centuries, men and women had been promised the miracle of a messianic coming; but the messiah hadn't come. Now there was science, a new messiah, which responded to human inventiveness and fueled aspirations that seemed actually realizable. Darwin assured the world that evolution was embedded in the very nature of life itself. Herbert Spencer popularized "social Darwinism," the belief that every evolutionary development was for the better. University faculties invented the discipline of history, which chronicled the movement of human society beyond medieval darkness to the enlightenment of modern times. It seemed only a matter of time until human innovation alone would make all things possible.

The message of progress reverberated with special immediacy for Jews, especially those in Germany, who brought the conviction of better times with them to the New World. Most of them arrived after the Civil War, to find a booming industrial economy throughout the victorious North. They remained east along the Atlantic coast or boarded railroads that deposited them throughout the expanding frontier—in either case, opening stores, running newspapers, and (sometimes) building economic empires. A second American revolution, this one economic, industrial, and ideological, was being born.

The ideological part was a hesitance by successful entrepreneurs like the founders of Goldman Sachs, Salomon Brothers, Macy's, Levi Strauss, and the *New York Times* to think of themselves as inherent sinners dependent utterly on the beneficence of God. Most of them attended Reform synagogues, where they received a message of human capability, progress, and hope. Their Yom Kippur liturgies retained the traditional confessions, but toned down, shortened, and elaborated with other liturgical staples that affirmed human potential and called on those with power and means to invest themselves in making the world a better place. More even than the words was the ambience in which High Holy Day services were held—the elevated register of the English, the grand music emanating from a magnificent organ and choir, and the high formality of style, all of which gave an unmistakable message of the heights to which human beings might aspire. It is best seen in the *Union Prayer Book*, Reform Judaism's liturgy as of 1894—which also featured prophetic calls to use our human potential to remake the world into a just, compassionate, and loving society for all. This was a far cry from calling on God to save us because we have no good works to offer! Penitential piety was out; the piety of human potential was in.

This version of Judaism, which we nowadays call classical Reform, is insufficiently appreciated, because of what the world has become in the hundred years after the *Union Prayer Book* (the *UPB*) was promulgated. The 1890s were a heady time, and in 1894, a new century that promised nothing but continued progress was only six short years away. It was a time when all things seemed possible.

But not all things possible came to pass, and some of what came to pass was not what people had thought possible. Looking back, we can see that the *UPB*'s optimism was a monument to the past, not a manifesto for the future. Internally speaking, classical Reform Judaism did not prove sustainable. Without sufficient emphasis on Jewish particularism—a Jewish People, language, and homeland—future generations of German Jews often abandoned Judaism altogether and joined, instead, a universal alternative without the trappings of Jewish minority status. An early example was the Society for Ethical Culture, founded in 1876 by Felix Adler, who probably would have succeeded his father, Samuel Adler, as the rabbi of New York's Temple Emanu-El had he not advocated dispensing with Judaism's cultural specificity in order to concentrate instead on its universal ethics. Other options were liberal brands of Christianity—Unitarianism (later, Universal Unitarianism), for example, which underplayed its Christian doctrine and emphasized the universality of human good that classical Reform too had heralded.

But the piety of human potential was defeated by outside forces more than by inside ones, because the world of 1894 was moving anywhere but toward human betterment. The same science that gave us modern medicine produced modern weaponry, too—machine guns (1885), barbed wire (1887), tanks (1912)—and by 1914, the world was engaged in unimaginable war. A brief respite in the 1920s was replaced by international economic depression and a second world war of even more ghastly consequence. Then came word of Stalin's excesses—the purges, gulags, and indiscriminate killings of millions. By the closing decades of the twentieth century, it became more and more difficult to believe in the inevitability of progress. If the nineteenth century passed judgment on a medieval God who had failed, then the twentieth issued an even harsher verdict on humans. Maybe we were more sinful that we had thought. We were certainly incapable of delivering our own messianic age; instead, we had brought only devastation, murder, and tragedy on a scale beyond anything ever conceived in human history.

What kind of piety was even possible for an age that had failed in its human endeavor but had little capacity for throwing it back into the lap of God? That has been our challenge now for a generation or so. Can we believe in anything anymore? What anthropology of human nature do we hold?

The Piety of Authenticity and the Piety of Nobility

One of Shakespeare's greatest lines is the advice Polonius gives his nephew, Laertes, in *Hamlet*: "To thine own self be true."[4] We like its resonance with our passion for personal authenticity, a stance that has become basic to the way baby boomers and the generation after them see the world.[5] But it meant something different to Polonius than it does to us.

When Shakespeare had Polonius urge truth to oneself, he meant being authentic to the sincere and honest self that is assumed to lie below the roles one tries on as a member of society: professional, consumer, employer, neighbor, and so forth.[6] The sixteenth century was the period when society as we know it came into being, when impersonal relationships multiplied, and when people dealt with each other for what they claimed to be, in the social settings that society presupposes. It was therefore exceptionally attuned to people who pretended to be what they were not. Machiavelli positively advised it: to rule successfully, one *must* dissemble, he cautioned. The word "villain" came precisely to mean someone who never tells the truth[7]—like Hamlet's mother, of whom Hamlet says:

> O most pernicious woman!
> O villain, villain, smiling, damnèd villain!
> . . . . .
> That one may smile, and smile, and be a villain.
> (ACT 1, SCENE 5, LINES 105–8)

Originally, a villain was a rural serf, the lowest rung on the social ladder in the era that concentrated power in an upper courtier class and demanded fawning pretense from those with no power at all. The word was easily transferred to anyone at all who played at being honest, virtuous, and loyal but who was not. Shakespeare specialized in such villains, not just Hamlet's mother, but Iago, who frames Othello, and Cassius, who manipulates Brutus to join in killing Julius Caesar.

The assumption was that people customarily play roles, say what is expected of them, and do what is necessary to get ahead. "To thine own self be true" meant keeping faith with the inner and real self that lay beneath these utilitarian outward appearances.

Because the sincere soul remains true to that deeper and better self that cannot tell a lie, the second half of Polonius's advice then holds: not just "To thine own self be true," but also "It must follow, as the night the day, / Thou canst not then be false to any man."[8] It is this second half that has fallen out of fashion today. Baby boomers were raised on the virtue of inner authenticity, according to which we have the right to nurture our internal selves. But their concern was hardly that in nurturing our own authentic selves we would then be false to no one else. For boomers, the self exists for its own sake. Living an authentic life for one's own sake became the goal.

This was also a tenet enshrined in the popular understanding of Jean Paul Sartre's existentialist novel *Nausea*, which became practically a cult classic when the early boomers were going to college. Its protagonist is beset by an inexplicable fit of nausea until he admits that he is on his own in life, without history, tradition, or God to justify or guide him. "Things are entirely what they appear to be and behind them ... there is nothing."[9]

How different this is from the perspective of Judaism's *Al Chet*. For Judaism, things are not just what they appear to be, and behind them there is something else—a set of ideals, values, and the commanding presence of God.

As popularly practiced, the new authenticity has no moral force to it. It is purely expressive, a kind of romantic individualism by which individuals claim the absolute right to express themselves in order to make themselves into the people they are meant to be. Authenticity has nothing to do with remaining true to an authentic tradition of which one is a part or an authentic set of values to which one owes obedience; it may even demand that one defy tradition and the past. Its compelling appeal is evident in the commercial devised by the U.S. Army from 1980 to 2001: not a call to defend the homeland, not a moral reminder to do one's duty, but "Be all that you can be: join the Army." The new authenticity summons us to be all that we can be, whatever we think that is.

It goes hand in hand with another trend of the past several decades: self-help books and the therapeutic culture. We further ourselves, take care of ourselves, and express ourselves, because the self is the only authentic thing we have.

But if the self is all we have and if the ultimate goal is self-expression, then it is hard to see how anything can be a sin, at least in the old-fashioned sense of being an affront to God. God, as it were, becomes irrelevant. To be sure, we think other people too have the right of self-expression, so we are not completely free to do whatever we want. John Stuart Mill is famous for his utilitarian ethic that advocated "the greatest happiness for the greatest number." What we have, then, is an expressive version of utilitarianism: "the greatest self-expression for the greatest number." We "sin" against others if we let our freedom of expression hamper others in their right to be expressive also; we sin against ourselves if we do not take care of ourselves or stop short of expressing our authentic way of being all that we can be.

The result is a society of laissez-faire, self-realization, and therapeutic care. It is hard to gainsay any of the three. But one wonders whether that is all there is. Do we exhaust life's meaning by the stipulation not to encroach on the mutuality of self-expression? Is there nothing greater than nurturing our inner self? The piety of authenticity runs counter to the Jewish notion that there is something that is truly and awfully wrong, base, despicable, even loathsome, and that, by extension, there is the opposite: something supremely good, worthy, purposeful—even noble—toward which to aspire.

I began by asking whether people even believe in sin anymore. I am not sure they do, not in the sense that the liturgy does. The liturgy, as we have it, says clearly, "We are not so arrogant and insolent as to say before You, Adonai our God and our ancestors' God, we are righteous [*tzaddikim*] and have not sinned. Truly, we and our ancestors have sinned." And, as we saw (see p. 9), the original manuscript copies go farther still: they read, "We *are* so arrogant and insolent as to say before You, Adonai our God and our ancestors' God, we are righteous [*tzaddikim*] and have not sinned...." It is not just a case that we have sinned, then, but that we even wish to say that we have not.

I am not arguing for a return to penitential piety. For most of us, the Enlightenment did that in—and we should not wish to return to the Middle Ages where superstition ruled religion as much as it did everything else. But I think we have something to gain from a return to the piety of the Enlightenment, with its faith in a higher order of things, its commitment to the possibility of bettering the world, and the belief that acting for human betterment is the right and noble thing to do. It is mandated, moreover, not just offered to people as an alternative that they might find useful in their personal projects of self-realization.

In 1818 there was still no such thing as modern-day Germany. In its place were a variety of polities, including Hamburg, a free port city, independently governed and cosmopolitan in outlook, thanks to the many ships from foreign lands that docked in its harbors. By 1818, its Jews had dedicated "the New Israelite Temple," and the very next year, they issued a Reform prayer book, the first of its kind. The work evoked dismay among traditionalists and sparked an exchange of views on the limits of proper Jewish worship. Among other things, the Hamburg Temple featured regular sermons, an innovation that conservatives opposed.

One of Hamburg's founding rabbis was Gotthold Salomon, known especially for his preaching skill. His sermonic message, however, was often something on which both Reform Jews and their modern Orthodox opposition could agree. Both were children of the Enlightenment, the optimistic frame of mind that twentieth-century cruelty did so much to undermine.

We may have gone too far in rejecting Enlightenment ideals. In 1824, Rabbi Salomon published a sermon titled "What Is Our Calling?"—a manifesto for a Judaism that celebrated the nobility of the human spirit. Almost two hundred years later (despite the understandable nineteenth-century sexist reference to God), it sounds newly fresh with promise—exactly what the romantic view of authenticity as self-expression for its own sake lacks:

> All of us feel, to one extent or other, that, in spirit and soul, we belong to a higher order than the ephemeral. We feel that we are human in the most noble sense of the word … that we are closely connected to the Father of all existence, and that we could have no higher purpose than to show ourselves worthy of this relationship.[10]

We saw above how another nineteenth-century advocate of Enlightenment Judaism defined sin as "the power of evil dwelling in no other being but man." Nobility is its opposite, for, as Salomon tells us, nobility too is distinctively human. Admission of one entails admission of the other.

Our culture of expressive individualism and therapeutic care admits no sin, but then must also do without nobility. Jewish tradition has overwhelmingly urged us to take cognizance of both. Even in the days of penitential piety, our sin, though elemental, was not original. The Bible taught the doctrine of a covenant with God—yes, God, no less, who, the Rabbis argued, wanted us to be a partner in creation. No matter how far we have fallen short of God's expectations, no matter how much our sin weighed us down or kept us in debt, we were always to remember that we were made in God's image, little lower than the angels, and able to effect great change by the abundance of good deeds of which, at our best, we are capable. Perhaps we are on our way to a new piety: the possibility of sin but the parallel possibility of nobility.

Sin, Sanction, and Confession in the Bible

Dr. Marc Zvi Brettler

The Bible is rich in sin and in sin terminology. It is said that some native peoples in the Arctic have many different words for snow; similarly, the Bible has many words for sin, including, most commonly, *avon* (appearing 233 times), *pesha* (93 times), and *chet* (34 times). The words are often used interchangeably, however, making it difficult to know whether each expresses a different nuance. Etymologically, each comes from its own metaphorical sphere: *avon* is related to words for "twisting, erring"; *pesha* to "rebel"; and *chet* to "miss the mark," but once the words are formed, they take on their own meanings not necessarily related to their metaphoric origins. In any event, other words for sin—some general, others more specific—emerge as well from these and other roots.

From the biblical perspective, all people sin; in the words of Solomon's prayer (1 Kings 8:46), "There is no person who does not sin." The same inevitability of sin is expressed poetically in Psalm 51:7: "Indeed I was born with iniquity; with sin my mother conceived me"—an idea that

---

Dr. Marc Zvi Brettler is the Dora Golding Professor of Biblical Studies at Brandeis University and has published and lectured widely on metaphor and the Bible, the nature of biblical historical texts, and gender issues and the Bible. He contributed to all volumes of the *My People's Prayer Book: Traditional Prayers, Modern Commentaries* series, winner of the National Jewish Book Award, and to *My People's Passover Haggadah: Traditional Texts, Modern Commentaries, Who by Fire, Who by Water—Un'taneh Tokef,* and *All These Vows—Kol Nidre* (all Jewish Lights). He is coeditor of *The Jewish Annotated New Testament* and *The Jewish Study Bible*, which won the National Jewish Book Award; and author of *How to Read the Jewish Bible*, among other books and articles. He has also been interviewed on National Public Radio's *Fresh Air* by Terry Gross.

early Christianity would develop more fully in its concept of original sin. Recognizing this ubiquity of human frailty, the Bible offers remedies to relieve the burden; unrectified sin can weigh us down—as it does Cain, whose sin was "too heavy to carry" (Genesis 4:13)—and this burden must be relieved.

Not all these remedies continue in Rabbinic and contemporary Judaism—those dependent on the sacrificial system of the Jerusalem Temple were either stopped or modified with the Temple's destruction. But those that survived the Temple's fall and became rooted in Rabbinic Judaism found their way into the *machzor.*

With the demise of sacrifice, post-biblical Judaism developed new remedies for sin as well as new terms for the post-sacrificial system of seeking pardon. The word *t'shuvah*, for example, does appear in the Bible, but never in the sense of repentance. *T'shuvah* as repentance is a post-biblical (or, Rabbinic) term.

The concept of confession goes back to the Bible, but the Bible does not always suppose that everyone who is suffering is guilty of sins and must confess. The clearest example of this is Job, whom the book's prologue introduces as "blameless and upright; he feared God and shunned evil" (1:1, 1:8, 2:3). Much of the book's center portrays Job either asking for demonstration of his guilt or insisting on his innocence (see esp. chap. 31). Psalm 6 is similar: the complainant, who is both ill and beset with enemies (signs of God's punishing rage, presumably), objects to God's unjust anger and nowhere admits he has sinned. Instead, he offers reasons why God should assuage God's wrath: God should consider the psalmist's downtrodden position (v. 4); God should remember God's own divine *chesed* (v. 5) (a very difficult word to translate, but often rendered "loving-kindness"); God should improve the person's situation because God will thereby benefit—if God kills the psalmist, the psalmist will be unable to offer God praise (v. 6). Such psalms describe what looks like punishment but lack confession of sin. This sort of psalm is commonplace, although there are other psalms, such as Psalm 51, that recognize sins and contain confessions of it.

Sometimes, the sin is presupposed, confession is considered desirable, but the culprit fails to make amends, so punishment is deemed inevitable. According to Jeremiah 25, for example, the people of Judah have been warned for decades to repent, but they have not done so; punishment by the Babylonians is bound to follow, and confession at this late date would be of no use.

In the Bible, then, punishment inevitably occurs if sin goes unremedied. But it is equally true that people are sometimes punished through no fault of their own, as when God punishes people from following generations for their ancestors' sins—and the Rabbis will have none of that. Rabbinic Judaism is convinced that all sinners benefit from restitution for misdeeds. Hence, the tremendous power of *t'shuvah*, the Rabbinically ordained method of repentance.

But since the Bible knows sin and divine punishment, a great number of biblical texts suggest various remedies for sin, including confession. It is not confession, however, but sacrifice that is primary.

The most significant such sacrifice is the *chatat*, once translated as "sin offering," but now understood by most scholars as a purification offering. This is based on the idea that various sins make parts of the Tabernacle (the *mishkan*)—and later, the Temple—impure; these offerings, more specifically their blood, act as a ritual detergent to remove that impurity. The ritual of the high priest (described in Leviticus 16) is an annual "housecleaning," intended to "clean up" the Temple/Tabernacle from sins that continue to haunt its precincts because the requisite sacrifice was not offered at the time by the sinning individual. The day on which this happens is Yom Kippur, the Day of Purgation. This is the meaning of the Hebrew root *k.p.r*, which is also etymologically connected to "cover" (as in the notion of "covering up" sins). We understand Yom Kippur today as granting atonement for sin, not, as in Leviticus, as purging the Temple from the impurities caused by those sins. Leviticus 4, which describes the *chatat* ritual, makes it clear that the blood purifies, in and of itself. There is no mention of any accompanying word or confession.

But the Bible is a complex document, with not one but several approaches to most issues. In contrast to Leviticus 4, the great rebuke at the end of Leviticus 26 gives greater importance to confession. After subjecting Israel to ever-escalating punishments, God promises that the people will be exiled. In exile:

> Those of you who survive shall be heartsick over their iniquity in the land of your enemies; more, they shall be heartsick over the iniquities of their fathers; and they shall confess their iniquity and the iniquity of their fathers, in that they trespassed against Me, yea, were hostile to Me. When I, in turn, have been hostile to them and have removed them into the land of their enemies, then at last

> shall their obdurate heart humble itself, and they shall atone for their iniquity. (Leviticus 26:39–41)

This text favoring confession is likely from the Babylonian exile, by which time sacrifices were not, at least in exile, the road to expiation. The Babylonian exile had no Temple for people's sins to pollute, after all. So a new system for understanding forgiveness had to take effect, a system in which confession became central.

Deuteronomy 30, another text that probably derives from the Babylonian exile, also suggests non-sacrificial methods for attaining forgiveness. That text imagines Israel in exile:

> If you take them [the divine punishments] to heart amidst the various nations to which Adonai your God has banished you, and you return to Adonai your God, and you and your children heed his command with all your heart and soul, just as I enjoin upon you this day, then Adonai your God will restore your fortunes and take you back in love. (Deuteronomy 30:1b–3a)

The language of confession is missing here, but the concept of returning (*shuv*—hence, later, *t'shuvah*) is present.

So the Bible does know confession, but its confessions have no standardized form. They are never in acrostic form and are unlike, therefore, the single acrostic *Ashamnu* or the double-acrostic *Al Chet.* Confessions are still ad hoc, made up on the spot by the sinner from various synonyms related to verbs of sinning. Some are very short—for example, 2 Samuel 12:13. David sleeps with Bathsheba, impregnating her, and has her husband Uriah killed. After being confronted by the prophet Nathan, David says just two Hebrew words: *Chatati l'adonai* ("I have sinned against Adonai"). This simple confession is effective, for the prophet responds, "Adonai has indeed transferred your sin; you shall not die."

David's success stands in stark contrast to Saul's longer confession in 1 Samuel 15:24–25: "I did wrong to transgress Adonai's command and your instructions; but I was afraid of the troops and I yielded to them. Please, forgive my offense and come back with me, and I will bow low to Adonai." Neither Samuel nor God forgives; the prophet replies, "I will not go back with you; for you have rejected Adonai's command, and Adonai has rejected you as king over Israel" (v. 26). Unlike the sacrificial system of the priests, which seems to work automatically, God judges confessions on their own merit, tinged, perhaps, by divine whim.

Some sections of the Torah that emphasize sacrifice do not, however, utterly ignore confession. An individual must offer a confession along with his *asham* offering, according to Leviticus 5:5, though no formula for that confession is offered. In the Yom Kippur scapegoat ritual, "Aaron shall lay both his hands upon the head of the live goat and confess over it all the iniquities [plural of *avon*] and transgressions [plural of *pesha*] of the Israelites, whatever their sins [plural of *chata'ah*, a biform of *chet*], putting them on the head of the goat; and it shall be sent off to the wilderness through a designated man" (Leviticus 16:21). Like other priestly rituals, this text suggests that if performed properly, the ritual works automatically; in this case, the sins are transferred to the goat and thereby removed from the civilized world to the wilderness, where they will have no affect on the populace. They are literally carried away elsewhere.

The careful reader will observe that the same physical understanding of sin as something concrete that can be transferred, removed, or otherwise dispelled as something no longer present stands behind the David and Bathsheba episode in 2 Samuel 12. The text there says that after his adulterous union with Bathsheba, David's sins are "*he'evir*ed"—"moved" or "transferred," to the guiltless offspring that results. "Indeed," Nathan tells David, "the child about to be born to you will certainly die" (2 Samuel 12:14b). Four verses and seven days later, he does. So even when a biblical confession is efficacious, punishment may still result, in this case, following the principle of intergeneration retribution (see, e.g., Exodus 34:7, "visiting the iniquity of parents upon children and children's children, upon the third and fourth generations"). Chapter 24 of 2 Samuel presents a similar case. David must be punished for arranging a census of the Israelites, but pleads, "I have sinned grievously in what I have done. Please, Adonai, transfer the guilt of your servant, for I have acted foolishly" (2 Samuel 24:10b). Quite remarkably, in this case, the prophet Gad gives David three choices (vv. 12–13): seven years of famine, three months of flight before enemies, or three days of plague. The sin that David committed is assigned a certain metaphoric "weight." Each of these three punishments is the equivalent of that weight, albeit transferred to others who bear the weight on behalf of David, who had committed the weighty sin to begin with.

We see here the predominant biblical understanding of sin as deserving a punishment that is equivalent to (as heavy as) the sin itself.

This metaphor is seen again, for example, in the image of Micah 7:18–19, which is recited as the main part of the *tashlich* ceremony. The translation below is intentionally overliteral, so that the passage's metaphorical world of forgiveness becomes clear:

> Who is a God like You, who carries (away) iniquity [*avon*] and passes by transgression [*pasha*]: who has not maintained his wrath forever against the remnant of his own people, because He loves graciousness! He will return and have compassion on us; He will wash away our iniquities [plural of *avon*], You will hurl all our sins [plural of *chat'ah*] into the depths of the sea.

Here, the prophet imagines a remission, not a transfer, of sin, but here too, sin is something concrete, an actual item that can be carried, moved, removed, or transferred. Remission can be accomplished in any number of ways: God can carry the sins away (compare the scapegoat ritual) so they are no longer connected to (and no longer have an affect on) the sinner; God can pay them no attention by passing them by; God can moderate God's anger, change God's mind, exercise compassion, and forgive or ameliorate punishment; God can wash away the sins, so they disappear like a laundered stain; God can throw them far away into the water, where they will have no impact. What a wonderful conflation of images for forgiveness, even when deserving of punishment.

I began with the biblical semantics of sin; let me move for a moment to its semantics of forgiveness. God can, as we just saw, mitigate God's anger and exercise compassion. Divine punishment often has the purpose of directing people toward good, so that if they repent, God may relent (*nicham*)—as God does with the Ninevites: "God saw what they did, how they turned back from their evil ways. And God renounced [*nicham*] the punishment He had planned to bring upon them, and did not carry it out" (Jonah 3:10). Most significantly, God—and in the Bible, *only* God—can *salach* (typically rendered "pardon"). This is never a human attribute. Since we understand most divine attributes through analogy to their human equivalents—for example, divine compassion (*rachamim*) is like human compassion (but better)—it is difficult to understand the nuance of words related to *salach* other than to say that it is to pardon in a way that only God can. It is not always clear whether it implies total forgiveness, as in Micah 7:18–19 (above), or whether it still includes transferred or reduced punishment. Its use in Psalm 103:3 along with "heal" (*rofei*), "He forgives [*sole'ach*] all your sins, heals all your diseases," suggests that it may refer to complete forgiveness, comparable to complete healing.

Vidui, verbal confession, as we have it in Rabbinic Judaism, takes as a given the biblical notion of God as *salach*, "forgiving." The Rabbinic *Vidui* of our Yom Kippur liturgy also draws elsewhere on various biblical confessions. We have already seen how our liturgical *Vidui* is anticipated by David's words, "I have sinned against Adonai"—though that is in the singular, not the plural (like the Rabbinic *Vidui* of our *machzor*). We see the plural form elsewhere in the Bible, however, in Deuteronomy 1:41, for instance: after the escapades of the spies, the people confess, "*We* have sinned against Adonai." Even more comparable are three biblical confession texts that use three or more words in the plural. Psalm 106:6, a late psalm, notes, "*We* have sinned like our forefathers; *we* have gone astray, done evil." An exilic text, 1 Kings 8:47, imagines the Israelites confessing in exile: "*We* have sinned, *we* have acted perversely, *we* have acted wickedly." Daniel 9:5, from the second century BCE, one of the latest texts of the Hebrew Bible, pictures the people recounting in a more lengthy form: "*We* have sinned; *we* have gone astray; *we* have acted wickedly; *we* have been rebellious and have deviated from your commandments and your rules." This tendency of more and more lengthy confessions continues and is expressed in the two forms of *Vidui* found in our *machzor*.

Much of the Bible prefers sacrifice to confession, especially as long as the Temple stands. Some texts, especially in the Prophets, insist that people remedy their behavior, insisting on neither sacrifices nor confession:

> Wash yourselves clean; put your evil doings away from my sight. Cease to do evil; learn to do good. Devote yourselves to justice; aid the wronged. Uphold the rights of the orphan; defend the cause of the widow. (Isaiah 1:16–17)

Nonetheless, the biblical understanding of sin influences Rabbinic thought, as does its understanding of confession. The Rabbis add a great deal to what the Bible has to say, for example, changing the predominant image of sin as a burden or weight to that of sin as a monetary obligation that must be repaid. It also extends and develops the form of the biblical confessions. These developments are part of the lengthier enterprise that the Rabbis call *t'shuvah* and forms the centerpiece, therefore, of the Yom Kippur prayer service.

The Problem of Repentance

A Dilemma in Late Medieval Sephardic Preaching

Rabbi Marc Saperstein, PhD

The various formulas for confession of sin in the Yom Kippur liturgy provide the central theme of this season. They are introduced on the Sabbath preceding the Day of Atonement and continue until the shofar blast that concludes the final *N'ilah* service. That theme is *t'shuvah*, repentance. Without an awareness and articulation of sin leading to genuine remorse and a sincere appeal for forgiveness, repentance is impossible. The liturgical confession is therefore just a first step to a larger goal, just a means to an end beyond itself: the return to God, cleansed of sin and committed to a life of goodness.

Obviously, repentance is not limited to this one time of year, but this is when it becomes paramount for the entire Jewish community. It is therefore not surprising to find repentance being addressed in sermons delivered during the Days of Awe, especially on the Sabbath between

---

Rabbi Marc Saperstein, PhD, formerly principal of Leo Baeck College, currently serves as professor of Jewish history and homiletics at Leo Baeck College and as professor of Jewish studies at King's College London. Previously he taught for twenty-nine years at three leading American universities. He has published four books on the sermon as source for Jewish history and culture, and contributed to *Who by Fire, Who by Water—Un'taneh Tokef* and *All These Vows—Kol Nidre* (both Jewish Lights).

Rosh Hashanah and Yom Kippur, Shabbat Shuvah, "The Sabbath of Return."

It is worth noting that the idea of repentance, so critical to Jewish religious thought, seems to have become especially problematic for Jews in the generation of the expulsion from Spain. As part of the introduction to this volume focusing on the liturgy of sin and repentance, we do well to highlight the larger context when it came so profoundly into focus.

There seems to be no question of the importance of the doctrine of repentance to Jewish thought ever since Rabbinic Judaism began. Don Isaac Abravanel and Isaac Arama, two cultural giants of the generation of the expulsion, describe it as "the peg upon which redemption is hung, the cure for all ills and the repair of all curses."[1] Still, the extent to which it appears to have become deeply problematic for these Spanish Jews is striking. Since repentance is understood to be one of the commandments of the Torah, we are not surprised to find Jewish thinkers wondering whether to classify it as "rational" or "traditional"—a dichotomy that had been introduced by Saadiah Gaon in the early tenth century—or whether God's acceptance of repentance is an act of justice or of totally unmerited divine grace. What *is* surprising, however, is the insistence by almost all Jewish thinkers that the efficacy of repentance is *not* rational, *not* just—a decision that leaves them and their listeners in something of a quandary.

Thus, in a sermon on the theme of repentance, the mid-fifteenth-century courtier-philosopher Joseph ibn Shem Tov insists that the atonement for sins sought from God "is not according to law and justice, but rather total grace from God."[2] Among his arguments he claims that according to the standards of justice, sins against God require "punishment for eternity, without any atonement; that is the law without doubt." Rational consideration must inevitably conclude that divine pardon due to repentance cannot be justified by law; it can arrive only by divine grace and mercy.[3]

A generation later, Joseph's son, Shem Tov ibn Shem Tov—a philosopher like his father—wrote a book containing eight sermons on repentance. For him, the problem arises through the aphorisms and tales that constitute well-known Rabbinic *aggadot*, such as the statements that as a result of repentance, willful sins are transformed into merits (Talmud, Yoma 86b) and that "in the place where the penitent stand, the totally righteous cannot stand" (Talmud, Berakhot 34b). Shem Tov calls these statements "absolutely strange." Here is how he continues:

> How can it be said that perversion and evil become virtues and merits? This is something difficult to say, all the more so to believe. And how can it be said that the stature of a person who has sinned is higher than one who never sinned throughout his life and who served God truthfully and faithfully? Human reason cannot tolerate the idea that a woman who has sinned and betrayed, and then returns in repentance, can sit with the righteous women and be of a higher level than they are in holiness and purity. This is not right; it cannot be![4]

This does not sound like someone who is indulging in an intellectual exercise by making a case that he knows can be easily refuted. To me this sounds like an anguished Jew wrestling with a real problem.

After reviewing various attempts to answer this quandary by providing a plausible, rational exegesis of these statements,[5] Shem Tov eventually gives up, throwing the matter back on tradition and faith: "What the sages said, they received from the prophets and the holy spirit. It is their *tradition* that the penitent are on a higher level than the righteous and the ministering angels. But human intellect is unable to know this mystery...." The one thing he insists on is that the righteous who have no need for repentance will not be disenfranchised by the glorified status of the penitent: "There is no doubt that God will reward the righteous according to the fruit of their deeds."[6]

Isaac Arama, author of *Akedat Yitzchak*, one of the most popular and influential homiletic works of the period, discusses the aggadic dictum about "the place where the penitent stand" in a manner rather similar to Shem Tov, actually going further in specifying the conflict with philosophical tradition: "Now indeed this view conflicts with what is found in the writings of the Philosopher [Aristotle], in chapters 1 and 12 of the 7th book of the *Ethics* ... and in chapter 11 of the first book.... Maimonides, in the 6th chapter of his introduction to Avot mentioned this view [of Aristotle] and supported it with the following verse.... He then challenged [Aristotle] with the Rabbinic statements.... Then he reconciled the two positions...." But Maimonides's reconciliation is not satisfying to Arama, who ends—as does Shem Tov—unable to make peace between the two traditions: "The words of Torah and the words of philosophy are irreconcilable."[7] Unlike Shem Tov, Arama uses this conflict to expose the inadequacy of reason and philosophical analysis for him. Yet for many, this discussion would have left the Rabbinic statement about repentance as a puzzle and a problem.

Similar problems can be seen in the work of other preachers and commentators from the generation of the expulsion. Isaac Caro, uncle of the celebrated Joseph, recapitulates the position we have heard from Joseph ibn Shem Tov: "The efficacy of repentance is total grace. Why should it avail a murderer that he makes repentance? The soul of the dead person will not return to its body by means of this repentance! If one profanes the Sabbath, it will not return re-sanctified as a result of repentance! It is certainly nothing but total grace."[8] Isaac Aboab, another of the leading Talmudists of the generation, raises the same issue in strikingly similar terms in one of his sermons. By law, repentance should be of no avail. "For what is the use of repentance made with the mouth for one who has denied God through his deeds? Furthermore, who can annul the reality of things that have already occurred? Who can set right what they have perverted? ... The sages taught ... that according to reason and strict justice, the sinner should not be able to achieve atonement through a verbal utterance."[9]

Finally, we have an extraordinary discussion of repentance from a preacher known only by the title of his manuscript sermon collection, *Dover Mesharim*. The discussion is in the form of a "disputed question," one of the most characteristic modes of scholastic argumentation, which increasingly finds its way into fifteenth-century Spanish Jewish discourse. In this form, two antithetical positions on a theological question are supported with arguments from reason and authority, before a resolution is reached. Our preacher realizes that this is a controversial preaching technique, and he begins his sermon by justifying its use in the pulpit. Then he turns to the issue at hand: "Whether God forgives the penitent." Taking his cue from the theme verse of *Parashat Nitzavim*, "The Eternal will not be willing to forgive him," the preacher proceeds to bring an argument from "experience": we see in the example of Saul, that "even though he admitted his transgression and said 'I have sinned' several times, his repentance was not accepted."

More provocative is the argument from *reason*:

> Assume that God decrees at the time of the commission of the sin that the evil person shall die, or be given whatever punishment is appropriate. Then if it is true that afterward

> He decrees that the one who is supposed to die because of his sin will be pardoned, and He removes from upon him what has already been decreed, the result is that God changes from wanting something to not wanting it. But whoever thinks this has thought something monstrously heretical, attributing a significant defect to God's stature.

There follows a straightforward philosophical argument: change entails movement; movement can occur only in time; if God changes, God must be subject to time; but that is false, as God created time. In conclusion, "the assumption that God accepts the penitent entails the conclusion that God changes, and this is total heresy. Therefore, we must necessarily conclude that God does not pardon and does not accept the penitent."[10] Of course the preacher does not leave it at this; he proceeds to argue the other side and then to resolve the conflict. But why does he make such a strong argument against the efficacy of repentance to begin with?

Virtually alone, Abraham Saba insists the opposite: that the efficacy of repentance is totally rational. It seems as if he is arguing explicitly against the position we have seen: "What you say—that once a person has sinned and transgressed there is no remedy for it—that is a lie.... That was the position in which Adam erred ...; he had doubt about repentance, thinking that having sinned against God, there was no remedy ... but Cain did repentance" and Adam learned of its efficacy from Cain. And in another comment, "Therefore this passage [from *Parashat Nitzavim*] comes to remove this error from the hearts of people who think that repentance cannot benefit one who has sinned against God.... 'It is not distant' from reason, for reason requires that if one admits his sins, feels sorrow for them, and never repeats them, God will accept his repentance."[11] His very insistence on this matter indicates his recognition of a troubling problem.

What are we to make of this problematizing of repentance in the sermons and commentaries from the generation of the expulsion? What does it mean, as a cultural statement, to insist that the efficacy of repentance is irrational, in conflict with reason and justice? I have no conclusive answer, but I will suggest some possible approaches.

It is possible—though I personally do not believe it to be so—that the material I have cited might serve as evidence for what Yitzhak Baer and others, based on some contemporary sources, viewed as the corrosive effects of philosophical study on the foundations of Jewish belief. Philosophical analysis penetrates here into pulpit discourse that insists on using it as a touchstone; it thereby undermines the simple faith in one of Judaism's core values.[12]

Another possibility is that these passages reveal the power not of philosophy but of the Christian theology of grace, recalling classical Christian teachings denigrating the centrality of good deeds as a means to salvation, insisting that sins against God cannot be atoned by finite human efforts, and promising to the sinner God's favor as an expression of totally unmerited love. Thus one influential fifteenth-century Christian preacher wrote that even with one thousand mortal sins, if the person only thinks contrition and mercy, God will pardon him and he will not go to hell. God's *greatest* wonder is *incarnation*, but the second—the preacher maintains—greater even than creation of the world, is the *conversion of the sinner*.[13] If Christian theology could promise its sinners divine favor *beyond* what reason and justice could validate or explain, should Jewish teaching promise less?

A third context in which to evaluate this material is that of the conversos. Most discussions of repentance in this period have focused on this theme, analyzing the positions of Abravanel, Arama, and others on the relevance of repentance for those living as Christians.[14] Does the problem lurk in the background even of our material? Is the emphasis on the irrationality of repentance a way of appealing to the conversos—perhaps through their familiarity with the Christian doctrine—by saying that even though it makes no apparent sense, God will accept your return? Or a way of addressing the Jews who may have been thinking, "It's not *fair* that we have continued to sacrifice to live as Jews, while *they* can be on the same level, indeed even a *higher* level, simply by a deathbed repentance"?

Finally, we should realize that repentance was not the only aspect of Judaism that was being problematized in this period. Virtually *everything* about the Bible and the aggadic literature was. Abravanel and Arama are well known for their exegetical technique of raising a series of "doubts" or intellectual problems with every passage they discuss and then resolving them. What is not as well known, as I have shown in a different study, is that this technique was *omnipresent* in that generation, appearing in all of the writers I have cited, and many more, in contexts that have nothing to do with repentance.[15] Apparently, it was considered intellectually and aesthetically de rigueur to raise doubts about the tradition in this way, so long as one could provide resolutions—despite the danger that the listeners or readers might remember the doubts and forget the resolutions. In this sense as well, the discussions of repentance would be part of a larger cultural trend.

Whatever may serve best to illuminate this anguished puzzlement over repentance, the commentaries and sermons were certainly not limited to the *theory* of repentance, overlooking its practical manifestations. I end, therefore, with another brief passage from the philosopher Shem Tov ibn Shem Tov, which invokes repentance not as an intellectual problem but as a moral challenge. It is a sermon for Yom Kippur, and the preacher makes use of the afternoon haftarah from Jonah. After discussing some conceptual and exegetical matters, he makes the application to his listeners: "And now you, O congregation of Israel, hear in how many ways the repentance of the nations is different from the repentance of Israel!" As expected in the tradition of sermonic self-criticism (*tokhechah*), the Jews come off second best. Unlike the Ninevites, the Jews failed to repent despite the rebukes of many prophets.

The homiletical climax comes in the final contrast, no longer in the biblical past but in the present:

> Fourth, Israel repents only by fasting, and weeping, and affliction, but not by deeds.... No Jew has ever repented by returning what he has stolen. But the nations, before anything else, made repentance and returned what they had stolen. No, *even on this sacred fast*, every Jew seeks out a place where he will be honored. In this way, our atonement needs atonement, and this Day of Atonement needs something that will atone for the sins and the transgressions that are performed on it![16]

No matter how problematic the theory of repentance may have become, it could still serve to inspire a primary function of the preacher—in the words of Isaiah: "to tell my people its sin" (Isaiah 58:1).

Six Understandings of Confession for Our Time

Dr. Annette M. Boeckler

The history of Judaism is interwoven with confession of sin. The idea of verbal confession arises because our ancestors in the Babylonian exile (sixth century BCE) believed they were being punished for their evil behavior in pre-exilic times. The prophets, whom they had ignored, had indeed been right. God is just and powerful enough to protect the weak; they had oppressed the needy and were themselves responsible for being overrun and carried off into captivity.

Living in exile, however, they had no choice but to transform a religion dependent on land, the Davidic dynasty, Jerusalem, and the Temple to the Judaism we know today. They thus turned to verbal confessions rather than sacrifices—like the confessions we now read in Daniel (chapter 9), Nehemiah (chapter 9), and Ezra (chapter 9). This new theology of sin and punishment re-created Judaism in exile, giving us a model for a whole host of diasporas in the future—a dynamic form of Judaism that could survive without land, Temple, and Davidic kingship.

This theology works as long as one believes in a close connection between transgression and destiny. But what happens when that relationship gets thrown into question? What if history is not moral? If even personal destiny has no moral component to it? These and similar questions

---

Dr. Annette M. Boeckler is senior librarian and lecturer for Jewish biblical interpretation and Jewish liturgy at Leo Baeck College in London. She has a PhD in Bible and studied *chazanut*, both privately (with cantor Marcel Lang, *z"l*, and cantor Jeremy Burko) and at the Levisson Instituut in Amsterdam. She contributed to *All These Vows—Kol Nidre* (Jewish Lights).

appear regularly throughout time, but especially in the era that dawned with modernity. This essay provides an overview of six different ways for us to understand confessions of sins in Judaism.[1]

1. **Confessing sins to repair the world**: understanding the *Ashamnu* and *Al Chet* within a magical worldview, in which God and destiny are linked. The *vidui* is understood as having the potential to change destiny for good.
2. **Confessing sins to justify God**: understanding the *Ashamnu* and *Al Chet* as defiant trust in God despite one's destiny. The *vidui* functions as a traditional theological statement.
3. **Confessing sins to improve oneself**: understanding the *Ashamnu* and *Al Chet* as psychotherapeutical tools for personal growth. Even before psychotherapy, however, this view was possible—as a rationalist perspective on the way to amend our character. The *vidui* is here understood as a moral compass for character improvement.
4. **Confessing sins to create community among Jews**: understanding the *Ashamnu* and *Al Chet* within a group-oriented worldview. From a philosophical perspective, the *vidui* is a mystical/moral exercise that creates unity within the Jewish People and, conceivably, even beyond—that is, unity not just among people, but unity with God as well. From a less cosmic and more sociological perspective, it becomes an exercise in group dynamics that strengthens the feeling of belonging.
5. **Confessing sins to create community within humanity**: understanding the *Ashamnu* and *Al Chet* against the backdrop of philosophical universalism. The *vidui* becomes a philosophical statement about the nature of human beings.
6. **Confessing sins as poetry**: understanding the *Ashamnu* and *Al Chet* poetically, using the tools of literary analysis that derive from tracing citations in our confessions to earlier texts from the Bible on. The *vidui* is revealed as a piece of poetry to be appreciated aesthetically, the idea being that aesthetic understanding of liturgy does not necessarily demand any personal resonance with the text but is an appreciation of its sound and form.

This little essay may be upsetting in some parts, as it challenges presuppositions that are usually taken for granted, but any puzzlement that it may create is intended to point the way to new ways of appreciating it. None of these six options should be judgmentally dismissed: they all have Jewish pedigrees, so to speak, in that they have all been tried in one *machzor* or another over time, and each one has its own unique value. Each way will be introduced by providing its philosophical roots, followed by examples taken from *machzorim* of different Jewish denominations in usage today.

1. Confessing Sins to Repair the World: The Cultic/Magical View

In ancient times, things happening on earth were explained as deeds performed by gods or demons. It follows that confessing sins and performing rituals can secure a good life. In this magical worldview, confession is a natural reaction to something that goes wrong in life: an illness, a national misfortune, a natural catastrophe (e.g., floods, droughts), and so on. The confession aims to repair the breach in behavior that brought the dire circumstance to pass. It repairs the broken world that sin has occasioned, thereby addressing the misfortune that is otherwise unexplainable. In ancient times confessions accompanied sacrifices or rituals in a temple. The sacrifice or ritual was the main factor. The Torah calls these sacrifices *asham* and *chatat* (Leviticus 4:3–5:7).

Confessing sins, however, predates Judaism. It goes all the way back to the appearance of Semitic peoples, generally, in history. The oldest known confessions in humanity are Babylonian-Assyrian texts from about three thousand years ago, invoking gods to forgive—which often meant to heal from an illness or, in general, to restore a previous preferable situation, as the following Babylonian example shows:

> O warrior Marduk, whose anger is the deluge,
> whose relenting is that of a merciful father,
>
> . . . .
>
> Who has not been negligent,
> which one has not committed no sin?
> Who can understand a god's behavior?...
> Forget what I did in my youth, whatever it was,
> let your heart not well up against me!
> Absolve my guilt, remit my punishment,
> Clear me of confusion, free me of uncertainty,

> Let no guilt of my father, my grandfather,
> my mother, my grandmother,
> my brother, my sister,
> my family, kith or kin
> approach my own self, but let it be gone!...
> O warrior Marduk, absolve my guilt, remit my guilt!...
> Like my real father and my real mother
> Let your heart be reconciled to me.
> O warrior Marduk, let me sound your praises![2]

This particular text does not provide the reason for the confession, but elsewhere, Babylonian confessions often contain something like, "A terrible headache has come over me" or "This and that illness or disaster has happened to me or my family." There then follows the confession as a prayer for healing.

The Bible partly shares this worldview. During a drought, for example, the prophet Jeremiah prayed:

> Nobles sent their servants for water; they came to the cisterns, they found no water. They returned, their vessels empty.... Though our iniquities testify against us, act, Adonai, for the sake of your name; though our rebellions are many and we have sinned against You. (Jeremiah 14:3, 14:7)

A similarly motivated confession can be found in King Solomon's Temple dedication prayer (1 Kings 8:33–39), where he lists all kinds of disasters for which confessions may be appropriate, and asks God to accept any such future confessions that may be uttered in this Temple. Both Jeremiah and Solomon believed that deeds are linked to destiny: bad things are punishments, and confessing sins can rectify fate.

An example of this way of understanding today is the Orthodox view expressed in the ArtScroll edition of the *Vidui*:

> Every good deed has a reward, and every bad deed a punishment.... Everything we do has a consequence and, more often than not, a chain of consequences, though often they are not readily apparent. A wise political or economic decision may not bear fruit for years. In the realm of

> Mitzvah-performance, too, we hardly ever see the results immediately. Sin is not punished by a bolt of lightning and virtue is not acknowledged by nuggets falling from heaven. It takes a great deal of time, both in this world and in the next, for God's accounts to be settled.[3]

2. Confessing Sins to Justify God: The Traditional Theological View

During the Babylonian exile (sixth century BCE), our ancestors would meet to fast, lament, and recite confessions of sins.[4] The late biblical book of Daniel is a story told about someone said to be in exile. It uses models of confession that had been pioneered there. Eventually, it was used as a model for our *Ashamnu*:

> We have sinned; we have gone astray; we have acted wickedly; we have been rebellious and have deviated from your commandments and your rules, and have not obeyed your servants the prophets who spoke in your name to our kings, our officers, our fathers, and all the people of the land. With You, Adonai, is the right, and the shame is on us to this very day, on the men of Judah and the inhabitants of Jerusalem, all Israel, near and far, in all the lands where You have banished them, for the trespass they committed against You." (Daniel 9:5–7)

For Daniel, who lives in exile, there is no Temple, so prayer cannot accompany sacrifice; words alone must suffice, as they do for us. At stake here is not just the misfortune of being carted off to exile, but the spiritual crisis that resulted from that historical episode, which had shaken the foundations of the previous theology to the point of destroying them. God had promised King David, "Your throne will be established forever" (2 Samuel 7:16)—and this "forever" had only lasted from 1004 to 586 BCE. Now a Babylonian king ruled over Israel. God's presence was believed to be in the Temple, but that Temple, God's very home, was now destroyed. Jerusalem was believed to be under God's special protection (cf. Psalm 48), and now it lay in ruins.

The ancient default position in such a situation would have been to stop worshiping one's own weak god (who had apparently been defeated) and begin worshiping the obviously stronger gods of the conquerors. The Israelites in exile, however, retained their religion by taking personal responsibility for their destiny. Based on the prophecies of former prophets—who had been rejected in their lifetimes—the Israelites regarded themselves not as forsaken victims, but as responsible sinners. Their confession of sins was a justification of God. And according to the prophets, words were indeed a valid replacement for the sacrifices that were no longer even possible (cf. Hosea 14:3; Amos 5:22–25; Micah 6:6–8; Isaiah 1:11–17; Jeremiah 7:22–23). As recited by Jews in exile, the *Vidui* expresses the longing to return to the Land of Israel. Because of our sins we are banished from it, but God may forgive us, bring us back, restore God's presence among us, and reinstate the Davidic dynasty and God's own power in God's own land.

Traditional Jewish liturgy expresses this theology, not in terms of the first exile but in terms of the second. What goes for the Babylonian destruction of the First Temple goes equally for the Roman destruction of the Second. We are in exile no less than our Babylonian forebears were. We too are at fault, and we too must confess our sins if we are to be reinstated in our land.

The traditional *Musaf Amidah* for the High Holy Days therefore says:

> Because of our sins we have been exiled from our land and removed far away from our country, and we are unable to perform our duties in the house of thy choice, the great and holy house called by thy Name, because of the hand that hath been stretched out against thy sanctuary. May it be thy will, Adonai our God and God of our fathers, merciful King, again in thine abundant mercy to have compassion upon us and upon thy sanctuary; O speedily rebuild it and magnify its glory.... Lead us in triumph unto Zion thy city, and unto Jerusalem, the place of thy sanctuary, with everlasting joy.[5]

3. Confessing Sins to Improve One's Character: The Rationalist/Spiritual View

In the Islamic culture of the twelfth century, the state-of-the-art natural science of the time was based on the rationalistic views of the ancient Greek philosopher Aristotle, who had been translated into Arabic. Moses

Maimonides (1135–1204) did what progressive Judaism followed six hundred years later: he tried to combine Jewish tradition with modernity. He adapted the scientific views of his time and shared the Aristotelian belief that God is perfect and therefore beyond the simple sort of deity who might be cajoled into changing God's mind. This rationalist position threw the whole notion of prayer as petition into question and required a new rationale for confession. Maimonides therefore regarded the publicly proclaimed confession as a fixed part of personal *t'shuvah*; its purpose was not to impact God but to change the character of the worshiper:

> If an individual transgresses any commandment of the Torah, whether it be a positive commandment or a negative commandment, whether it be on purpose or accidentally, when he repents and turns away from his sin, he is obligated to confess his guilt before the Holy One of Blessing, as it is written, "And they shall confess their guilt for their transgression" [Numbers 5:7]; this is a confession of guilt with words. This confession of guilt is a positive commandment. How does one confess his guilt? He says, "Please, O Lord [*ana Adonai*], I have sinned [*chatati*], I have transgressed [*aviti*], I have rebelled before You [*pashati l'fanekha*], and I have done such and such [*v'asiti kakh v'khakh*]. Behold, I am remorseful and I am shamed by my deeds. I shall never return to this action." This is the main part of verbal confession, and expanding on it is praiseworthy.[6]

This confession, Maimonides further explains, must be said with the right attitude—that is, with shame and contrition and the honest intention to change one's ways of acting in the future. One should confess in public and describe the sin in detail.[7]

To be sure, Maimonides does not say expressly here that the impact of confession is purely a change in the worshiper, but he never says that God will be changed by it either. In principle, however, his position is clear. Confession alters the character of the confessor.

The latest American Conservative *machzor, Mahzor Lev Shalem*, concurs, in a marginal gloss to *Ashamnu*:

> The liturgical list is alphabetical, with the hope that it will help us find our own words to name our transgressions.

> We might concentrate on one particular failing in our lives.[8]

Or, in other words, in a gloss next to *Al Chet*:

> No list of sins can ever be complete. By beginning with *alef* and ending with *tav*, we express our intention to include in our confession everything of which we are guilty, from A to Z. However, this form of the Al Het does not relieve us of our individual obligation to confess the particular sins of which we are each personally responsible.[9]

The British Reform *machzor, Forms of Prayer (Seder Ha-T'fillot)*, volume 3, is more precise. Each *Vidui* during Yom Kippur is provided with a short reflection, where the characterological notion of confession is explicit. Confession is all about personal healing and enlightenment:

> Before a man is healed, he must acknowledge his illness.
> Before a woman is healed, she must acknowledge her illness.
> Before a person finds light he/she must know his/her own darkness.
> Before a people is forgiven it must confess its sins.[10]

This *machzor* provides many modern versions of confessions newly designed to deal with today's issues. They are intended as a checklist for our behavior during the past year and a goad to improve our behavior in the future. The new texts sometimes conflate both old and modern poetry,[11] but also provide altogether new creations, like this one:

> We ask Your pardon not only for the great sins, but for the small ones as well.... For not listening to Your voice within us, for denying the needs of our soul, for making this world a god: Forgive us, pardon us and grant us atonement. For not doing ourselves justice, for giving our money and withholding ourselves, for shrugging our shoulders: Forgive us, pardon us and grant us atonement. For passing the blame to others, for using them for our own ends, for not taking responsibility: Forgive us, pardon us and grant

> us atonement. For not growing up, for believing only in this life, for forgetting eternity: Forgive us, pardon us and grant us atonement.[12]

Vidui here becomes an individualistic meditation provoking deep personal self-reflection, the rationalist-characterological approach of Maimonides transformed by modern psychology into an exercise in self-betterment.

The *machzor* of the American Reform congregations, *Gates of Repentance*, expresses this psychological perspective clearly:

> In my individuality I turn to You, O God, and seek your help.... Therefore while around me others think their own thoughts, I think mine.[13]

Gates of Repentance also provides a more cosmic understand of the Yom Kippur confessions in that they are also steps on the way back to the original praise of God in the time of creation. Renewal of self becomes a mirror image of an entire universe renewed, a case of positioning oneself as part of the purity that characterized a bygone era. The service titled "From Creation to Redemption" reveals this intent. The purpose of confessing sins from this higher framework of thought is "that the House of Israel, purified, reconciled, and reconsecrated, may again become worthy to stand in Your presence, and to be the messenger of Your word, O Eternal God, God Most High."[14]

This characterological understanding of confession begins, therefore, in Maimonides and medieval philosophical rationalism but continues in our own psychological understanding of human nature. Interestingly, its accent on personal process can at the same time turn into a spiritual exercise, too. The *machzor* of an American Jewish Renewal congregation, *Machzor Eit Ratzon*, therefore suggests an alternative to *Al Chet*, called *Al Hamitzvot*, which is said to care for the development of our souls by reflecting on the virtues we have achieved. It sounds like a modern educational approach to improve character by highlighting our strengths, not focusing on our mistakes:

> For the righteous deeds we have done before you: ... in feeding the hungry ... in sheltering the homeless ... in raising the spirits of those who were depressed ... in helping those in need of assistance ... in telling the truth when that

> was appropriate ... in remaining silent when the truth was hurtful ... in helping to fix the world ... in giving tzedakah ... in walking humbly before God ... in seeking justice for the oppressed ... in pursuing peace ... in standing up for ourselves ... in standing up for others ... in honoring our elders ... in honoring our teachers ... in helping other people's parents ... in treating other people with respect ... in affirming the divine in every person ... in acknowledging our blessings ... in thanking You for them regularly ... in feeling awe at the world you created ... in asking for Your assistance ... in asking what You expect of us ... in seeking Your counsel ... in avoiding harmful speech ... in living modestly ... in reflection on our actions ... in improving our behavior ... in respecting the laws of the land ... in working to change the laws of the land ... in envisioning a better world and working to achieve it ... in using our resources wisely ... in taking care of our world ... in taking care of ourselves ... in taking care of our families ... in expanding our Jewish education ... in observing our traditions ... in challenging our traditions ... in contributing to our communities ... in strengthening our institutions ... in supporting our people in Israel and elsewhere ... [others may be added here]. For all of these righteous deeds, God of righteousness, let us be counted among the righteous.[15]

4. Confessing Sins to Create Community among Jews: The Mystical/Moral View

Mystical expressions of religion stress the nature of religion as relationships, both with God and with fellow believers. Yitzchak ben Shlomo Luria Ashkenazi (or, the *A*shkenazi *R*abbi *I*tzchak, the *Ari*; 1524–1572) therefore asked:

> Why was the confession couched in the plural form so that we say, "We have sinned," and not "I have sinned"? This is because all Israel is one body, and each individual Jew is a limb of this body. And when his fellow commits a sin, it is as if he himself had committed it. Therefore, even if he has not committed any particular sin he must confess it, for when his fellow sins, it is as if he himself had transgressed.[16]

Samson Raphael Hirsch (1808–1888), the founder of modern Orthodoxy, continued this way of thinking but added a moral aspect, thus sharing the typical moral understanding of religiosity of the nineteenth century: *Ashamnu* is a kind of checklist of possible sins that helps us discover the sins we have actually committed, as well as the sins of which others may be guilty but which we might have prevented them from doing:

> The confession of sins ... is an enumeration of all the many sins and errors known to mankind. It is entirely in the plural form. For these are sins which certainly will not be lacking in the collective life of the community of Yisrael as such. Moreover, in keeping with the principle "All Israelites are responsible for one another" (*Kol yisrael arevim zeh lazeh*), even he who is not aware of having been guilty of such a sin himself should seriously consider whether he himself had not sinned by neglecting to do anything in his power that might have kept his fellow-Jew from committing the transgression. For, according to our Sages, may they rest in peace [Talmud, Avodah Zarah 4a, Shabbat 55a], all those who, though by no means sure that such attempts on their part would have ended in failure, have not even tried to restrain their brother from wrongdoing by warning and exhortation, share in their brother's sin.[17]

Ashamnu, especially, lists sins that the average person certainly did not commit, but by mentioning them, each individual links him- or herself to the community of *k'lal yisrael* ("all Jewry") and becomes conscious of the sins the commission of which he or she could have prevented but did not.

A *machzor* that follows this approach is the Reconstructionist movement's *Kol Haneshamah*. It explains *Al Chet* by saying:

> It is customary for people to gently tap their chests with their fists once for each transgression of the *Vidui*. Even though the *Vidui* is stated in the plural, this tapping reminds us that each of us must ask ourselves not only which of these sins we have committed, but which of these sins we have failed to prevent others from committing.[18]

Many Progressive and Conservative *machzorim* combine this moral understanding with the individualistic one just described. The British Reform *machzor* ends the reflection before each *Vidui* with:

> We can confess our sins and those of our fellowmen/
> fellow women,
> for we are responsible each for the other.[19]

5. Confessing Sins to Create Community within Humanity: The Universal View

Franz Rosenzweig (1886–1929), too, stressed the collective aspect of confession, but enlarged the collective to include the whole of humanity:

> And so "We" in whose community the individual recognizes his sin, can be nothing less than the congregation of mankind itself.... For everyone is a sinner.[20]

The confessing congregation is, according to Rosenzweig, not narrowly particularistic. Rather, through confession of all manner of sins that reflect human weakness in general, it asserts its solidarity with humanity as a whole.[21] Confession thereby teaches us our place in humanity and the more expansive meaning of human life that comes from our understanding of ourselves as universals created by God. This understanding of sin may sound similar to many Christian understandings of sin because it may emphasize sin as a state of being that results in bad deeds, rather than simply the deeds themselves.

Jewish prayer books that adopt this view tend to combine it with Hirsch's statement of universal responsibility. The British Liberal *Machzor Ruach Chadashah* tries somewhat to do so. It balances personal reflection with universal consideration for the nature of society as a whole, stressing our ethical responsibilities toward others. One of its newly composed confessions says:

> The Day of Atonement demands that we examine not only our personal lives, but also the life of the society about us. Before God we must confess our share of responsibility for the evils which destroy its harmony and inflict hardship and loneliness on so many of its members.[22]

The American Conservative *Mahzor Lev Shalem* ends its explanation on *Al Chet* with the following:

> And we are also called upon to contemplate those sins which are especially prevalent in our world today.[23]

6. Confessing Sins as Poetry: The Literary View

Ashamnu is not an isolated text. It is embedded in a context that enables it to draw meaning from the texts that precede it.

In its traditional context, *Ashamnu* is preceded by a prayer by Mar Zutra, "Let our prayer come before You" (Talmud, Yoma 87b). It contains the core sentence that in any case has to be said to make a "valid" confession: "But we have sinned" (*aval anachnu chatanu*).[24] According to its literary context, *Ashamnu* functions as poetic embellishment of this statement. More than simple affirmation, however, the list demonstrates that our sins do not originate solely with ourselves, because each and every one of them was committed first by our ancestors. That message is provided by the simple fact that none of the transgressions is made up *de novo*—each and every one of them is drawn from biblical citations, generally prophetic or other accusations of Israel in biblical times.[25]

It is not our personal sins that we list therefore, but the sins that represent the tradition of our ancestors who did all this long before we did. They were consequently banished from their land, just as we are, according to the traditional perspective that sees us living in exile once again.

We normally like to refer to our ancestors positively, emphasizing, that is, the positive aspects of the tradition that they have bequeathed us. We say, "As their children, we have inherited their spiritual legacy."[26] Our confessions provide the negative side of that equation, because part of this legacy is our ancestors' sins.

Traditional liturgy provides this perspective. A model prayer book from which we might cite is the classic compilation *Seder Avodat Yisrael*, edited by Seligman Baer in 1868. It has an extensive scholarly commentary in the vein of nineteenth-century scholarship; for twelve of the twenty-four sins of *Ashamnu* a biblical proof text is given.[27]

After *Ashamnu*, we get a quote from Nehemiah 9:33, one of the prayers of the people in the Babylonian exile: "Surely You are in the right with respect to all that has come upon us, for You have acted faithfully, and we have been wicked."

The transition to *Al Chet* is made by a medieval poem by Solomon ibn Gabirol (*Malkhut Keter*) and by Rav's prayer (Talmud, Yoma 87b)—the one we use, stating, "You know the secrets of the universe, and the hidden enigmas of all that lives"; then follows *Al Chet* with its litany describing the motivations for sins, presented in the typical format of medieval penitential lists.

Seen from a literary perspective, *Ashamnu* is the echo of the ancestors of antiquity, and *Al Chet* is the voice of medieval Jews. One can regard these texts as literature without feeling any need to update them with one's own shortcomings. As poetry, the liturgy becomes akin to the great poems of world literature: some speak to us, others don't.

Conclusion

Each of these six different ways of understanding confession has had its own value in certain times and circumstances. Our task is to find the one that best fits our own era. The high priest in the Temple confessed three times on the Day of Atonement, once very personally for himself, once very particular only for his family, and then once again, generally, for all Israel. We too may find different approaches to *Ashamnu* and *Al Chet* both possible and necessary.

Al Chet in Israeli Culture

Israeli Confessions over Everything

Rabbi Dalia Marx, PhD

In Elul of 1890, the month of repentance and introspection then as now, a sensitive and imaginative seventeen-year-old from a village in the Pale of Settlement (today's Ukraine) wrote a desperate letter to his teachers and friends. Having just recently arrived at the Volozhin Yeshivah, the prestigious Lithuanian house of study, sometimes referred to as the "mother of all yeshivahs," the young man was depressed, lonely, and disappointed. He had left home hoping to obtain a comprehensive modern Jewish education, only to discover that Volozhin provided only little beyond traditional Talmudic studies. The boy's name was Chayim Nachman Bialik, later to be referred to as the national poet of the State of Israel. Toward the end of his lengthy letter, Bialik included a heart-wrenching confession of his inner state of being that began with the conviction that "my heart is dying within me."

Rabbi Dalia Marx, PhD, is a professor of liturgy and midrash at the Jerusalem campus of Hebrew Union College–Jewish Institute of Religion and teaches in various academic institutions in Israel, the United States, and Europe. Rabbi Marx earned her doctorate at the Hebrew University in Jerusalem and her rabbinic ordination at HUC–JIR in Jerusalem and Cincinnati. She is involved in various research groups and is active in promoting progressive Judaism in Israel. Rabbi Marx contributed to *Who by Fire, Who by Water—Un'taneh Tokef* and *All These Vows—Kol Nidre* (both Jewish Lights). She writes for academic journals and the Israeli press, and is engaged in creating new liturgies and midrashim.

[1] מת לבי בקרבי... וגם אני הנני הולך למות... [2] קצתי בחיי ואהיה עלי למשא... אך אתודה־נא טרם מותי, [3] אתן תודה על שגיאותי וחטאי, כי מודה ועוזב יְרחם, [4] אכה כף על ירך ואתופף על לבי ואומר: על חטא שחטאו אבותי באנס וברצון, [5] ועל חטא שחטאו לפנַי באמוץ הלב; [6] על חטא שחטאו לפני בבלי דעת, [7] ועל חטא שחטאו לפני בגלוי שבסתר... [8] וע"ח שחטאו לפני בדעת ובמרמה, [9] וע"ח שחטאו הורי ומורי בזלזולי, [10] וע"ח שחטאו בחזק־יד, [11] וע"ח שחטאו בטפשות הלב, [12] וע"ח שחטאתי ביודעים ובלא יודעים, [13] ועל כלם אֱלוֹהַּ סליחות סלח להם, מחל להם, כפר להם.

[1]My heart has died within me ... and I am going to die.... [2]My life has become loathsome and a burden ... but let me confess before I die. [3]I'll offer confession for my mistakes and sins, because confession and renunciation bring mercy. [4]With solemnity and reverence I say: "For the sin my ancestors committed through force or through choice, [5]for the sin they committed against me through haughtiness of heart, [6]for the sin they committed against me through lack of knowledge, [7]for the sin they committed against me through the exposed within the concealed ... [8]for the sin they committed against me through knowledge and through deceit, [9]and for the sin my parents and teachers committed through demeaning me, [10]and for the sin they committed through strength of hand, [11]and for the sin they committed through foolish hearts, [12]and for the sin I committed through knowledge and through lack of knowledge: [13]for all of these, God of forgiveness, forgive them, pardon them, absolve them.

[Editor's note: We are grateful to the authors of the Hebrew texts cited here for allowing us to include their work. Their Hebrew was translated into English by Dr. Joel M. Hoffman, after which, when requested, we altered the translations to accord with author preferences. We apologize for any instances in which we fail to reproduce the fullness of the original Hebrew or where we may have misconstrued the author's intentions.]

[14]and for the sins for which my punishment is a burnt offering ...	[14]ועל חטאים שאני עולה עליהם עולה כליל...
[15]and for the sins for which my punishment is not a sin offering ...	[15]ועל חטאים שלא אני חיב עליהם חטאת...
[16]and for the sins for which my punishment is to go lower and lower ...	[16]ועל חטאים שנתחיבתי עליהם רק יורד ויורד...
[17]and for the sins for which my parents' punishment surely is a guilt offering	[17]ועל חטאים שהורי בודאי חייבים עליהם אשם.
[18]and for the sins for which I was subjected in this life to lashings and beatings, whether I deserved it or I didn't deserve it: for all of these, forgive and pardon and absolve them, for you are the one who forgives and pardons etc. etc. etc.	[18]ועל חטאים שהֻכיתי בחיים מלקות ומכות מרדות, בין שהייתי חיָב, ובין שלא הייתי חיָב[...] על כלם תסלח ותמחול ותכפר להם, כי אתה סלחן ומחלן וכו' וכו' וגו'.[1]

Young Bialik did not die. Shortly after sending off his desperate letter, he moved to Odessa, the cultural capital for Eastern European Jewry, and eventually emigrated to Israel. The productive poet, journalist, translator, and editor passed away in 1934.

Let us look more carefully at Bialik's distress letter. The talented youth could have expressed his feelings in many ways, yet in order to convey his pain, he used the format of the *Vidui*, the traditional Jewish confession that he knew so well from his years of attending synagogue. But the way he used the traditional language does the opposite of what the *Vidui* is meant to do—instead of beating on his own chest seeking atonement and forgiveness, he used the long-established formula as a charge sheet to accuse his parents and teachers.

He turns the traditional line "for the sin we have committed through demeaning parents and teachers" to "for the sin my parents and teachers committed through demeaning me." Thinking about domestic offenses and abuse, I find the line "for the sin they committed against me through the exposed within the concealed" especially unsettling. What, one wonders, are those sins that the adults in Bialik's life committed against him "through the exposed within the concealed"? In this long list, he puts himself in the place of the victim, the object against whom the sins and transgressions were committed.

Bialik was transforming the *Vidui* into a parody of itself. He deliberately denied the original content of the text while maintaining its form and structure, thereby creating a thought-provoking tension between substance and form.

Was the bright but still young poet-to-be doing it deliberately, hoping to evoke from his reader a sense of unease, or was he doing it unconsciously, just accessing automatically the language he knew, the linguistic and poetic arsenal of prayer that he "owned" as a matter of course? I believe both possibilities may apply. As the following examples show, Bialik was not alone in his very untraditional use of a very traditional poetic staple. *Ashamnu* and *Al Chet* have become part of the Jew's natural idiom, a sort of foundational "inner language," as it were, for those who recite them annually at the holiest occasions in the Jewish year, and even to those who don't.

The following pages discuss some new versions of *Al Chet*, created in recent years in Israel. The texts, written in very different styles and literary capabilities, reflecting diverse agendas, reveal an interesting phenomenon: Israelis need the classic liturgical religious language even when they want to say utterly non- (and sometimes even anti-) religious things.

Before we turn to the less expected versions, let us turn to *Al Chet* as it appears in the Israeli Reform *machzor*, *Kavanat Halev* (1991). Due to the length of the traditional *Vidui,* the editors kept its alphabetical order but printed only one line per letter (not the double acrostic, typical of traditional Ashkenazi liturgy). In keeping with Reform theology, which severs our contemporary connection to the sacrificial cult of old, they also omitted the lines referring to various offerings of Temple times.

In the concluding service (*N'ilah*) of Yom Kippur, two alternative confessions are added; the first is a modern composition by Rabbi Moti Rotem, the first Reform rabbi to be ordained in Israel. Its content differs little from the traditional text and the alphabetical acrostic but it uses modern language and contemporary symbolic idioms:

1 We closed our ears to the cry of the poor and wretched.	1 אָטַמְנוּ אָזְנֵינוּ מִזַּעֲקַת דַּל וְאֻמְלָל.
2 We disdained people of honesty and integrity.	2 בָּזִנוּ לִישַׁר דֶּרֶךְ וּנְקִי כַפַּיִם.
3 Our heart was haughty.	3 גָּבַהּ לִבֵּנוּ.
4 We excluded good manners from our lives.	4 דָּחִינוּ דֶּרֶךְ אֶרֶץ מֵחַיֵּינוּ.
5 We agreed with entrenched power holders.	5 הִסְכַּמְנוּ עִם בַּעֲלֵי מֵאָה.
6 We gave up on holiness.	6 וִתַּרְנוּ עַל הַקְּדֻשָּׁה.
7 We sanctified the golden calf.	7 זָבַחְנוּ לְעֵגֶל הַזָּהָב.
8 We set our sights on "only by might and only by power."	8 חָרַטְנוּ עַל דִּגְלֵנוּ "רַק בְּחַיִל וְרַק בְּכֹחַ".
9 We daubed with plaster the flimsy chambers of our hearts.	9 טַחְנוּ תָּפֵל אֶת חַדְרֵי לְבָבֵנוּ.
10 We were able but unwilling.	10 יָכֹלְנוּ אַךְ לֹא רָצִינוּ.
11 We dug a pit for those who walk in innocence.	11 כָּרִינוּ בּוֹר לִתְמִימֵי דֶרֶךְ.
12 We stared with enmity at others.	12 לָטַשְׁנוּ עַיִן אֶל זוּלָתֵנוּ.
13 We were quick to raise our voices and our hands with aggression.	13 מִהַרְנוּ לְהָרִים קוֹל וָיָד.
14 We took advantage of every opportunity to exploit.	14 נִצַּלְנוּ כָּל הִזְדַּמְּנוּת לְנַצֵּל.
15 We were self-satisfied.	15 סָמַכְנוּ עַל עַצְמֵנוּ.
16 We worshiped foreign idols.	16 עָבַדְנוּ אֱלִילֵי נֵכָר.
17 We were afraid to proclaim the truth out loud.	17 פָּחַדְנוּ לְהַכְרִיז עַל הָאֱמֶת בְּקוֹל.
18 We laughed at and mocked the unfortunate.	18 צָחַקְנוּ וְלָעַגְנוּ לָרָשׁ.
19 We sanctified the unholy and the materialistic.	19 קִדַּשְׁנוּ אֶת הַחוֹל וְאֶת הַחֹמֶר.
20 We saw and did not testify.	20 רָאִינוּ וְלֹא הֵעַדְנוּ.
21 We forgot what was not convenient to remember.	21 שָׁכַחְנוּ אֶת שֶׁלֹּא נָעַם לָנוּ לִזְכֹּר.
22 We reached for more but ended up with less.	22 תָּפַשְׂנוּ מְרֻבֶּה לֹא תָפַשְׂנוּ.[2]

The second text is by teacher and poet Aryeh Uri, a member (and undertaker, in fact) of Kibbutz Maagan Michael. The poem is titled *Tachanun* ("Supplication"):

[1]On the eve of holidays and
before battles
[2]He would recount his sins
[3]For the sin I have committed
[4]While of sound mind
[5]That I didn't dare to reach out
[6]That I didn't listen to all sounds
[7]That I didn't care for children
[8]For my sin of not tasting all wines
[9]That I didn't abhor trivialities
[10]That I didn't decode secrets
[11]That I didn't rise above anxieties
[12]For my sin of not wiping the
tears of babies
[13]That I didn't listen to silence
[14]That I didn't discern between
desires
[15]For my sin of not loving all loves
[16]For my sin of not cheering up
the afflicted
[17]That I didn't do the bidding of
the elderly
[18]For my sin of silencing the
screams

[1]בְּעֶרֶב מוֹעֵד וּבְטֶרֶם קְרָב
[2]הָיָה מוֹנֶה אֶת חֲטָאָיו
[3]עַל חֵטְא שֶׁחָטָאתִי
[4]בְּיִשּׁוּב הַדַּעַת
[5]שֶׁלֹּא הֵעַזְתִּי לָגַעַת
[6]שֶׁלֹּא הֶאֱזַנְתִּי לְכָל הַצְּלִילִים
[7]שֶׁלֹּא טִפַּחְתִּי אֶת הָעוֹלָלִים
[8]עַל חֵטְא שֶׁלֹּא טָעַמְתִּי מִכָּל
הַיֵּינוֹת
[9]שֶׁלֹּא בַּזְתִּי לְקַטְנוּנוֹת
[10]שֶׁלֹּא פִּעְנַחְתִּי אֶת הַסּוֹדוֹת
[11]שֶׁלֹּא גָּבַרְתִּי עַל הַחֲרָדוֹת
[12]עַל חֵטְא שֶׁלֹּא מָחִיתִי
דִּמְעַת הַתִּינוֹקוֹת
[13]שֶׁלֹּא הִקְשַׁבְתִּי לַשְּׁתִיקוֹת.
[14]שֶׁלֹּא הִבְחַנְתִּי בֵּין הַתַּאֲווֹת
[15]עַל חֵטְא שֶׁלֹּא אָהַבְתִּי אֶת
כָּל הָאֲהָבוֹת
[16]עַל חֵטְא שֶׁלֹּא שִׂמַּחְתִּי אֶת
הַנַּעֲנִים
[17]שֶׁלֹּא קִיַּמְתִּי דְּבָרָם שֶׁל הַזְּקֵנִים
[18]עַל חֵטְא שֶׁשָּׁתַקְתִּי אֶת
הַזְּעָקוֹת

[19]For my sin of not mocking smooth talkers	[19]עַל חֵטְא שֶׁלֹּא בָּזִיתִי אֶת דּוֹבְרֵי הַחֲלָקוֹת
[20]For my sin of not plucking musical strings	[20]עַל חֵטְא שֶׁלֹּא פָּרַטְתִּי עַל הַמֵּיתָרִים
[21]For my sin of not being startled by hidden crying	[21]עַל חֵטְא שֶׁלֹּא נֶחֱרַדְתִּי לַבְּכִי בַּמִּסְתָּרִים
[22]For my sin of not remembering that we can't forget	[22]עַל חֵטְא שֶׁלֹּא זָכַרְתִּי אֶת שֶׁאֵין לִשְׁכֹּחַ
[23]For my sin of not forgetting in order to forgive.	[23]עַל חֵטְא שֶׁלֹּא שָׁכַחְתִּי כְּדֵי לִסְלֹחַ.[3]

The speaker in this poem regrets not living life to its fullest, not exhausting the pleasures, feelings, and excitement that life has to offer ("For the sin of not tasting all wines"), but simultaneously, he laments not being more attentive to the sufferings of others ("For the sin of not wiping the tears of babies"). This is not an explicitly religious text in the narrow sense of the word, and there is nothing essentially Jewish about it. Yet, the poem acknowledges some manner of (divine?) judgment, for it begins with a person who would count his sins "on the eve of holidays and before battles"—intertwining and juxtaposing sacred holidays and the battlefield. In a way, the Day of Atonement is a kind of battle,[4] and going to the battle is a form of being judged. The Israeli experience brings to mind the somber memories specifically of the Yom Kippur War in 1973.[5]

The kibbutz movement was once the bastion of the socialist and secular young State of Israel. And yet, some of the boldest and most creative expressions of religiosity nested within it. Mekhon Shitim, the archive and educational center of the kibbutz movement, located on Kibbutz Bet Hashitah, has recently published a version of *Al Chet*, titled "Confession for Our Time":

[1]For the sin we have committed through violence,
[2]And for the sin we have committed through cold-heartedness.
[3]For the sin we have committed through wasting natural resources,
[4]And for the sin we have committed through ignoring Israel's treasures.
[5]For the sin we have committed through haughtiness,
[6]And for the sin we have committed through racism.
[7]For the sin we have committed through suppressing the other,
[8]And for the sin we have committed through rejecting efforts for peace.
[9]For the sin we have committed through privatization,
[10]And for the sin we have committed through violating human rights.
[11]For the sin we have committed by abandoning values,
[12]And for the sin we have committed through squabbling.
[13]For the sin we have committed through demeaning parents and teachers,
[14]And for the sin we have committed through the degradation of human life.
[15]For the sin we have committed through materialism,

[1]על חטא שחטאנו באלימות,
[2]ועל חטא שחטאנו באטימות לב.
[3]על חטא שחטאנו בבזבוז משאבי טבע,
[4]ועל חטא שחטאנו בבורות באוצרות עם ישראל.
[5]על חטא שחטאנו בגאווה,
[6]ועל חטא שחטאנו בגזענות.
[7]על חטא שחטאנו בדיכוי האחר,
[8]ועל חטא שחטאנו בדחיית המאמץ לשלום.
[9]על חטא שחטאנו בהפרטה,
[10]ועל חטא שחטאנו בהפרת זכויות אדם.
[11]על חטא שחטאנו בויתור ערכי,
[12]ועל חטא שחטאנו בווכחנות.
[13]על חטא שחטאנו בזלזול הורים ומורים,
[14]ועל חטא שחטאנו בזילות חיי אדם.
[15]על חטא שחטאנו בחומרנות,

[16]And for the sin we have committed through poor education.
[17]For the sin we have committed through the stupidity of our mouths,
[18]And for the sin we have committed through fussiness.
[19]For the sin we have committed through the evil inclination,
[20]And for the sin we have committed through despair.
[21]For the sin we have committed through surrendering to reality.
[22]For the sin we have committed through kneeling to money and power,
[23]For the sin we have committed through gossiping tongues.
[24]And for the sin we have committed through mocking the poor,
[25]For the sin we have committed through favoritism.
[26]And for the sin we have committed through fraud,
[27]For the sin we have committed through exploitation and through alienation.
[28]And for the sin we have committed through dangerous driving,
[29]For the sin we have committed through trafficking women.

[16] ועל חטא שחטאנו בחינוך קלוקל.
[17] על חטא שחטאנו בטיפשות פה,
[18] ועל חטא שחטאנו בטרחנות.
[19] על חטא שחטאנו ביצר הרע,
[20] ועל חטא שחטאנו בייאוש.
[21] על חטא שחטאנו בכניעה למציאות,
[22] ועל חטא שחטאנו בכריעת ברך לממון ושררה.
[23] על חטא שחטאנו בלשון הרע,
[24] ועל חטא שחטאנו בלעג לרש.
[25] על חטא שחטאנו במשוא פנים,
[26] ועל חטא שחטאנו במרמה.
[27] על חטא שחטאנו בניצול וניכור,
[28] ועל חטא שחטאנו בנהיגה מסכנת.
[29] על חטא שחטאנו בסחר בנשים,

[30] ועל חטא שחטאנו
בסילוף.
[31] על חטא שחטאנו בעושק
עניים,
[32] ועל חטא שחטאנו
בעבודת אלילי אדם וחומר.
[33] על חטא שחטאנו בפערים
חברתיים,
[34] ועל חטא שחטאנו
בפגיעה בחלש.
[35] על חטא שחטאנו בציניות,
[36] ועל חטא שחטאנו
בצריכה מופרזת.
[37] על חטא שחטאנו
בקשיחות לב,
[38] ועל חטא שחטאנו בקלות
ראש.
[39] על חטא שחטאנו
ברכילות,
[40] ועל חטא שחטאנו
ברשלנות.
[41] על חטא שחטאנו
בשחיתות,
[42] ועל חטא שחטאנו
בשנאת חינם.
[43] על חטא שחטאנו
בתעמולת שקר,
[44] ועל חטא שחטאנו
בתאוות בצע.[6]

[30]And for the sin we
have committed through
misrepresentation,
[31]For the sin we have committed
through oppressing the poor.
[32]And for the sin we have committed through worshiping
human and
materialistic gods,
[33]For the sin we have committed
through social inequity.
[34]For the sin we have committed
through attacking the weak.
[35]For the sin we have committed
through cynicism,
[36]And for the sin we have
committed through excessive
consumption.
[37]For the sin we have committed
through hearts of callousness,
[38]And for the sin we have
committed through heads of
superficiality.
[39]For the sin we have committed
through gossip,
[40]And for the sin we have committed through negligence.
[41]For the sin we have committed
through corruption,
[42]And for the sin we have committed through pointless hatred.
[43]For the sin we have committed
through spreading lies,
[44]And for the sin we have committed through avarice.

This text, too, stresses society's ills, but in contrast to Rotem's, the sins mentioned in it are specific to contemporary Israeli society, not the human condition in general. Some of the wrongdoings, organized alphabetically, are cited directly from the traditional confession, yet others denote the current Israeli condition, especially that of the kibbutzim. After many decades of practicing *arvut hadadit*, "mutual [economic, emotional and social] care," most of the kibbutzim went through a process of privatization (line 9), graded salaries, and decrease in collective social responsibility (line 33). This process was very painful, at least in some of the kibbutzim, and caused much alienation and loneliness (line 27). Now, only a few years later, many kibbutzniks feel they have given up their values in exchange for very little (line 11).

At first glance this poem seems quite traditional—a list of sins in acrostic format. But it deviates from the traditional confession in an important structural way: it lacks the word *l'fanekha* ("before You"). Self-criticism remains, but it is purely the individual who stands in judgment; there is no divine "You" before whom one stands. Paradoxically, it is precisely the religious seriousness of the text that necessitated the omission of the Divine. Intending it as a religious statement, the author could not afford the luxury of words that would put it beyond the pale of the secular mind-set of the kibbutz society for whom it was composed.

Prayer and Politics: Which Serves Which?

Writing about the liturgical or semi-liturgical compositions of today, rather than ancient times, has the advantage of our being able to observe the extent to which people find them relevant to their lives. While normally we can only guess at the political or ethical causes that prompted prayers in antiquity, we can be quite certain of them today. In many cases, we can even speak with those who created them. The only disadvantage of exploring new liturgies is that we do not know how they will be accepted in the long run. The examination I am offering here is first and foremost an exploration of contemporary culture. Some of the cited texts do not have impressive literary qualities, but they are significant nonetheless, as cultural and social markers.

Rabbis for Human Rights (RHR, founded in 1988) is an extraordinary organization on the divided Israeli scene; it is the only organization in Israel that incorporates Orthodox, Conservative, and Reform rabbis and is committed to speaking "in the voice of Jewish tradition about issues of human rights."[7] For some years, before the High Holy Days, the organization has been publishing a pre–High Holy Day confession, updated annually. Looking back over the years, we can see that the content remains roughly the same but is increasingly expansive.

In structure, the RHR confession is not unusual: it quotes lines from the traditional *Vidui* and applies them to contemporary Israeli reality. In content, it stands out by condemning the treatment of the poor and the sick, the Palestinians, and people seeking refuge in Israel, but it is not, however, altogether "left wing," because it also demands justice for the Jewish settlers who lost their homes in the Gaza Strip during the disengagement process in 2005. In terms of other social issues, it also speaks against political corruption, submission to religious coercion, sex trafficking, and more.

The RHR confession has both Hebrew and English versions and is read during the Day of Atonement in various synagogues in Israel and in the diaspora. Rabbi Arik Asherman, the general secretary of the organization, who writes the *Vidui*, told me that people eagerly anticipate each new version, which "many people use for personal meditation and reflection."

The final section of the 2011 English version reads:

[1]For the sin which we have sinned against You by thinking to ourselves and by whispering in closed rooms about that which we should have shouted from the rooftops.
[2]And for the sin which we have sinned against You through short-sightedness, ignoring education and long-term change, and believing we could repair the world instantly.
[3]For the sin which we have sinned against You by smugly disparaging those whose concept of justice is different than ours.
[4]And for the sin which we have sinned against You by lack of faith in You, in ourselves, and in our society, when we said that *Tikun Olam* (Repairing the World) is "in the heavens" or "across the sea," and thus beyond our capability.
[5]For all these and more, God of forgiveness, we ask forgiveness, pardon, and atonement.
[6]May the words and the intentions of our prayer bring us to true *t'shuvah* and lead us forward to acts of righteousness and *tz'dakah*, in order to make our world a place in which *Shechinah* can dwell.[8]

The Rabbis for Human Rights are not the first to publish a political confession. In the early 1980s, Yesh G'vul ("There Is a Limit" or "Enough Is Enough"), a movement that was initiated by veteran combat soldiers who refused to serve in Lebanon, published a political poster against the war. It contained a confession by Michael Brizon, a left-wing publicist, literally known as Bet Michael. The text was constructed as an *Al Chet*, numbering the sins and transgressions of Israelis, ending with the following words:

[1]For the sin we have committed against You through degrading the human image, theirs and ours.
[2]For the sin we have committed against You through worshiping the ground.
[3]For the sin we have committed against You through corrupting the souls of young soldiers.
[4]For the sin we have committed against You through resigning ourselves to "we have no choice."
[5]And for the sin we have committed against You through indifference.
[6]And for the sin we have committed against You through following orders that serve the style of the occupation.
[7]And for all of these we have no right to ask forgiveness, because we didn't recognize the humanity of others.

[1] ועל חטא שחטאנו לפניך בהשפלת צלם אנוש, שלהם ושלנו.
[2] על חטא שחטאנו לפניך בסגידה לאדמה.
[3] על חטא שחטאנו לפניך בהשחתת נפשם של חיילים צעירים.
[4] על חטא שחטאנו לפניך בהצטדקות של "אין ברירה".
[5] ועל חטא שחטאנו לפניך באדישות.
[6] ועל חטא שחטאנו לפניך בציות לצווים שמשרתים את סגנון הכיבוש.
[7] ועל כל אלה אין לנו רשות לבקש מחילה, כי לא הכרנו באנושיותם של אחרים.

While the RHR text is meant to empower people to become socially and politically active, the Yesh G'vul text was meant merely to shock Israelis with its unflattering mirror, but it does not explicitly call for action, let alone for religious action. And while the RHR text is intended for liturgical use in synagogues, Bet Michael of Yesh G'vul had no ritual application in mind.

These two confessions, RHR and Yesh G'vul, have a similar structure and political views but belong to two separate and maybe even contradictory worlds. For the Yesh G'vul text, ancient and sacred words serve a contemporary political end; while for RHR, contemporary words are chosen to enhance our prayer experience through relevant calls to action on issues that should concern us. Yesh G'vul bends the ancient formula of Jewish confession to proclaim a modern political vision, but does so out of context—no actual Yom Kippur confession is intended; RHR co-opts both the traditional text and its original intent, for purposes of serving a modern political and social agenda. Old and new—Yom Kippur confession as a staple activity for the Jewish soul (on one hand) and a contemporary social agenda of some controversy and consequence (on the other)—reinforce and strengthen each other and elaborate each other.

Confessing Everything

Almost every year before Yom Kippur, the Israeli press publishes a series of new and innovative confessions, constructed according to the formula of *Al Chet*. Here are some rather unexpected examples.

Modern Hebrew is considered, by many, one of the most successful achievements (if not the greatest of all) of the Zionist project. An ancient language that had not been spoken for almost two millennia came back to life as a living vernacular. Yet, many lament what they consider the decline and corrosion of Hebrew's elemental purity, especially among young people. Ruvik Rosenthal, a Tel Aviv journalist and language expert, wrote what he called a "Linguistic Confession"; here are the first three verses of the text:

[1] עַל חֵטְא שֶׁחָטָאנוּ לְפָנֶיךָ
בְּעִלְּגוּת לָשׁוֹן
וְעַל חֵטְא שֶׁחָטָאנוּ לְפָנֶיךָ
בְּהֶרֶס הַבִּנְיָן

[1] For the sin we have committed against You through stuttering tongues.
And for the sin we have committed against You through destroying grammar.

For mixing up "i" and "e" so there's no more "e" in the language of Hibriw.
[The original Hebrew poem highlights a grammatical form in which the sound "i" is mispronounced as "e." Rather than translate the Hebrew grammatical forms and wordplays literally, here and below we find similar wordplays in English to mimic the impact of the original.]
And for not internalizing our Hebrew grammar lessons.
What can we say? This time we've overdone et.
For all of these, God of forgiveness, forgive us, pardon us, absolve us.
[2]For the sin we have committed against You through conjugation in the throat.
And for the sin we have committed against You through lazy pronunciation.
So the shame of our sins becomes the same as our shins.
[Our example of bad pronunciation involves the word "sin" from "for the sin...." The original Hebrew poem similarly has a wordplay on "sin." In Hebrew, the word for "sin" is chet, *which happens also to be the name of a letter.* Chet *is a guttural sound, and most speakers pronounce the gutteral* chet *the same as the palatal* khaf, *a fact that the poem laments by citing an idiom that uses both letters.]*
And the "r" is hard to hear—who got the idear that's there's nothing to fea?
[The Hebrew involves the guttural letter ayin, *which most Israelis no longer pronounce, and the specific example is the*

עַל כִּי אֶת הָהִפְעִיל לְהֶפְעִיל הָפַכְנוּ
וְאֶת הַחִירִיק מִן הָעִבְרִית הֶשְׁלַכְנוּ
וְאֶת שִׁעוּרֵי הַדִּקְדּוּק לֹא הֶפְנַמְנוּ
מַה יֵּשׁ לְדַבֵּר, הַפַּעַם הֶגְזַמְנוּ
וְעַל כֻּלָּם, אֱלוֹהַּ סְלִיחוֹת,
סְלַח לָנוּ, מְחַל לָנוּ, כַּפֵּר לָנוּ.
[2]עַל חֵטְא שֶׁחָטָאנוּ לְפָנֶיךָ בִּנְטִיַּת גָּרוֹן
וְעַל חֵטְא שֶׁחָטָאנוּ לְפָנֶיךָ בְּעַצְלוּת הַהֶגֶה
עַל כִּי הָיְתָה הַחֵית לְכָף
וְהַסַּחַר לְמֶכֶר
וְהָיְתָה הָעַיִן לְאָלֶף וְהֶעָפָר לְאֵפֶר
נֶאֱלְמָה גַּם הָהֵא, לָאַשְׁפָּה תִּתְנָאֵל
וְעִמָּהּ גַּם הַיּוֹד: אֵל אֶל אִיסְרָאֵל.
וְעַל כֻּלָּם, אֱלוֹהַּ סְלִיחוֹת,
סְלַח לָנוּ, מְחַל לָנוּ, כַּפֵּר לָנוּ.

*phrase "dust and ashes," the words for which in Hebrew—*efer *and* afar*—differ mostly in that one has an* ayin *and the other doesn't.]*
The "h" has disappeared, too, so
worry and don't be appy.
[Modern Hebrew, like some dialects of Hebrew, generally no longer has the sound "h."]
For all of these, God of forgiveness,
forgive us, pardon us, absolve us.
[3]For the sin we have committed against
You through insolence or through error
and for the sin we have committed
against You through switching number
and switching gender.
[The Hebrew just mentions gender, but, because English doesn't have grammatical gender, we use examples of mismatched number.]
There's three girls who went to the store
And two shekels is what they used
To buy theirselves a plethora of snacks.
Then they laid down to eat them.
For all of these, God of forgiveness,
forgive us, pardon us, absolve us.

[3] עַל חֵטְא שֶׁחָטָאנוּ לְפָנֶיךָ
בְּזָדוֹן וּבִשְׁגָגָה,
וְעַל חֵטְא שֶׁחָטָאנוּ לְפָנֶיךָ
בְּחִלּוּפֵי מִינִים
שְׁלֹשָׁה יְלָדוֹת הָלְכוּ לַמַּתְנָ"ס
הוֹצִיאוּ שְׁתֵּי שֶׁקֶל מִתּוֹךְ
הַמִּכְנָס
קָנוּ לְעַצְמָם מִינֵי תַּרְגִּימָה,
מִשֶּׁמָּה פָּנוּ הֵם לְצֹמֶת הוּמָה,
וְעַל כֻּלָּם, אֱלוֹהַּ סְלִיחוֹת,
סְלַח לָנוּ, מְחַל לָנוּ, כַּפֶּר לָנוּ.[9]

In witty and funny language (which is almost impossible to translate) that mocks Israeli slang and grammatical mistakes, Rosenthal specifies our language-related sins. In a conversation I had with the author, he told me that the confession was written many years back but did not create resonance until a few years ago, when the principal in his son's school asked him whether he had anything interesting that he might distribute among the students before Yom Kippur. Rosenthal gave him the text, and within one week it was widely circulated by e-mail and online publications. People make no liturgical use of the Rosenthal *Vidui*, but it is used for educational purposes.

A major problem in Israeli today is road safety. Anxious and hasty drivers combine with poor road conditions to cause many tragic accidents. A few years ago, a confession for "drivers, bikers, and pedestrians" was published. It too is organized alphabetically like the traditional *Vidui*. Here is the verse of the anonymous text, written for *alef*, the first letter in the Hebrew alphabet:

[1]We didn't stop at red lights.
[2]We didn't lower our high-beam lights.
[3]We were aggressive on our trips.
[4]We didn't turn on our lights during winter [as required by Israeli law; the winter is the rainy season in Israel, and this law is similar to American laws that require a driver to turn on the headlights whenever the windshield wipers are in use].
[5]We didn't wear our reflective vests [when we stopped by the side of the road, as required by Israeli law].

[1]אור אדום לא עצרנו
[2]אורות גבוהים לא הנמכנו
[3]אגרסיביים היינו בנסיעותינו
[4]אורות בחורף לא הדלקנו
[5]אפוד זוהר לא לבשנו.

The unsigned text, which was published on some Internet forums, ends with the promise, "From now on, we commit ourselves not to do this anymore."

Rivka Lubitch is a feminist Orthodox activist who struggles against the monopoly of the Orthodox and ultra-Orthodox rabbinic courts, which discriminate against women. In 2001, in her weekly column on YNET, a popular Israeli online news website, she published a confession for the judges in rabbinic courts, many of whom are notoriously known as sexist and prejudicial.

In a conversation I had with her, Lubitch said that she directs her writings to the larger public, aiming to shake it from its indifference; she intended her confession, therefore, as an exercise in heightening public awareness, but eventually she realized that it also served as an announcement to the religious authorities that they have sins for which they must atone. The rabbis secretly follow her work, she maintains, and she has never experienced such angry responses as she did for the publication of this *Vidui*. How dare she, said many, to use sacred words to attack religious authorities. Here is part of her text:

[1]*What can we say to You, the One who sits on high? And what can we tell You, the One who dwells in the heavens? For You know that which is concealed and that which is revealed.*

[2]*For the sin we have committed against You through force or through choice*—force, because we looked over our right shoulder and saw there rabbis who insist on strict interpretation of Jewish law, and we felt forced to be strict. And choice, because sometimes even without looking over our shoulder, we wanted to be strict and make things worse for people.

[3]*For the sin we have committed against You through ignorance*—we didn't always know how great the suffering of family members was when we delayed and dragged our feet over many years.

[4]*For the sin we have committed against You through exposing nakedness*—as, for example, in the case where we said a husband doesn't have to grant his wife a divorce, because the things he did to his daughter aren't connected to matters between him and her and don't constitute grounds for divorce.

[1]*מה נאמר לפניך יושב מרום, ומה נספר לפניך שוכן שחקים, הלא כל הנסתרות והנגלות אתה יודע.*

[2]*על חטא שחטאנו לפניך באונס וברצון* — אונס — משום שהסתכלנו מעבר לכתף הימנית וראינו שם רבנים מחמירים, והרגשנו אנוסים להחמיר. וברצון — משום שלפעמים, גם מבלי להסתכל מעבר לכתף, רצינו להחמיר ולהקשות על אנשים.

[3]*על חטא שחטאנו לפניך בבלי דעת* — שלא תמיד ידענו מה גודל סבלם של בני המשפחה כאשר התמהמהנו וסחבנו את התיק במשך שנים רבות.

[4]*על חטא שחטאנו לפניך בגלוי עריות* — כמו למשל במקרה ההוא שאמרנו שאין מקום לחייב את הבעל בגט, כי המעשים שעשה לילדה שלו לא קשורים לעניין שבינו לבינה, ואינם מהווים עילה לגט.

[5]*For the sin we have committed against You through our mouths' speech*—as when we told a woman, "You're preventing yourself from getting divorced," even though she fled from him after two months of marriage and for more than seven years she's unsuccessfully tried to divorce him.

[6]*For the sin we have committed against You through the heart's meditations*—as, for example, those among us who refuse to look at women but must arbitrate between a man and his wife.

[7]*For the sin we have committed against You through the confessions of our mouths*—as when we demanded that a woman retract her accusations that her husband cheated on her in order to get a divorce (the woman prepared a letter in which she retracts the accusations but even so the husband didn't agree to grant her a divorce).

[8]*For the sin we have committed against You through profaning God's name*—this page can't include an elaboration of this sentence, nor is there any need to elaborate or explain it.

[9]*For the sin we have committed against You through mockery*—that we sometimes laughed at converts and asked them stupid questions,

[5]*על חטא שחטאנו לפניך בדיבור פה* — כמו כשאמרנו לאשה "את מעגנת את עצמך", למרות שהיא ברחה ממנו אחרי חודשיים של נישואים, וכבר למעלה משבע שנים היא מנסה להתגרש ממנו ללא הצלחה.

[6]*על חטא שחטאנו לפניך בהרהור הלב* — כמו למשל מי מבינינו שלא מסתכל על נשים אבל צריך לפסוק בין איש ואשתו.

[7]*על חטא שחטאנו לפניך בוידוי פה* — כמו כשדרשנו מאשה להסכים לחזור בה מן ההאשמות שבעלה בגד בה תמורת הגט (האשה הכינה מכתב בו היא חוזרת בה אולם הבעל ממילא לא הסכים לתת את הגט).

[8]*על חטא שחטאנו לפניך בחילול ה'* — הדף לא יכול להכיל פירוט של המשפט הזה, וגם אין צורך לפרט או להסביר אותו.

[9]*על חטא שחטאנו לפניך בלצון* — שלפעמים קצת צחקנו על גרים ושאלנו

as, for example, when we asked a convert who was an artist what would happen if we took one of her pictures off the wall and used it to serve a cup of coffee—would that be a violation of Shabbat (ha ha ha).

[10]*For the sin we have committed against You through food and through drink*—as, for example, when we decided that a husband can impose conditions for a divorce that have to do with what the wife wears or eats.

[11]*For the sin we have committed against You through legs running to do evil*—the times when we ended things early because we were in a hurry to get home (even if it was for afternoon prayers), and we didn't have time to hear out people who had waited half a year for the ten lousy minutes we'd dedicated to them.

[12]*For the sin we have committed against You through pointless hatred*—for example, when we callously commented on a new immigrant from Russia who was trying to prove his Jewishness that "they're all trying to lie to us."

[13]*For all of these, God of forgiveness, forgive us, pardon us, absolve us.*

אותם שאלות שטותיות. כמו למשל כששאלנו גיורת אומנית מה יקרה אם נוריד תמונה שלה מהקיר ונגיש עליה כוס קפה -האם זה יהיה מוקצה בשבת (חה חה חה).

[10]*ועל חטא שחטאנו לפניך במאכל ובמשתה* — כמו למשל כשפסקנו שבעל יכול להתנות תנאים תמורת הגט שנוגעים ללבוש או למאכל של האשה.

[11]*על חטא שחטאנו לפניך בריצת רגליים להרע* — בפעמים שסגרנו את הדיון מוקדם כי מיהרנו ללכת הביתה (אפילו אם זה היה לתפילת מנחה), ולא היה לנו פנאי לשמוע אנשים שחיכו חצי שנה לעשר הדקות המסכנות שהקדשנו להם.

[12]*על חטא שחטאנו לפניך בשנאת חינם* — למשל כשזרקנו הערה על עולה מרוסיה שניסה להוכיח את יהדותו — "הם כולם מנסים לשקר אותנו".

[13]*ועל כולם אלוה סליחות סלח לנו מחל לנו כפר לנו.*[11]

Lubitch begins with the traditional text but then adds her own unorthodox interpretation. As I spoke with her to receive her permission to publish her *Vidui*, she said that each line reminded her of a story that she had encountered during her work. This *Vidui* may not find its way into synagogue usage, but it draws its satirical efficacy from being modeled on the traditional liturgical text.

Not all creative Israeli texts come from the left. The following instance was published in 2011 by the right-wing LeHaVa, an acronym for *irgun lim'ni'at hitbol'lut b'eretz hakodesh*, "Organization for the Prevention of Assimilation in the Holy Land." The organization, whose aim is to prevent social and professional encounters between Jews and non-Jews, especially Arabs, put the confession in the mouths of those who encourage, as they call it, assimilation. It is not entirely clear who stands behind this initiative and how established the organization is, but its provocative and blunt style attracts much attention from the media.

A Prayer for Pardon for Those Who Encourage Assimilation

[1]For the sin we have committed against You through hiring enemies and not brethren.
[2]For the sin we have committed against You through encouraging assimilation.
[3]For the sin we have committed against You through renting houses to enemies.
[4]For the sin we have committed against You through employing non-Jews [literally, *goyim*] with Jews.
[5]For the sin we have committed against You through ignoring those who sounded the alarm.
[6]For the sin we have committed against You through hiring non-Jewish packers.

בקשת מחילה למעודדים התבוללות

[1]על חטא שחטאנו לפניך בהעסקת אויבים ולא אחים
[2]על חטא שחטאנו לפניך בעידוד ההתבוללות
[3]על חטא שחטאנו לפניך בהשכרת בתים לאויבים
[4]על חטא שחטאנו לפניך בהעסקת גוים עם יהודיות
[5]על חטא שחטאנו לפניך בהתעלמות מאלה שהתריעו
[6]על חטא שחטאנו לפניך שהעסקנו אורזנים גויים

[7]For the sin we have committed against You through having seen Arabs harassing girls and having kept quiet.
[8]For the sin we have committed against You through hiring Arab drivers to drive Jewish girls.
[9]For the sin we have committed against You through encouraging national service with non-Jews.
[10]For the sin we have committed against You through having seen the mother's tears and having kept quiet.
[11]For the sin we have committed against You through encouraging get-togethers with Jewish and Arab youth.
[12]For the sin we have committed against You through knowledge and through lack of knowledge.
[13]For all of these, God of forgiveness, forgive us, pardon us, absolve us.

[7]על חטא שחטאנו לפניך
שראינו ערבים מטרידים
בנות ושתקנו
[8]על חטא שחטאנו לפניך
שעודדנו שירות לאומי עם
גוים
[9]על חטא שחטאנו לפניך
שראינו את דמעות האם
ושתקנו
[10]על חטא שחטאנו לפניך
שהעסקנו נהגים ערבים
בהסעת בנות יהודיות
[11]על חטא שחטאנו לפניך
בעידוד מפגשים נוער יהודי
וערבי
[12]ועל חטא שחטאנו לפניך
ביודעים ולא יודעים
[13]ועל כולם אלוה סליחות,
סלח לנו, מחל לנו, כפר
לנו.[12]

The writer warns against all forms of interreligious and intergroup contacts, the implicit assumption being that working together, volunteering together, or even having non-Jews as packers in the supermarket produces mixed marriages and "a mother's tears." The text does not pretend to literary quality—it is repetitious (for example, four of the twelve lines refer to hiring non-Jews) and mixes language registers—as if to say that this is no time for subtle and refined speech; we must instead shout out warnings in any way possible. Still, one may wonder whether the low literary quality of the text was intentional …

The text first appeared in some online news publications and attracted much response, both praise and condemnation. Interestingly, many of these responses themselves were written in the format of the *Al Chet Vidui*, some adding more lines, even more hateful than those of the original text; some writing an alternative text, calling for atonement for the sins of those who composed the original one. Here, too, the field of the discussion was the traditional format of the *Vidui*.

Al Chet in Israeli Poetry

Phrases from the *Al Chet* recur in numerous Israeli poems and songs, such as this example by Moshe Meir.

A Poem in the Middle. For the poems. For the sin.

[1]For the sin I have committed before You
[2]if my poems came before You
[3]after the smoke of the furnaces that wondered if children came before You
[4]Is there still a place to ask about the poems?
[5]For the sin I have committed before You.
[6]Striking the purity of the poem.
[7]Is it ludicrous?
[8]Is it yearning through the ashes of the day?
[9]In any event—
[10]A poetic certainty—
[11]Before You.
[12]For the sin I have committed before You through rising up to write my poems.

שיר בתווך. על השירים. על חטא.

[1]על חטא שחטאתי לפניך
[2]אם באו שירי לפניך
[3]אחר עשן כבשנים התוהים
— הבאו בנים לפניך
[4]היש עוד מקום לשאול על השירים?
[5]על חטא שחטאתי לפניך.
[6]מכה בתומת השיר.
[7]הנלעגת?
[8]הנכספת באפר היום?
[9]מכל מקום —
[10]ודאות שירית —
[11]לפניך.
[12]על חטא שחטאתי לפניך
— בהתנשאי לכתוב שירי.

[13]For the sin I have committed before You through taking up letters that You used to create heaven and earth	[13]על חטא שחטאת לפניך — בנוטלי אותיות שבראת בהן שמים וארץ
[14]To write my poems.	[14]לכתוב שירי.
[15]For the sin I have committed before You through taking up the letters of your Torah and your prophets	[15]על חטא שחטאתי לפניך — בנוטלי אותיות תורתך ונביאיך
[16]and dropping them into the abyss of the poem's fundamentals	[16]בהטילי אותן לתהומות יסודי השיר
[17]Out of your tremendous love I did this.	[17]מאהבתך כי עצמה עשיתי
[18]For not having any words without your words I did this.	[18]מאין בי דבר ללא דברך עשיתי
[19]Pained at not having any words without your words I did this.	[19]בכאב על כי אין בי דבר ללא דברך עשיתי
[20]Longing for when I will know heaven and earth and dust and clods of earth and woman without your words I did this.	[20]ביחול מתי אדע שמים וארץ ורגבים ואישה ללא דברך עשיתי
[21]Joyful at knowing that I will not know without your words I did this.	[21]בשמחה על כי אדע כי לא אדע ללא דברך עשיתי.
[22]For the sin I have committed before You—by composing my poems—laughing, mocking.	[22]על חטא שחטאתי לפניך — באחדי שירי — בצחוק, בלעג.
[23]Because of the blazing fiery furnace	[23]מפאת כבשן האש היוקדת
[24]I made a shield and protector.	[24]עשיתי לי צינה ומגן
[25]I made laughter	[25]עשיתי לי צחוק.
[26]For the sin I have committed before You.	[26]על חטא שחטאתי לפניך.
[27]How sweet are my sins!	[27]מה מתקו חטאי.
[28]I who have vowed before You	[28]אני שנדרתי לפניך

29 not to sin before You
30 to keep your laws
31 with all their layers,
32 and the layers of their layers
33 My poem was to me the scope of sin
34 Expansive skies of sin
35 in which I float, shouting joyously.
36 Don't forgive my sins.
37 Just please
38 plea--se
39 Let my sins come before You
40 Because
41 only in them
42 am I too
43 before You.

29 לא לחטוא לפניך
30 לשמור חוקותיך
31 על פצלותיהן
32 ופצלות פצלותיהן —
33 היתה לי שירתי מרחב החטא
34 שמים גדולים של חטא
35 ואני דואה בהם בצווח חדווים.
36 אל תמחל על חטאי.
37 רק אנא
38 א — נא
39 עשה שיהיו חטאי לפניך
40 כי
41 רק בם
42 גם אני
43 לפניך.[13]

The poem explicitly refers to a post-Holocaust reality (after the smoke of the furnaces), asking whether there is still room for poetry—a response perhaps, to Theodor Adorno, the German philosopher, who said in 1949, "To write poetry after Auschwitz is barbaric." Still, Meir writes his poem and confesses to the sin of writing. Writing the confession becomes the sin itself. (My poem was to me the scope of sin.) The poet seeks no forgiveness; on the contrary, his sin of poetry is what presents him *l'fanekha* (before You [God]). He is not asking for his sin to be wiped away; on the contrary, he asks only that his sin appear before God.

Interestingly, using the same liturgical text, Meir does in his poetry the opposite of what most of the writers cited above did. While they used the traditional phrase as religious or as a cultural icon, which draws its efficacy and authority from its familiarity, he reread it, deconstructed it, and inserted new meaning to the metaphor of standing before God.

Al Chet as Conversation

One certain sign of the cultural centrality of the Yom Kippur confessions is the fact that the wording of *Al Chet* has entered popular conversation. The phrase *l'hakot al chet* ("to beat on [the chest for] one's sin") is often used in Israel, especially in the press, when referring to people's public remorse. In the original context, of course, one beats on one's own chest; Israeli discourse sometimes reverses the intent by referring to the need for others to beat their chests for taking the wrong side of a debate. Those who opposed the 2011 negotiations that brought about the release of a large number of terrorists in exchange for the freedom of kidnapped soldier Gilad Shalit, for example, often used the phrase "for the sin we have committed against You through negotiations." From the opposite camp one often heard the call "for the sin we have committed against You through lack of compassion," due to the dragged and ineffective negotiations with those who held Shalit.

Even when addressing an utterly nonreligious (or even antireligious) context, Hebrew speakers draw rhetorical power from the familiarity of *Al Chet*. I call this language of the Jewish People our foundational core, or the "inner language." People may not always know the source of some of the phrases that they draw upon, but they constitute the common linguistic "property" of the Jewish heritage. Israelis who are not religious may be alienated from the Yom Kippur ritual itself—standing in the synagogue, beating the chest, and reciting a long sequence of things for which we atone. But the prayer itself, which references primarily social and interpersonal offenses, does not seem problematic to them. They can readily adapt it to new circumstances as they arise.

Some new texts are meant to be recited in a worship context, especially in the synagogue in Yom Kippur. Others are composed only for political, ideological, or literary use. The former (those texts that are meant for actual use in the synagogue) sometimes differ most from the original version: the kibbutz text omits the word *l'fanekha* (before You [God]), precisely to preserve its secular understanding of sin as acknowledging one's faults, with no divinity to whom one is accountable. Texts without liturgical purpose, by contrast, specifically select exact phrases from tradition so as to borrow the authority of that prayer for controversial, even radical, ends.

Liturgical Innovation in Israel

Like their non-Orthodox siblings in the diaspora, Israeli Jews too use the vernacular in their worship, but for them, that vernacular is the sacred language of Hebrew. Diasporan Jews can easily "translate away" difficulties in the Hebrew text—they provide interpretive "translations" that hide the original intent of the Hebrew. Israelis, who read the prayers in their original language, have no access to that strategy. Diasporan Jews who, in many cases, do not even understand the Hebrew can recite it as if the Hebrew is a symbolic icon; Israelis do not wish, and indeed are not able, to do so—they cannot easily see the words of a language they actually speak as a mantra in which meaning is secondary to symbolic significance.[14] The allegiance to Hebrew explains both the relative traditionalism of Israeli liturgy and the need for enormous creativity. Needless to say, the two stand in tension (if not in contradiction). This may explain, at least in part, the aversion many Israeli Jews have toward prayer, prayer books, and synagogue life altogether.

Finally, there is the ongoing debate in Israel regarding the Hebrew literary-liturgical style. Editors and authors of prayer books for Israelis must make constant language-based decisions. They wish to use edifying and artful language that draws on traditional texts, but in a way that makes those textual allusions accessible to speakers of Modern Hebrew. If they choose a high linguistic register, they may create distance from the text; if they choose a more pedestrian style, they may cause people to treat it as less than sacred and spiritual.

The omnipresence of Hebrew in the life of the worshipers, inside and outside of the synagogue, creates a uniquely Israeli issue with worship. Questions of authenticity, relevancy, meaning, and clarity are asked in a direct fashion, on the spot and at every moment. It is impossible to ignore them (as one may do in the diaspora, where people dispense with Hebrew when the official conversation about a prayer is over). For worshipers in Hebrew, contact with the tradition is direct, ever present, and ever suggestive—so, also, extremely problematic and even painful. This helps explain the fact that in many circles in Israeli society, the mere willingness to attend worship in a synagogue (any synagogue) is considered an overt political statement. And yet, there is today an exciting new openness in Israeli society to worship, liturgy, and religiosity. More and more people want to grapple with their Jewish identity and with Jewish texts and rituals, and they are not willing any more to consume the kind of Orthodox or secular forms of "ready-made Judaism" that have been their sole options thus far. Some of the texts presented here attest to this phenomenon, and I believe that we will see more, in quantity and quality, in the near future.

Part II

Ashamnu and *Al Chet*

The Yom Kippur Liturgy of Confession

Editor's Introduction

Rabbi Lawrence A. Hoffman, PhD

The Yom Kippur liturgy of confession varies somewhat from place to place and even from service to service. All Jews and all services contain a short confession, *Ashamnu*, and (except for in the *N'ilah*) a long one, *Al Chet*. In addition, the two confessions always appear with introductions and conclusions. In most services, a general preamble introduces the whole. But this general framework does allow for minor (and sometimes major) variations.

To begin with, Sephardi and Ashkenazi Jews have somewhat different texts, and there are subdivisions within these two categories as well. Sephardi practice began with Jews in the Iberian Peninsula prior to the 1492 expulsion from Spain. One branch of exiles went north to the Netherlands and then, later, to England and the New World. Another branch went east to the Turkish (Ottoman) Empire, which included the Land of Israel. These two branches have somewhat different liturgies.

Ashkenazi practice too varies somewhat. The word "Ashkenaz" refers to Northern and Central Europe, largely France and Germany, where Ashkenazi practice began. But by the sixteenth century, Ashkenazi Jews were emigrating to Eastern Europe, primarily present-day Poland. The Western branch in Germany proper is known technically as *Minhag Rhinus* ("Rhineland Custom"); the Eastern branch in Poland is called *Minhag Polin* ("Polish Custom").

Because the vast majority of Jews in North America and an overall majority worldwide hail from Eastern Europe, we have chosen here to reproduce Ashkenazi practice in general and the Polish custom in particular.

We had to contend, as well, with the fact that the liturgy of confession occurs in all five of the services that constitute Yom Kippur. Also, it is said individually during the silent recitation of the *Amidah*, but then again, aloud, during the prayer leader's repetition of that prayer. Minor changes occur from occasion to occasion. We chose here to reproduce the major part of the liturgy that occurs regularly throughout the services, modified somewhat to allow for limitations in space and for our desire to include whatever readers would be most likely to find familiar and want to know about.

Translator's Introduction

Dr. Joel M. Hoffman

Most of *Al Chet* is built around the poetry and impact of synonyms, sometimes just a few (such as three Hebrew words that mean "forgive" coupled with three that mean "sin"), sometimes more. This creates a double challenge for the translator.

First, words often have fewer synonyms in English than in Hebrew. When that is the case, so that there is no natural English for all of the Hebrew synonyms, we must choose between accuracy and naturalness. But the poetic force of the Hebrew comes less from the nuance of each word than from the cumulative impact of the combined string of synonyms, so a non-natural translation for a specific word impacts not only that word but the words around it as well.

A parallel example would be this familiar phrase from Shakespeare's *Comedy of Errors* (act 2, scene 2):

> Was there ever any man thus beaten out of season,
> When in the why and the wherefore is neither rhyme nor reason?

Dr. Joel M. Hoffman lectures around the globe on popular and scholarly topics spanning history, Hebrew, prayer, and Jewish continuity. He has served on the faculties of Brandeis University in Waltham, Massachusetts, and Hebrew Union College–Jewish Institute of Religion in New York. He is author of *And God Said: How Translations Conceal the Bible's Original Meaning* and *In the Beginning: A Short History of the Hebrew Language*, and has written for the international *Jerusalem Post*. He contributed to all ten volumes of the *My People's Prayer Book: Traditional Prayers, Modern Commentaries* series, winner of the National Jewish Book Award; to *My People's Passover Haggadah: Traditional Texts, Modern Commentaries*; and to *Who by Fire, Who by Water—Un'taneh Tokef* (all Jewish Lights).

A "translation" of the second line along the lines of "when in the why and the cause of what happened is neither poetic assonance nor reason" matches in some regards but misses the mark in others. Much of our translation suffers from similar drawbacks, detracting from the text, sometimes subtly, sometimes more severely. The notes to the translation indicate those cases where the English is particularly insufficient.

Second, many of the synonyms or near synonyms are also technical terms, enjoying a range of general and more specific meanings. The English word "crime" is illustrative, in that it refers generally to things that are undesirable ("What a crime that it's raining during our picnic!"), specifically to illegal acts of all sorts, and even more specifically to only certain kinds of illegal acts in particular. (Technically, parking violations in most places are "civil infractions," not crimes.) Our Hebrew is similar, with, for example, words like *chet*, *avon*, and *pesha*. All of them mean "sin," in general, but they are not entirely synonymous because each one has its own specific and technical meaning.

In general, it is nearly impossible to translate technical terms from Hebrew into English unless English has similar technical terms, and for most of the technical terms in *Al Chet*, it does not. Some of the nuances of the technical terms are discussed on pages 96–108.

Annotated Translation

Dr. Joel M. Hoffman

A. Preamble to Confession (*Ki Anu Amekha*, "For We Are Your People")

[1]Our God and our ancestors' God, forgive us, pardon us, absolve us.
[2]For we are your people, and You are our God.
[3]We are your children, and You are our parent.
[4]We are your servants, and You are our master.
[5]We are your community, and You are our lot.
[6]We are your possession, and You are our destiny.
[7]We are your flock, and You are our shepherd.
[8]We are your vineyard, and You are our vintner.
[9]We are your work, and You are our creator.
[10]We are your bride, and You are our lover.
[11]We are your prize, and You are our God.
[12]We are your people, and You are our king.

[1] אֱלֹהֵֽינוּ וֵאלֹהֵי אֲבוֹתֵֽינוּ,
סְלַח לָֽנוּ, מְחַל לָֽנוּ, כַּפֶּר לָֽנוּ.
[2] כִּי אָֽנוּ עַמֶּֽךָ, וְאַתָּה אֱלֹהֵֽינוּ.
[3] אָֽנוּ בָנֶֽיךָ, וְאַתָּה אָבִֽינוּ.
[4] אָֽנוּ עֲבָדֶֽיךָ, וְאַתָּה אֲדוֹנֵֽנוּ.
[5] אָֽנוּ קְהָלֶֽךָ, וְאַתָּה חֶלְקֵֽנוּ.
[6] אָֽנוּ נַחֲלָתֶֽךָ, וְאַתָּה גוֹרָלֵֽנוּ.
[7] אָֽנוּ צֹאנֶֽךָ, וְאַתָּה רוֹעֵֽנוּ.
[8] אָֽנוּ כַרְמֶֽךָ, וְאַתָּה נוֹטְרֵֽנוּ.
[9] אָֽנוּ פְעֻלָּתֶֽךָ, וְאַתָּה יוֹצְרֵֽנוּ.
[10] אָֽנוּ רַעְיָתֶֽךָ, וְאַתָּה דוֹדֵֽנוּ.
[11] אָֽנוּ סְגֻלָּתֶֽךָ, וְאַתָּה אֱלֹהֵֽינוּ.
[12] אָֽנוּ עַמֶּֽךָ, וְאַתָּה מַלְכֵּֽנוּ.

[13]We are your declaration, and You are our declaration.
[14]We are arrogant, and You are forgiving.
[15]We are insolent, and You are patient.
[16]We are full of sin, and You are full of compassion.
[17]We are the ones whose days are like a passing shadow, and You are the One whose years are unending.

[13] אָנוּ מַאֲמִירֶיךָ, וְאַתָּה מַאֲמִירֵנוּ.
[14] אָנוּ עַזֵּי פָנִים, וְאַתָּה רַחוּם וְחַנּוּן.
[15] אָנוּ קְשֵׁי עֹרֶף וְאַתָּה אֶרֶךְ אַפַּיִם.
[16] אָנוּ מְלֵאֵי עָוֺן, וְאַתָּה מָלֵא רַחֲמִים.
[17] אָנוּ יָמֵינוּ כְּצֵל עוֹבֵר, וְאַתָּה הוּא וּשְׁנוֹתֶיךָ לֹא יִתָּמּוּ.

B. *Vidui Zuta*: The Short Confession (*Ashamnu*, "We Have Been Guilty ...")

Introduction

[1]Our God and our ancestors' God, let our prayer come before You, and do not ignore our pleas, for we are not so arrogant and insolent as to say before You, Adonai our God and our ancestors' God, we are righteous and have not sinned. [2]But we and our ancestors have sinned.

[1]אֱלֹהֵינוּ וֵאלֹהֵי אֲבוֹתֵינוּ, תָּבֹא לְפָנֶיךָ תְּפִלָּתֵנוּ, וְאַל תִּתְעַלַּם מִתְּחִנָּתֵנוּ, שֶׁאֵין אֲנַחְנוּ עַזֵּי פָנִים וּקְשֵׁי עֹרֶף לוֹמַר לְפָנֶיךָ, יְיָ אֱלֹהֵינוּ וֵאלֹהֵי אֲבוֹתֵינוּ, צַדִּיקִים אֲנַחְנוּ וְלֹא חָטָאנוּ. [2]אֲבָל אֲנַחְנוּ וַאֲבוֹתֵינוּ חָטָאנוּ.

The Confession (*Ashamnu*)

[1]We have been guilty of failure, betrayal, gluttony, malice, misguidance, evil, presumptuousness, destruction, mendacity, deceit, lying, mockery, treachery, incitement, stubbornness, iniquity, sin, hostility, insolence, wickedness, corruption, depravity, straying, and deception.

[1]אָשַׁמְנוּ, בָּגַדְנוּ, גָּזַלְנוּ, דִּבַּרְנוּ דֹפִי, הֶעֱוִינוּ, וְהִרְשַׁעְנוּ, זַדְנוּ, חָמַסְנוּ, טָפַלְנוּ שֶׁקֶר, יָעַצְנוּ רָע, כִּזַּבְנוּ, לַצְנוּ, מָרַדְנוּ, נִאַצְנוּ, סָרַרְנוּ, עָוִינוּ, פָּשַׁעְנוּ, צָרַרְנוּ, קִשִּׁינוּ עֹרֶף; רָשַׁעְנוּ, שִׁחַתְנוּ, תִּעַבְנוּ, תָּעִינוּ תִּעְתָּעְנוּ.

[1]*Failure*: The Hebrew has twenty-four verbs here. We translate with nouns because Hebrew allows both verbs and nouns with no object, while English allows only nouns. So, for example, in Hebrew one can say, "I betrayed," meaning "I betrayed people/others/someone/etc.," but not in English. However, English does allow the nearly identical "I have been guilty of betrayal." Our first verb, however, *ashamnu*, means "we were guilty." Because we use "guilt of" to introduce the nouns, we use the general "failure" here.

Conclusion

[1]We have veered from your commandments and from your good laws and we are worthless. [2]You have been righteous throughout all that has happened to us, for You have done justly with us and we are the ones who did evil. [3]What can we say to You, the One who sits on high? And what can we tell You, the One who dwells in the heavens? For you know that which is concealed and that which is revealed!

[1]סַרְנוּ מִמִּצְוֹתֶיךָ וּמִמִּשְׁפָּטֶיךָ הַטּוֹבִים, וְלֹא שָׁוָה לָנוּ. [2]וְאַתָּה צַדִּיק עַל כָּל הַבָּא עָלֵינוּ, כִּי אֱמֶת עָשִׂיתָ וַאֲנַחְנוּ הִרְשָׁעְנוּ. [3]מַה נֹּאמַר לְפָנֶיךָ יוֹשֵׁב מָרוֹם? וּמַה נְּסַפֵּר לְפָנֶיךָ שׁוֹכֵן שְׁחָקִים? הֲלֹא כָּל הַנִּסְתָּרוֹת וְהַנִּגְלוֹת אַתָּה יוֹדֵעַ!

[1]*Veered*: We might prefer "strayed," but the Hebrew here (*sarnu*) is not related to the verb we just translated as "straying" (*ta'inu*).

[1]*From your good laws*: Our English, like the Hebrew, is ambiguous. The point is "your laws, which are good," though the grammar also allows for the (probably unintended) reading "your laws, but only the good ones."

[2]*You have been righteous throughout all that has happened to us, for You have done justly with us and we are the ones who did evil*: Nehemiah 9:33.

[3]*To you*: Literally, "before you." We omit "before" to make "tell you" possible next.

[3]*Heavens*: Hebrew, *sh'khakim*. This same word forms the "sky" in the Modern Hebrew equivalent of "skyscraper."

C. *Vidui Rabbah*: The Long Confession (*Al Chet*, "For the Sin ...")

Introduction

[1]You know the secrets of the universe, and the hidden enigmas of all that lives. [2]You scrutinize and examine every detail of our organs. [3]Nothing is hidden from you, and nothing is enigmatic to You. [4]So let it be your will, Adonai our God and our ancestors' God, that You forgive all our sins, pardon all our iniquities, and absolve all our misdeeds.

[1]אַתָּה יוֹדֵעַ רָזֵי עוֹלָם, וְתַעֲלוּמוֹת סִתְרֵי כָּל חָי. [2]אַתָּה חוֹפֵשׂ כָּל חַדְרֵי בָטֶן, וּבוֹחֵן כְּלָיוֹת וָלֵב. [3]אֵין דָּבָר נֶעְלָם מִמֶּךָּ, וְאֵין נִסְתָּר מִנֶּגֶד עֵינֶיךָ. [4]וּבְכֵן יְהִי רָצוֹן מִלְּפָנֶיךָ, יְיָ אֱלֹהֵינוּ וֵאלֹהֵי אֲבוֹתֵינוּ, שֶׁתִּסְלַח לָנוּ עַל כָּל חַטֹּאתֵינוּ, וְתִמְחַל לָנוּ עַל כָּל עֲוֹנוֹתֵינוּ, וּתְכַפֶּר־לָנוּ עַל כָּל פְּשָׁעֵינוּ.

[1]*Hidden*: In a wordplay we cannot duplicate in English, the word for "universe" and "hidden" both come from the same root in Hebrew, *ayin.lamed.mem*.

[2]*Scrutinize and examine every detail of our organs*: Literally, "scrutinize every chamber of the stomach and examine the kidneys and the heart." But, all three organs—stomach, kidney, and heart—function differently in Hebrew than they do in English, so translating literally would lead the English reader astray.

[3]*Enigmatic to You*: Literally, "before your eyes."

The Confession (*Al Chet*)

[1]For the sin we have committed against You through force or through choice,
[2]and for the sin we have committed against You through haughtiness of heart.
[3]For the sin we have committed against You through ignorance,
[4]and for the sin we have committed against You through the expression of our lips.

[1] עַל חֵטְא שֶׁחָטָאנוּ לְפָנֶיךָ
בְּאֹנֶס וּבְרָצוֹן,
[2] וְעַל חֵטְא שֶׁחָטָאנוּ לְפָנֶיךָ
בְּאִמּוּץ הַלֵּב.
[3] עַל חֵטְא שֶׁחָטָאנוּ לְפָנֶיךָ
בִּבְלִי דָעַת,
[4] וְעַל חֵטְא שֶׁחָטָאנוּ לְפָנֶיךָ
בְּבִטּוּי שְׂפָתָיִם.

[1]*Through*: The Hebrew here, and in each line following, is the more general prefix *b-*, variously "through," "with," "in," and so on. We try to keep "through" throughout to better preserve the impact of the repetition in Hebrew.
[1]*Force or through choice*: It is tempting to spell this sentence out, perhaps along the lines of "... under duress or of our own free will." But the Hebrew, like our English, is both pithy and slightly odd, in that we are the object of the first noun ("someone forces us to do something") but the subject of the second ("we choose to act").
Additionally, the words here, and in the following lines, were chosen not just for their meaning but also because they form an extended acrostic.
[2]*Haughtiness of heart*: Or just "haughtiness." The Hebrew includes the word *lev* ("heart") as part of an expression. We include the organ in translation here because it forms an occasional pattern with "lips," below, then "mouth," and so on.
[4]*Our lips*: Hebrew, "the lips." Body parts in English commonly take possessives, while in Hebrew they do not. (This has some surprising consequences. For example, the literal translation of "I broke my arm" in Hebrew—*Shavarti et ha-yad sheli*—only means "I broke my arm in the way that I might break something that's not a body part, like a table, for example, by hitting it with a hammer on purpose." The way to convey in Hebrew what we mean by the English "I broke my arm" is the equivalent of "I broke the arm.")

[5]For the sin we have committed against You through exposing nakedness,
[6]and for the sin we have committed against You through exposed and secret acts.
[7]For the sin we have committed against You through knowledge and through deceit,
[8]and for the sin we have committed against You through our mouths' speech.
[9]For the sin we have committed against You through cheating our friends,
[10]and for the sin we have committed against You through the heart's meditations.
[11]For the sin we have committed against You through whoremongering,
[12]and for the sin we have committed against You through the confessions of our mouths.

[5]עַל חֵטְא שֶׁחָטָאנוּ לְפָנֶיךָ בְּגִלּוּי עֲרָיוֹת,
[6]וְעַל חֵטְא שֶׁחָטָאנוּ לְפָנֶיךָ בְּגָלוּי וּבַסָּתֶר.
[7]עַל חֵטְא שֶׁחָטָאנוּ לְפָנֶיךָ בְּדַעַת וּבְמִרְמָה,
[8]וְעַל חֵטְא שֶׁחָטָאנוּ לְפָנֶיךָ בְּדִבּוּר פֶּה.
[9]עַל חֵטְא שֶׁחָטָאנוּ לְפָנֶיךָ בְּהוֹנָאַת רֵעַ,
[10]וְעַל חֵטְא שֶׁחָטָאנוּ לְפָנֶיךָ בְּהַרְהוֹר הַלֵּב.
[11]עַל חֵטְא שֶׁחָטָאנוּ לְפָנֶיךָ בִּוְעִידַת זְנוּת,
[12]וְעַל חֵטְא שֶׁחָטָאנוּ לְפָנֶיךָ בְּוִדּוּי פֶּה.

[6]*Exposed*: The Hebrew, like our English, nearly matches the previous line.
[10]*Heart's meditations*: The Hebrew, though it uses the word "heart," is broader, including what we would call the "mind." Yet we opt for "heart" in translation to continue the pattern of occasional body parts.
[11]*Whoremongering*: Or, "gathering for whoredom."

[13]עַל חֵטְא שֶׁחָטָאנוּ לְפָנֶיךָ
בְּזִלְזוּל הוֹרִים וּמוֹרִים,
[14]וְעַל חֵטְא שֶׁחָטָאנוּ לְפָנֶיךָ
בְּזָדוֹן וּבִשְׁגָגָה.
[15]עַל חֵטְא שֶׁחָטָאנוּ לְפָנֶיךָ
בְּחֹזֶק יָד,
[16]וְעַל חֵטְא שֶׁחָטָאנוּ לְפָנֶיךָ
בְּחִלּוּל הַשֵּׁם.
[17]עַל חֵטְא שֶׁחָטָאנוּ לְפָנֶיךָ
בְּטֻמְאַת שְׂפָתָיִם,
[18]וְעַל חֵטְא שֶׁחָטָאנוּ לְפָנֶיךָ
בְּטִפְּשׁוּת פֶּה.

[13]For the sin we have committed against You through demeaning parents and teachers,
[14]and for the sin we have committed against You through insolence or through error.
[15]For the sin we have committed against You through strength of hand,
[16]and for the sin we have committed against You through profaning God's name.
[17]For the sin we have committed against You through the impurity of our lips,
[18]and for the sin we have committed against You through the stupidity of our mouths.

[13]*Demeaning parents and teachers*: Our English is unfortunately ambiguous, meaning either "by us demeaning parents and teachers" or "by parents and teachers who are demaning." The Hebrew is clearly the former. (Other examples of this kind of ambiguity include "flying planes can be dangerous" and various jokes that start "visiting in-laws can be....")
[14]*Error*: Hebrew, *sh'gagah*, which refers to errors, but also more specifically to sins committed in error.
[15]*Strength of hand*: Or, just "strength," but, again, we try to include "hand" to continue the pattern of body parts.
[16]*Profaning God's name*: Literally, "profaning the name," a common expression in Hebrew.

[19]For the sin we have committed against You through the evil inclination,
[20]and for the sin we have committed against You through knowledge and through lack of knowledge.
[21]And for all of these, God of forgiveness, forgive us, pardon us, absolve us.
[22]For the sin we have committed against You through deception and through lying,
[23]and for the sin we have committed against You through handing bribes.
[24]For the sin we have committed against You through mockery,
[25]and for the sin we have committed against You through gossiping tongues.

[19] עַל חֵטְא שֶׁחָטָאנוּ לְפָנֶיךָ
בְּיֵצֶר הָרָע,
[20] וְעַל חֵטְא שֶׁחָטָאנוּ לְפָנֶיךָ
בְּיוֹדְעִים וּבְלֹא יוֹדְעִים.
[21] וְעַל כֻּלָּם, אֱלוֹהַּ סְלִיחוֹת,
סְלַח לָנוּ, מְחַל לָנוּ, כַּפֶּר לָנוּ.
[22] עַל חֵטְא שֶׁחָטָאנוּ לְפָנֶיךָ
בְּכַחַשׁ וּבְכָזָב,
[23] וְעַל חֵטְא שֶׁחָטָאנוּ לְפָנֶיךָ
בְּכַפַּת שֹׁחַד.
[24] עַל חֵטְא שֶׁחָטָאנוּ לְפָנֶיךָ
בְּלָצוֹן,
[25] וְעַל חֵטְא שֶׁחָטָאנוּ לְפָנֶיךָ
בְּלְשׁוֹן הָרָע.

[19]*The evil inclination*: This is a technical term in Hebrew, so we use the most common English translation.
[20]*Through knowledge and through lack of knowledge*: The most natural translation of this line would be "knowingly and unknowingly," but we want to continue the pattern of starting with "through."
[23]*Handing bribes*: The Hebrew has the noun "hand": the hand of bribery. This is as close as we can come in English.
[25]*Gossiping tongues*: Literally, "the tongue of evil." We would normally prefer just "gossip," but, once again, we preserve the pattern of body parts, even though in this case the Hebrew really has little to do with the tongue but rather more generally with "language" (like "mother tongue" in English).

[26]For the sin we have committed against You through negotiations,
[27]and for the sin we have committed against You through food and through drink.
[28]For the sin we have committed against You through usury and through interest,
[29]and for the sin we have committed against You through pride.
[30]For the sin we have committed against You through the conversations of our lips,
[31]and for the sin we have committed against You through winking our eyes.

[26] עַל חֵטְא שֶׁחָטָאנוּ לְפָנֶיךָ בְּמַשָּׂא וּבְמַתָּן,
[27] וְעַל חֵטְא שֶׁחָטָאנוּ לְפָנֶיךָ בְּמַאֲכָל וּבְמִשְׁתֶּה.
[28] עַל חֵטְא שֶׁחָטָאנוּ לְפָנֶיךָ בְּנֶשֶׁךְ וּבְמַרְבִּית,
[29] וְעַל חֵטְא שֶׁחָטָאנוּ לְפָנֶיךָ בִּנְטִיַּת גָּרוֹן.
[30] עַל חֵטְא שֶׁחָטָאנוּ לְפָנֶיךָ בְּשִׂיחַ שִׂפְתוֹתֵינוּ,
[31] וְעַל חֵטְא שֶׁחָטָאנוּ לְפָנֶיךָ בְּשִׂקּוּר עָיִן.

[26]*Negotiations*: Literally, "giving and taking," which is the Hebrew expression for "negotiations." The Hebrew contains two opposites, as do so many other lines here. Our English does not. It is tempting to translate "give and take," but that's not what the Hebrew means.
[29]*Pride*: Literally, "outstretched necks." We have no way to include the word "neck" in our translation.

[32]For the sin we have committed against You through eyes of deceit,

[32] עַל חֵטְא שֶׁחָטָאנוּ לְפָנֶיךָ בְּעֵינַיִם רָמוֹת,

[33]and for the sin we have committed against You through vainglory.

[33] וְעַל חֵטְא שֶׁחָטָאנוּ לְפָנֶיךָ בְּעַזּוּת מֶצַח.

[34]And for all of these, God of forgiveness, forgive us, pardon us, absolve us.

[34] וְעַל כֻּלָּם, אֱלוֹהַּ סְלִיחוֹת, סְלַח לָנוּ, מְחַל לָנוּ, כַּפֶּר לָנוּ.

[35]For the sin we have committed against You through breaking free of our yokes,

[35] עַל חֵטְא שֶׁחָטָאנוּ לְפָנֶיךָ בִּפְרִיקַת עֹל,

[36]and for the sin we have committed against You through criminality.

[36] וְעַל חֵטְא שֶׁחָטָאנוּ לְפָנֶיךָ בִּפְלִילוּת.

[37]For the sin we have committed against You through incitement,

[37] עַל חֵטְא שֶׁחָטָאנוּ לְפָנֶיךָ בִּצְדִיַּת רֵעַ,

[38]and for the sin we have committed against You through narrowness of vision.

[38] וְעַל חֵטְא שֶׁחָטָאנוּ לְפָנֶיךָ בְּצָרוּת עָיִן.

[32]*Eyes of deceit*: Or, "deceitful eyes." We prefer our translation because, like the Hebrew, it changes the order of "eye" in the phrase between this line and the previous one.

[33]*Vainglory*: The Hebrew expression contains the word "forehead" in a way we cannot mimic in English.

[35]*Yokes*: That is, the yoke of God's rule. This is a common Jewish metaphor. A yoke, once common and now mostly rare, is the device by which a human controls an ox. Similarly, the general imagery is that we should be pleased to have God guide us.

[38]*Narrowness of vision*: Hebrew, "narrowness of eyes," but "narrow eyes" in English doesn't mean what we want it to.

[39] עַל חֵטְא שֶׁחָטָאנוּ לְפָנֶיךָ
בְּקַלּוּת רֹאשׁ,
[40] וְעַל חֵטְא שֶׁחָטָאנוּ לְפָנֶיךָ
בְּקַשְׁיוּת עֹרֶף.
[41] עַל חֵטְא שֶׁחָטָאנוּ לְפָנֶיךָ
בְּרִיצַת רַגְלַיִם לְהָרַע,
[42] וְעַל חֵטְא שֶׁחָטָאנוּ לְפָנֶיךָ
בִּרְכִילוּת.
[43] עַל חֵטְא שֶׁחָטָאנוּ לְפָנֶיךָ
בִּשְׁבוּעַת שָׁוְא,
[44] וְעַל חֵטְא שֶׁחָטָאנוּ לְפָנֶיךָ
בְּשִׂנְאַת חִנָּם.
[45] עַל חֵטְא שֶׁחָטָאנוּ לְפָנֶיךָ
בִּתְשׂוּמֶת־יָד,
[46] וְעַל חֵטְא שֶׁחָטָאנוּ לְפָנֶיךָ
בְּתִמְהוֹן לֵבָב.
[47] וְעַל כֻּלָּם, אֱלוֹהַּ סְלִיחוֹת,
סְלַח לָנוּ, מְחַל לָנוּ, כַּפֶּר לָנוּ.

[39]For the sin we have committed against You through heads of superficiality,
[40]and for the sin we have committed against You through necks of stubbornness.
[41]For the sin we have committed against You through legs running to do evil,
[42]and for the sin we have committed against You through slander.
[43]For the sin we have committed against You through empty promises,
[44]and for the sin we have committed against You through pointless hatred.
[45]For the sin we have committed against You through handing money,
[46]and for the sin we have committed against You through foolish hearts.
[47]And for all of these, God of forgiveness, forgive us, pardon us, absolve us.

[39]*Heads of superficiality*: This is the first of three successive body-part images. Of the three, "heads of superficiality" is the most forced in English, but we want to maintain the poetic impact.
[45]*Handing money*: Literally, "putting the hand," probably in the sense of "putting one's hand on money." The phrase comes from Leviticus 5:21, where it is included in a list of sins having to do with money.

[48]And for sins for which our punishment is a burnt offering [*olah*],
[49]and for sins for which our punishment is a sin offering [*chatat*],
[50]and for sins for which our punishment is an offering whose value varies with the means of the person offering it [*korban oleh v'yored*],
[51]and for sins for which our punishment is a guilt offering, either on account of the certainty of sin or on account of the possibility thereof [*asham vada'i v'asham talu'i*],
[52]and for sins for which our punishment is corporal punishment [*makat mardut*],
[53]and for sins for which our punishment is forty lashings [*malkut arba'im*],
[54]and for sins for which our punishment is death by the hand of heaven [*mitah bidei shamayim*],
[55]and for sins for which our punishment is being cut off or childless [*karet va'ariri*].

[48] וְעַל חֲטָאִים שֶׁאָנוּ חַיָּבִים עֲלֵיהֶם עוֹלָה,
[49] וְעַל חֲטָאִים שֶׁאָנוּ חַיָּבִים עֲלֵיהֶם חַטָּאת,
[50] וְעַל חֲטָאִים שֶׁאָנוּ חַיָּבִים עֲלֵיהֶם קָרְבָּן עוֹלֶה וְיוֹרֵד,
[51] וְעַל חֲטָאִים שֶׁאָנוּ חַיָּבִים עֲלֵיהֶם אָשָׁם וַדַּאי וְאָשָׁם תָּלוּי,
[52] וְעַל חֲטָאִים שֶׁאָנוּ חַיָּבִים עֲלֵיהֶם מַכַּת מַרְדּוּת,
[53] וְעַל חֲטָאִים שֶׁאָנוּ חַיָּבִים עֲלֵיהֶם מַלְקוּת אַרְבָּעִים,
[54] וְעַל חֲטָאִים שֶׁאָנוּ חַיָּבִים עֲלֵיהֶם מִיתָה בִּידֵי שָׁמָיִם,
[55] וְעַל חֲטָאִים שֶׁאָנוּ חַיָּבִים עֲלֵיהֶם כָּרֵת וַעֲרִירִי.

[56]and for sins for which our punishment is the four kinds of death sentences assigned by the court: stoning, burning, beheading, and strangling. [57]For the positive commandments and the negative commandments (whether they can be mitigated or not); regarding what is revealed to us and what is not revealed to us. [58]What is revealed to us we have already confessed before You and acknowledged to You, and what is not revealed to us is revealed and known before You, as is said: [59]what is hidden is for Adonai our God, and what is revealed is for us and our descendants forever, that we might do everything in this Torah. [60]For You forgive Israel and pardon the tribes of Yeshurun in each and every generation, and other than You we have no king who can forgive or pardon us.

[56] וְעַל חֲטָאִים שֶׁאָנוּ חַיָּבִים עֲלֵיהֶם אַרְבַּע מִיתוֹת בֵּית דִּין, סְקִילָה, שְׂרֵפָה, הֶרֶג, וְחֶנֶק. [57] עַל מִצְוַת עֲשֵׂה וְעַל מִצְוַת לֹא תַעֲשֶׂה, בֵּין שֶׁיֵּשׁ בָּהּ קוּם עֲשֵׂה, וּבֵין שֶׁאֵין בָּהּ קוּם עֲשֵׂה, אֶת הַגְּלוּיִם לָנוּ וְאֶת שֶׁאֵינָם גְּלוּיִם לָנוּ. [58] אֶת הַגְּלוּיִם לָנוּ כְּבָר אֲמַרְנוּם לְפָנֶיךָ, וְהוֹדִינוּ לְךָ עֲלֵיהֶם, וְאֶת שֶׁאֵינָם גְּלוּיִם לָנוּ, לְפָנֶיךָ הֵם גְּלוּיִם וִידוּעִים, כַּדָּבָר שֶׁנֶּאֱמַר: [59] הַנִּסְתָּרֹת לַייָ אֱלֹהֵינוּ, וְהַנִּגְלֹת לָנוּ וּלְבָנֵינוּ עַד עוֹלָם, לַעֲשׂוֹת אֶת כָּל דִּבְרֵי הַתּוֹרָה הַזֹּאת. [60] כִּי אַתָּה סָלְחָן לְיִשְׂרָאֵל וּמָחֳלָן לְשִׁבְטֵי יְשֻׁרוּן בְּכָל־דּוֹר וָדוֹר וּמִבַּלְעָדֶיךָ אֵין לָנוּ מֶלֶךְ מוֹחֵל וְסוֹלֵחַ אֶלָּא אָתָּה.

[57]*Positive commandments*: A technical term, representing commandments to do something.
[57]*Negative commandments*: Also a technical term, representing commandments not to do something.
[58]*Confessed*: Hebrew, “said.”

Conclusion

[1]My God, until I was created I was unworthy, and now that I have been created it is as though I was not created. [2]I am dust as I live, all the more so on my deathbed. Before You I am like a vessel full of shame and humiliation. [3]May it be your will, Adonai my God and my ancestors' God, that I sin no more. [4]And in your great mercy erase my previous sins before You, but not through punishment or terrible disease.

[1]אֱלֹהַי, עַד שֶׁלֹּא נוֹצַרְתִּי אֵינִי כְדַי, וְעַכְשָׁו שֶׁנּוֹצַרְתִּי כְּאִלּוּ לֹא נוֹצַרְתִּי. [2]עָפָר אֲנִי בְּחַיַּי קַל וָחֹמֶר בְּמִיתָתִי: הֲרֵי אֲנִי לְפָנֶיךָ כִּכְלִי מָלֵא בוּשָׁה וּכְלִמָּה. [3]יְהִי רָצוֹן מִלְּפָנֶיךָ יְיָ אֱלֹהַי וֵאלֹהֵי אֲבוֹתַי שֶׁלֹּא אֶחֱטָא עוֹד. [4]וּמַה שֶּׁחָטָאתִי לְפָנֶיךָ מְחֹק בְּרַחֲמֶיךָ הָרַבִּים אֲבָל לֹא עַל יְדֵי יִסּוּרִים וָחֳלָיִם רָעִים.

[1]*Unworthy*: Presumably, not worthy of being created.

[2]*Deathbed*: Hebrew, just "bed."

[2]*Vessel full of shame and humiliation*: The Hebrew is poetic in a way we cannot capture in English. The Hebrew phrase "vessel full ..." starts with the sound *klima*, which also happens to be the word for "humiliation."

Part III

Ashamnu and *Al Chet* As Prayer Book Editors See Them

Finding Ourselves in God

Rabbi Elyse D. Frishman

Imagine two drawings. In one, you are in the center, some trees surround you, perhaps; you are outlined clearly against the bright blue sky. In the other, infinite sparks of light fill the vast heavens, and you are a speck of a speck of a speck within that grand cosmos.

The first is your point of view as someone in the center of the universe. In the second, you are infinitely less important, almost invisible. We normally see ourselves in picture number one: the person around whom the universe revolves. It takes a good deal of effort to imagine our existence in the infinite space of picture number two. It is possible, however, so our perspective vacillates between the two extremes: from utter self-importance to utmost humility. Both are real.

So where is the center of the universe? Physically, there is none. Space is curved and without an edge; traveling from one "end" to another, you'd wind up where you began—much like a sea voyager on our planet. Picture number one is wrong, but not because there is some physical presence other than ourselves that is the actual center; it is wrong because there is no physical center altogether. It's actually plausible that the center of the universe is *wherever you are*. But at the same time, of course, the center is where everyone else is also.

So perhaps the center is *everywhere*. That is the view of Jewish mystics who would say that the center of the universe is not in any one of ourselves, but in God, because God is everywhere. We call God *hamakom*, "the place," meaning "every place," for if God is everywhere, wherever there is "place" there is God. The infinite universe, then, has no physical

---

Rabbi Elyse D. Frishman is editor of *Mishkan T'filah: A Reform Siddur* and rabbi of The Barnert Temple in Franklin Lakes, New Jersey. She contributed to *Who by Fire, Who by Water—Un'taneh Tokef* (Jewish Lights).

center, but only a spiritual one, its God-ness, which is everywhere. In the first picture, we are the center; in the second picture, God is.

We sin when we confuse the centers, as if the only proper picture is the first one, with the sun, moon, or stars shining just for us. This egocentrism leads us astray, off target, away from God, the true center. This is *chet*, "missing the mark." "Missing the mark" is an idiom used commonly for "sin" in Jewish tradition. But thinking of it as an arrow aiming for a bull's-eye but going off target misses the point. Missing the mark means missing the reality of a God-centered universe and insisting instead on a self-centered one. We naturally think of ourselves as part of picture number one; in reality, we are part of picture two, part of a larger whole.

The whole of which we Jews most naturally consider ourselves is the Jewish *People*. Each individual has a place; each person is important—not so self-important that one imagines being a "master of the universe,"[1] as in picture number one; but important enough to feel needed and wanted as a necessary contributor to the welfare of all: a serious member of the whole, as in picture number two.

Through prayer and *mitzvot*, Jews deepen that understanding of purposeful relationship to the whole that is picture number two: the Jewish whole and the universal one, all peoples and even all that is—our planet, the cosmos, and, by definition, God. Jews try to focus on *we*, not *me*. Our default as human beings is picture number one: the center, the master of the universe. At our best, we Jews find our way to picture number two, at one with the whole.

The *I* of the individual flourishes in the context of *we*—*we* the Jewish People, *we* the human community, *we* in partnership with God, *Hamakom*, the Center. *I* never disappears, and shouldn't. But sin, *chet*, results from wanting to be master. *Chet* comes from focusing on *I*; *t'shuvah* reflects the effort to rejoin *we*.

In Hebrew, *I* is *anokhi*, the biblical word that best reflects a strong sense of self. Quite often in Torah, *anokhi* denotes a state of suffering. When Rebecca is in terrible pain, pregnant with twins, she demands of God, "If so, why do I [*anokhi*] exist?" (Genesis 25:22). What is the purpose of my pain? *Anokhi* feels radically alone, confused, uncertain, in despair.

When Esau comes home hungry from an unsuccessful hunt, he is overcome with the smell of his twin brother Jacob's stew, and he exchanges his birthright for the food. "*I* [*anokhi*] am going to die!" he exclaims. "What good is my birthright to me?" (Genesis 25:32). The human *anokhi* has no perspective beyond itself; it is disconnected from the whole.

Anokhi is born with Adam and Eve, who eat the fruit of the Tree of Knowledge of Good and Evil and thereby become self-aware. Having selves for the first time ever and needing to find their place in the universe, they mistakenly withdraw into themselves, overwhelmed and terrified. When God demands, "Where are you?" Adam responds, "I heard your voice in the garden, and I was awestruck because *I* [*anokhi*] am self-aware and I need to distinguish myself from You" (Genesis 3:9–10). A condition of *anokhi* is self-awareness.

Good news and bad news! We cannot be human without being self-aware. We cannot enter relationships without a self to do the entering. But too much emphasis on the self limits those very relationships—with others and with God. The result is loneliness and insecurity, self-absorption and short-sightedness, pain and suffering. With feelings centered only on the self, we lose sight of the whole, miss the mark of seeing ourselves in picture number two—which is to say, we sin. *Chet* is a consequence of the *anokhi* that sees itself only in picture number one and lacks, therefore, a sense of a center beyond itself, which is God.

How does one resume the search for a relationship with God as the center?

Interestingly, God too is *Anokhi.* (It's helpful to think of God's *Anokhi* with a capital *A,* and the human *anokhi* as lowercase.) God's *Anokhi* appears as part of Jacob's dream when Jacob too acknowledges his human *anokhi.* But Jacob's acknowledgment is not the self-centeredness of Rebecca's, Esau's, and Adam's. "Surely God is in this place and I, I [*anokhi*] didn't know it," Jacob declares (Genesis 28:16). Having been lost and alone in the physical expanse of the desert, Jacob discovers God's presence and is alone no more. He has moved from picture number one to picture number two—in relationship now with God, who promises Jacob, "*I* [*Anochi*] am with you" (Genesis 28:15). It is not just God and Jacob who are together, however, because God draws Jacob into an even larger whole, the covenant of the Jewish People. "I am the God of your father Abraham and the God of Isaac," God explains. "The land on which you are lying I will give to you and your descendants … through you and your descendants all the families of the earth will find blessing" (Genesis

28:13–14). God is found, not because Jacob is important, but because Jacob chooses to engage in the covenant of Israel.

It is as if Jacob himself, not just the angels, ascends the ladder. No longer alone, he is part of a people, centered on God, not on himself. He can now move forward and define the future. So too with us. When we sink into ourselves, we mess up. When we come out of ourselves, we discover a purposeful future.

Jacob, who becomes Israel, anticipates the story of the Jewish People as a whole, the tale that begins with deliverance from Egypt. There too God appears as the divine *Anokhi*, the Self that fills the universe and therefore history. The very first of the Ten Commandments reads, "I [*Anokhi*] am the Eternal your God who brought you out from Egypt" (Exodus 20:2). Ours is not a story of personal redemption alone, but of a people's. God lifted us up as one. We were redeemed together. We bear responsibility together. And we confess together: for the sin *we* have committed, as a people.

Al chet shechatanu l'fanekha, "For the sin we have committed against You." *Against God*—the center that embraces us. We return ourselves to the center, to God. We move from *I* into *we*—a *we* that knows and rejoices in a center other than ourselves.

It is natural to live a great deal of our lives in picture number one. Our consciousness of self even mandates it. The miracle of being human, however, gives us not just consciousness of self but consciousness of what is beyond that self and consciousness, therefore, of what it might be like to live in the ultimate reality of picture number two. No one is important enough to be the actual center of all that is. The true center, God, includes us all. And when one sins, all are affected, even God. So the language of confession reminds us: *Al chet shechatanu l'fanekha*—"For the sin *we* have committed *against You*."

It is the rebuilding of *we* that is at the heart of this prayer. We need each other to make sense of our lives. We need each other and God to make ourselves whole.

Multiplying the Sins

Rabbi Andrew Goldstein, PhD

As I survey the collection of *machzorim*, ancient and modern, lying open on my desk, a number of questions come to mind: why does Jewish liturgy tend to start out short and concise and, as time goes by, get longer and longer, with explanations, repetitions, and convolutions? *Al Chet* may have begun with as few as six sins in it, while the current Ashkenazi version has forty-four.

When I lead the congregation on Yom Kippur, making my way through these endless (it seems) additions, I find myself wondering which of the sins we are supposed to take seriously; looking at the faces in front of me, do I get the feeling that there is much repenting going on down there in the pews? Do any of the lines in the prayer move me to think about my own actions?

To be honest, as I look through the by now seemingly endless list of sins in *Al Chet*, I realize I might own up to having committed many of them. But I think then of the list of misdemeanors in Deuteronomy 27, the ones so wicked that they rain down curses on the perpetrators: everything from misdirecting the blind to having sex with beasts or one's mother-in-law! And what about Leviticus 18, the traditional Torah portion on Yom Kippur afternoon, with its seventeen or eighteen examples of forbidden sex—some of them quite mind-boggling. By comparison, the list in *Al Chet* seems quite anodyne: "arrogant, haughty, gossiping, levity, overeating...." The extensive list we have is not only overly long, then, but (worse, perhaps) it is less than startling; it is as domesticated a set of sinful wildness as one might imagine. I easily recognize many of these as part of my nature—maybe not the four or five sexual sins in the

---

Rabbi Andrew Goldstein, PhD, is the rabbinic advisor to the European Union for Progressive Judaism and coeditor of *Machzor Ruach Chadashah*. He contributed to *Who by Fire, Who by Water—Un'taneh Tokef* and *All These Vows—Kol Nidre* (both Jewish Lights).

long list, but even these get lost among all the other ones and appear in an English translation that makes them sound almost respectable.

If you agree that the sins of *Al Chet* are rather tame, does repeating them over the long Yom Kippur day, up to ten times in some rites, make them more effective? Or does confession just become an ever more boring redundancy? Come *N'ilah* (the concluding service), aren't we simply fed up with it all? Even inured to sin altogether by the constant reminder of all the petty wrong we might potentially do or have done? Wouldn't it be more effective to keep the list short and snappy, with a set of sins that are really sins? After all, *Al Chet* comes just after the other ancient confession: *Ashamnu, bagadnu, gazalnu*—a short, neat alphabetic formulation of sins.

The earliest version of *Al Chet* may have had just six sins: "For the sin we have committed against You ... under duress ... of our own will ... in secret ... in public ... unconsciously ... consciously." The Western Sephardim (the European Sephardim, as opposed the Sephardim who developed in the Mediterranean lands) keep to this number to this day. *Seder Rav Amram* (ninth century) extended the list to twelve and Maimonides (twelfth century) seems to have an acrostic of twenty-two lines. But *Machzor Vitry* (our best source for early Ashkenazi liturgy, France, eleventh to twelfth century) lists thirty-six. Did the authors of these works choose from preexisting lists or make up their own? The extension to twenty-two sins makes some sense, as it is a full alphabetic acrostic, but it eventually becomes a double acrostic of forty-four; liturgists do tend to get more long-winded over time.

In the Temple, on Yom Kippur, the high priest's spoken confession had but three words of regret, each one referring to a different kind of sin: *chatanu, avinu, pashanu* (Mishnah Yoma 3:8).[1] The early Rabbis (third century CE)[2] must have constructed their own, maybe silent, confession, making up their own list of sins—the list of six were just the headlines that developed eventually to aid individual meditation on specific sins that might come to mind. The trend, in any event, was to go from the extemporary to the fixed. We see it elsewhere, too—the "silent prayer" at the end of the *Amidah*, for instance: the Talmud (Berakhot 17a) cites several rabbis, each with his own private meditation, but gradually standard ones emerged for everyone to say. So it is that instead of a short but impactful statement of sin, we ended up with two fixed and lengthy lists that are recited by rote, repeated over and again, in time to stirring melodies. The melodies do add gravitas to the litany, but do they make us more conscious of the meaning, or does the music simply obscure the purpose of the words?

Moderating the tepid nature of the sins is a list of punishments, quite frightening punishments, with which the traditional liturgy concludes the list of sins: "For sins for which our punishment is corporal punishment ... forty lashes ... being cut off or childless ... death sentences [assigned by] the court: stoning, burning, beheading, and strangling!" I wonder how these words strike modern worshipers who say and understand them. Do they heighten the desire to repent, or do they sound like archaic nonsense? No wonder the custom is not to read them aloud.

Reform and Conservative prayer books leave out this chilling passage but not the trend of gradually lengthening the *Al Chet* litany. The American Reform *Union Prayer Book II* listed nine sins;[3] these were copied by Rabbi Israel I. Mattuck in his British *Liberal Jewish Prayer Book*, volume 2.[4] Its successor, *Gates of Repentance*, increased the list to eighteen, but then added thirty-six descriptions of contemporary expressions of our failings: "condemning in our children the faults we tolerate in ourselves ... nurturing racial prejudice and denying its existence ... shunting aside those whose age is an embarrassment to us ... waging aggressive war," and so on.[5] The American Reform *Gates of Prayer* adopted this list,[6] and other modern non-Orthodox prayer books have added similar selections of human failings as new crimes came to their editors' attention. The process was started in the Reconstructionist *High Holiday Prayer Book* of 1948; for example, "We sin ... when we ridicule ideas and belittle heroism ... when we make our cities a jungle, and make violence the law ... when we cast onto the waste-heap the precious heritage of our people."[7] Rabbi Ronald Aigen's *machzor* includes "for the sin of false and deceptive advertising ... building weapons of mass destruction," and so on.[8] The Conservative *Mahzor Lev Shalem*, the latest High Holy Day prayer book to be published by that movement, includes "for the sin of destroying species You saved from the flood" and other concerns on the ecological agenda.[9]

As new *machzorim* are published in the future, will the then current moral concerns be included: "for eating chicken we suspect has been factory farmed ... for wearing a T-shirt that must have been made by sweated labor ... for buying cheaply online books we perused at the local bookshop"? Do these up-to-date sins have more resonance with today's worshipers than those on the traditional list? I suspect they do have a genuine and immediate effect the first few times they are read, but very quickly seem shallow and out of date, whereas the traditional list will stand for all time. And note: this list is addressed to individual worshipers in their own life; the more modern additions often address society's woes. Surely it is more realistic to try to correct your own failings than to endeavor to personally save the planet (although you could argue that encouragement to *tikkun olam* is not to be taken lightly).

Perhaps there is a place for a variety of lists and formulas—maybe different selections in different services, just as the traditional liturgy included two lists of sins: *Ashamnu* and *Al Chet*, the former serving as a rousing introduction to the latter. Perhaps *Al Chet* should be preceded by instructions, written or verbal: "Say the list in unison with the other congregants, but tick off one or two in your mind, and concentrate on these and make them your particular aim in the coming year as you try to improve your conduct and personality." *The Complete ArtScroll Machzor* provides an appendix that personalizes each of the forty-four sins of *Al Chet*; for instance, "*Under duress* ... we have said we had no choice but to sin, we rationalize that we have no choice but to sin. For example, if we are afraid we may lose our jobs or customers, we may permit ourselves to do things we know to be wrong and would not condone in others."[10]

I myself, however, keep returning to the very beginning, the Rabbinic origin of our confession, where individuals were expected to construct their own list of relevant offenses. The unison congregational recitation of the two litanies may have their place, but I find most effective the silent reading of inspiring prose that really makes me think. There are some deeply moving passages in the *Union Prayer Book*,[11] individual confessions tailored specifically for the whole congregation and then one each for "the Aged, Women, Young People, Children." My teacher, Rabbi John D. Rayner, wrote a beautiful confessional meditation for *Gates of Repentance*;[12] of its many memorable paragraphs I end with one.

> I have been weak. I have too often failed to make the effort required of me to fulfill my obligations: to do my work conscientiously, to give my full attention to those who needed me, to speak the kindly word, to do the generous deed, to give my fellow men and women those evidences of my concern for them which would have made their lives happier, or less lonely, I have not loved enough, not even within my family circle.

For the Sin of "Unattempted Loveliness"

Rabbi Edwin Goldberg

In his book *The People of the Lie*, the late author M. Scott Peck argues that most evil in our world is committed through lack of awareness.[1] People don't wake up and say, "Gee, today I think I will commit a sin." They hurt other people because they are not aware of the damage they are doing. Of all the transgressions listed in the traditional *Al Chet*, therefore, the most important may be the wrong that we do "through lack of knowledge" (as per the translation in this volume), which I prefer to read as "thoughtlessness" (*b'li da'at*). The Hebrew words for "knowledge" (*da'at*) and "religion" (*dat*) are similar, so we might also read the sin as the harm we do others "through lack of religion."

Not that by itself religion will necessarily awaken people to follow the right moral path! But religion does play two important roles: it provides the knowledge of where we go wrong, and more than that, it tells us that we go wrong in the first place. This goes also for sins of omission—not just what people actually do wrong, that is, but what people fail to do right, the missed opportunities to practice righteousness, what is called "unattempted loveliness" by the poet Marguerite Wilkinson.[2]

No one gets up in the morning with the intention to attempt no loveliness all day either. Like sins of commission, sins of omission too

---

Rabbi Edwin Goldberg serves as coordinator of the Central Conference of American Rabbis (CCAR) editorial committee on the forthcoming CCAR *machzor*. He has a doctorate in Hebrew letters from Hebrew Union College–Jewish Institute of Religion and is a rabbi at Temple Judea in Coral Gables, Florida.

proceed from lack of awareness, making the sin of thoughtlessness the "gateway" sin to all the others. We need religion because religion provides the texts and practices that keep us from spiritual somnambulism.

I am especially concerned about the younger generation. I'm not saying that our youth are immoral or even amoral. They just don't know what to think when it comes to matters of morality. They are unaware of what it means to be good.

New York Times columnist David Brooks often writes about American young adults' moral relativism. In a September 13, 2011 column titled "If It Feels Right," he described a recent poll conducted by Notre Dame sociologist Christian Smith where interviewers asked twenty-somethings open-ended questions about moral dilemmas and the meaning of life.[3] From their answers it was clear to see that the young people were trying to say something sensible about their moral choices but they lacked the proper vocabulary.

When asked to describe a moral dilemma that had challenged them, more than half of the questioned youngsters either couldn't answer the question or mentioned problems that are not moral at all, such as whether they could afford to rent a certain apartment.

When asked about evil, they could generally agree that rape and murder are wrong. But in less extreme matters, moral thinking was not considered relevant. Even drunken driving or cheating on a test or on a lover did not make the cut. "I don't really deal with right and wrong that often," is how one interviewee put it. Most of the young people believed that moral choices are exclusively personal and therefore no one else's business.[4]

Our young adults have been given so little structure for understanding the difference between right and wrong. As far as they were concerned, the universe is morally neutral.

It is not hard to understand why they feel that way. High school students are consumed with getting into colleges. They expend enormous effort taking the next step forward in their upward mobility through life. Moral instruction—which is to say, matters of character, not of achievement—is irrelevant to that pursuit; it can sometimes even hamper it. Religion, the institutions designed to teach children about character, is abandoned as a needless drain on their precious time. It can only get in the way.

With the Rabbis of antiquity, I presume that people are born with a lack of moral awareness. Babies don't consciously refrain from crying in their crib because mommy needs a break. So when does awareness of the needs of others kick in? I think we have to be coached. Hence the recitation of sins on Yom Kippur.

But recitation is insufficient. We require also the discipline of mindfulness. That is why our Jewish tradition balanced the Talmud with specifically ethical literature known as *musar* as a nuanced nudge in awakening our dormant higher selves. The formal recitation of sin (on one hand) and the mindfulness of *musar* (on the other) are the Jewish way to the religion of awareness, awareness of our faults so that we might know enough to want to change them.

A personal confession, as an example: I know that I am not a great listener. I find myself too often thinking how I can work my way back into the conversation instead of listening to the conversation unfold. But at least I know this is a challenge for me, and knowing that, I can decide to improve. Paradoxically, reciting the line in *Al Chet* that reminds me of the sins we do thoughtlessly helps me realize how much my thoughtless failure to listen hurts others and allows me to want to confront this shortcoming.

This is all part of the larger task of refining our character. Thinking about the sins I commit without knowing it leads me to *musar* literature's discussion of the ethical practice of listening with attentiveness, *sh'mi'at ha'ozen*. That same literature suggests a regimen by which I can replace my bad habit with a good one. I now kiss the mezuzah as I enter my home to remind me of the first word within it: *Sh'ma*, "Listen." I enter my home with the intention of listening. Further, I keep by my side the following levels of listening:

Not listening
Listening to tell your story
Listening to judge
Listening to apply
Listening to understand[5]

I try to move up the ladder from not listening to listening to understand.

This taxonomy is a practical method for me to be aware of my fault and to do something about it. The problem is defined, and a solution is presented. Awareness is achieved. *Al Chet* cuts me to the quick, but the *musar* allows my character to be refined.

This very process transformed the great twentieth-century philosopher Martin Buber, as he went from being a terrible listener to appreciating the gift of personal presence. Buber grew up surrounded by Jewish study but also the modern world of German intelligentsia. He began as a professor of religion and philosophy, a teacher and writer on religious experience and mysticism. But in the middle decades of his life he experienced an event of momentous personal consequence.

He had been fully engaged in the deep religious intensity of meditation and prayer when there was a knock at the door. Interrupted from the spiritual moment, Buber went to answer the door. It was a young man, a former student and friend, who had come specifically to speak with him.

Buber was polite, even friendly, but could not wait to get back to his meditations. After a short conversation, the young man left. Buber never saw him again because he was killed in battle (or perhaps committed suicide—the story is not entirely clear).

Buber learned later, from a mutual friend, that the man had come because he had been perplexed about an issue involving the very meaning of his life and what life was asking of him. Buber had not recognized the young man's true intent at the time because he had been too concerned with returning to his prayers and meditation. He had been polite and friendly, he remembered, even cordial, but not fully present, not in the way that only one person can for another—sensing the questions and concerns of the other even before they themselves are aware of what their questions are.

Martin Buber had learned that profound listening enhances our ability to practice compassion. Sin can simply be unattempted loveliness. Moral awareness is an aversion to sin. Character is the commitment to moral awareness. Repentance is the pathway to character. Half the battle of repentance is knowing there is a battle at all, and the other half is finding a way to replace our selfish obliviousness with a renewed recognition of a world that needs our attention to be redeemed.

Manifesting as Jews

Rabbi Jonathan Magonet, PhD

Having written my PhD on the literary structure of the book of Jonah, that troublesome and puzzling character is never far from my thoughts on Yom Kippur. Jonah, too, makes a public confession, his own personal *al chet*, but it is not without its problems.

When the sailors discover that Jonah is responsible for the catastrophic storm that they are encountering, Jonah more or less confesses his role. But only more or less—not entirely. Twice the sailors refer to the event as "this evil" (Jonah 1:7–8) and then use an unusually late Hebrew construction regarding it: *b'shelmi*, they say; and then *ba'asher l'mi*: "On whose account has this evil come upon us?" Mentioning something twice in the Bible customarily sets up a "normative" meaning; a third time suggests we are supposed to look for something new. That third time comes in Jonah's confession: *b'sheli*, "through me," and the anticipated novelty arrives when he replaces the sailor's "this evil" with "this great storm" (1:12). It is as if he is willing to acknowledge some degree of responsibility (the storm), but not admit the true extent of what the storm represents (an *evil*). This pattern of reluctant confessions makes Jonah a kind of "anti-model" of what Yom Kippur expects from us.

This theme of half-truths and partial acknowledgment touches the problem and challenge of Yom Kippur confessions generally: their collective nature, based on the Rabbis' assumption that "all Israel are responsible, one for the other" (Talmud, Sh'vuot 39b). Even if we ourselves have not personally committed the sin to which we confess, it is assumed that other

---

Rabbi Jonathan Magonet, PhD, is emeritus professor of Bible at Leo Baeck College in London, where he was principal (president) from 1985 to 2005. He is coeditor of three volumes of *Forms of Prayer* (the prayer books of the British Movement for Reform Judaism) and editor of the eighth edition of *Daily, Sabbath and Occasional Prayers*. He contributed to *Who by Fire, Who by Water—Un'taneh Tokef* and *All These Vows—Kol Nidre* (both Jewish Lights).

Jews have done so, and as "Israel," we bear collective responsibility for them. But what sins should be included, and how far is the traditional list still relevant? Moreover, how effective is the exercise of confession itself? Victor Gollancz,[1] a publisher and explorer of spirituality, describes his annoyance as a child when confronted with sins he could never have committed, but acknowledgment as an adult of their relevance to his own life:

> Hardening of the heart; wronging our neighbour, sinful meditation; unclean lips; denying and lying; "the stretched forth neck of pride"; effrontery; envy; levity; stiff-neckedness; "confusion of mind" (certainly, but how could I help it?); even perhaps, on second thoughts, "wanton looks"—not only do I now know that most if not all of these things were ingredients in my character, as many of them still are.[2]

But he questions the efficacy of the exercise of confession anyway:

> Just as confessing a thing didn't and in some cases quite obviously couldn't imply that you'd done it, so confessing what in fact you *had* done didn't necessarily imply that you were aware of having done it; nor again did confessing what you couldn't help knowing you'd done necessarily imply that you sincerely repented of it and would not try to do it again.

In the face of such a critique, and given the distance so many Jews have traveled from the traditional understanding of confession's efficacy, modern prayer books have substituted contemporary lists of sins whose immediate relevance may more readily strike a familiar chord. These updated lists feature two broad areas of innovation.

The first addresses our responsibility for events in the global public arena, something only indirectly implied in texts belonging to the pre-Emancipation Jewish world. Today, we are more conscious of being citizens in the wider world, sharing responsibility with all others for the wrongs committed against the underprivileged or victims of society.

We thus see contemporary liturgies challenging the congregation to confront issues about everything from ethnic cleansing and genocide to threats to endangered species and climate change. Of course, the more up-to-date and immediate the sins acknowledged, the less likely they are to be relevant for more than a year or two, so these lists tend to appear in sheets distributed to the community for a given year and then be replaced by new sheets the year after. In addition, even though they are important wake-up calls to our conscience, the delicate line between liturgy and party-specific political propaganda is easily crossed. A further problem is that if the particular issue really hits home, its graphic detail may undermine the liturgical moment itself by introducing too much reality.

A special problem arises when it comes to sins concerning the State of Israel. Since they define our relationship to a Jewish state, they open up all the internal conflicts and wounds within Israel's political arena, most dramatically regarding attitudes toward and treatment of Palestinians and the Arab minority. Moreover, all such "confessions" stumble over the troubled relationship between Israel and the diaspora and the right of diaspora communities to criticize the actions of the State of Israel.

When working on our current High Holy Day *machzor* for the Reform Synagogues of Great Britain (now the Movement for Reform Judaism) in the 1980s, we were very much influenced by the 1972 *machzor* of the Rabbinical Assembly. *Ashamnu* was "translated" through a list of sins organized by the English alphabet. We drew the line at "we are xenophobic," on pronunciation grounds, preferring "we have practised extortion," but accepted for the letter "k" "we have killed." Confessing to "killing" marks a radical departure from the type of sin listed in the traditional confessions, yet it is an acknowledgement of the reality of Israel as a state at war with its neighbors.

The Israeli organization Rabbis for Human Rights has produced confessions for the Jewish New Year that are very powerful in admitting wrongs done by the Israeli government against Palestinians: expropriating land, demolishing homes, uprooting trees, using exceptional lethal force, and so on. For an organization that carries out active intervention and protest against such "sins," such a confession carries a degree of authenticity. But what about communities that do nothing to combat the "sins" in question—how legitimate is it for them to use it, even on the basis that "all Israel are mutually responsible"? Clearly such a confession can only be seen as "one-sided" and even a betrayal by those of a different political persuasion, within and beyond Israel.

Are the Yom Kippur confessions meant to produce real thought and self-examination, and indeed, change, or do they never move beyond a ritualized behavior? Are they merely, as Gollancz expresses it, "a kind of traditional performance, and at that level sincere; for by taking part in this performance Jews were simply manifesting as Jews, and nothing could have been sincerer than that"?

Insofar as liturgies define the values or self-understanding of the community that recites them, they are in the broadest sense "political." But is their role to reflect a status quo or to provoke change—the professed task of the entire penitential period? We should think of ourselves as modern-day Jonahs deciding how to respond to the charge against us: do we *confess* to being responsible for "this evil" or do we simply *acknowledge* the existence of "this great storm"?

We are on more comfortable ground with the second approach to "modernizing" the sins to which we confess, and that is to stay within the private sphere of our inward journey: the mistakes, foibles, and hindrances that we ourselves put in our way, even those that we feel reluctant about naming as "sins." Such a list was created for *Forms of Prayer* by Lionel Blue:

> For the sin we committed against You, through evading and avoiding, because we could not face the truth.
> For our flight into hypocrisy and deception because we did not dare to speak it.
> For the facts we dissembled, and all we glossed over, for the excuses we made.
>
> For feeding our bodies and starving our souls.
> For interfering with the souls of others, and neglecting their needs.
> For shifting our responsibilities, for reproaches and recriminations.
>
> For our foolishness, our folly and false standards.
> For seeing these things only in others, never in ourselves.
> For our complacency which blinds us, and our self-righteousness which lessens us.
>
> For calculating kindness and measuring out pity.
> For charity that is cold, and prayers without feeling.
> For sending in accounts for love.

For the appeals that we ignored, and the people whom we refused.
For the affection which died, and our lives that became bitter.
For the visions which faded, the ideals we neglected, and the opportunities we lost.

For the fear of change and renewal, and our unbelief.
For saying prayers aloud, but refusing to listen.
For being our own worst enemy.[3]

The cumulative effect of such a list is powerful enough to warrant devoting part of the service to contemplating each element, even though the driving power of the liturgical context, the need to move on to the next set piece, allows little time to do it. Nevertheless, such texts do at least complement the traditional lists of sins, speaking more directly about private and personal issues of which we are readily aware and can therefore not just acknowledge but even admit.

The weight of Yom Kippur is overwhelming. The confession of sins is only a small part of the extraordinary accumulated power of the day. Yet the tradition demands that even the catharsis that comes with the final shofar blast is not the end. For then, as a curious anticlimax, comes a hurried *Havdalah*, and for some the *Ma'ariv* service, to mark the return to another "normal" evening. Yet this raises an interesting question, because as we recite the daily *Amidah*, the sixth blessing entreats, "Forgive us, our creator, for we have sinned; pardon us, our sovereign, for we have disobeyed." To which comes the inevitable question, what possible sins could we have committed between the end of Yom Kippur and *Ma'ariv*? To which comes the reply, that confession is on behalf of the sin of all the people who did not stay to recite *Ma'ariv*!

From Staid Sins of Yesteryear to Wrongdoings of Today

Rabbi Charles H. Middleburgh, PhD

For the first, cognizant, years of my life, the High Holy Day *machzor* that we used in the Brighton and Hove Progressive Synagogue, on the Sussex coast where I grew up, was the *Liberal Jewish Prayer Book* (*LJPB*), volume 3, part of Rabbi Israel Mattuck's great liturgical work for the English Liberal Movement and inspired by the *Union Prayer Book* already in widespread use in America, ever since its promulgation in 1895—a few decades before Mattuck sat down to write his own volume.

My recollections of those early *Yamim Nora'im* are vague, but I do recall as a child looking around at familiar congregants sitting nearest to me, the men in suits with severe expressions, the women immaculately dressed, wearing hats and suitably serious faces, and wondering how any of them could possibly have committed any of the catalogue of sins that was recited in the great confessions of the Days of Awe. Such is the innocence of childhood!

Whether my fellows at the time were guilty of some or all of the sins in *Ashamnu* and *Al Chet* I never discovered, but there was something about the fastidious way in which they recited them that suggested to me that they believed that their neighbors at least, if not themselves, were confessing appropriate guilt.

Rabbi Charles H. Middleburgh, PhD, is rabbi of the Cardiff Reform Synagogue and director of Jewish studies at Leo Baeck College in London, where he has taught since 1984; and coeditor with Rabbi Andrew Goldstein, PhD, of the Liberal Judaism *Machzor Ruach Chadashah*. He contributed to *Who by Fire, Who by Water—Un'taneh Tokef* and *All These Vows—Kol Nidre* (both Jewish Lights).

In spite of the fact that a truncated form of *Al Chet* occurred in the *LJPB*, its text, together with *Ashamnu*, which preceded it, did not came alive for me until our successor volume, *Gates of Repentance* (*GOR*) was published in 1973. There were three reasons for this: one, I was older and much more in tune with my own faults and weakness; two, the *Ashamnu* acrostic for Yom Kippur morning was rendered most creatively and memorably in English, using the same alphabetic style but modern examples of sin, with which I resonated; and three, *Al Chet* itself had been extended from nine lines to eighteen.

John Rayner's *Ashamnu* acrostic of human failings read:

> We have been arrogant, bigoted and cynical; deceitful, egoistic and foolish; grudging, haughty and insolent; jealous, knavish and lustful; malevolent, niggardly and obstinate; possessive, quarrelsome and resentful; selfish, tyrannical and unforgiving; vindictive, weak-willed and xenophobic; we have yielded to temptation, and we have forgotten Zion.[1]

Here was a list of sins I could certainly understand, and over the years I am certain I have, to some degree or other, been guilty of them all.

The eighteen-line version of *Al Chet* was arranged thematically rather than in the alphabetic acrostic of the overblown medieval version; it also felt relevant because of its idiomatic translation, which, for me, is a key aspect of making this text pertinent and powerful to a modern worshiper.

So where the traditional text spoke of "throwing off your yoke," *GOR* spoke of "defying the moral law"; where the text once described "wronging a neighbor," *GOR* had "harming our fellow men in any way." Perhaps these changes are subtle, but especially to those not steeped in the traditional idiom language of prayer, they spark an instant comprehension of the sin involved, rather than requiring a pause for puzzlement or questioning ("What is a 'yoke' anyway?"), for neither of which the context allows time.

The other priceless innovation in *GOR*, which Rabbi Andrew Goldstein, PhD, and I included in the Liberal Movement's subsequent High Holy Day volume (*Machzor Ruach Chadashah* [*MRC*], 2003), was the text inspired by the version of *Al Chet* that Chaim Stern, *z"l*, originally wrote for *GOR* and subsequently included in *Gates of Repentance*, the volume he edited for North American Reform Jews after returning from England, where he had coedited our own *Gates of Repentance*: "We sin against You when we sin against ourselves."[2] It had no fewer than thirty-three verses, interspersed three times with the phrase that gives the whole text its name. Of the three key "confessional" pieces of liturgy, it is this that always strikes a chord within me, and while I did not grow up in the "breast-beating" tradition, this prayer inspires at least a mental blow with each and every line.

The other challenge of this section of the High Holy Day liturgy is that while what we might call "classic" sins retain, by definition, their perennial relevance, there is no doubt that they occasionally need an update as fresh sins, failings, and issues rear their ugly head. It is for this reason that in recent years I have taken to delivering a "fresh" take on *Al Chet* on Shabbat Shuvah (the Sabbath that falls between Rosh Hashanah and Yom Kippur), although the one I newly offer every year is always modeled on the traditional text in terms of style and (as much as possible) even content.

My freshly composed conceptions of sin in our time enable me to retain a properly acute sense of self-flagellation—an impossibility if I were to limit myself to a laundry list of yesterday's sins, even reasonably recent "yesterdays" such as those reflected in prayer books written nowadays to last for twenty to thirty years.

In 2011 my *Al Chet* read as follows:

> For the sin which we have committed by making unreasonable demands of God,
> And for the sin which we have committed by denying God's existence, in our thoughts and our deeds, when it suited us.
> For the sin which we have committed by restricting our Judaism to the synagogue rather than making it live in our homes,
> And for the sin which we have committed by forcing our children to live the Jewish lives we ignore.
> For the sin which we have committed by being steadfastly ignorant about our faith and its traditions,
> And for the sin which we have committed by pretending that we did not have time for study.

For the sin which we have committed by taking from our community rather than giving to it,
And for the sin which we have committed by praising the dedication of others instead of following their example.
For the sin which we have committed by believing ourselves to be superior to others,
And for the sin which we have committed by doing nothing to distinguish our behavior.

For all these sins, O God of forgiveness; forgive us, pardon us, grant us atonement.

For the sin which we have committed by denying our own responsibilities to society at large,
And for the sin which we have committed by finding fault with those who dedicate their lives to the welfare of others.
For the sin which we have committed by turning our backs on the poor and defenseless,
And for the sin which we have committed by narrowing our vision to ourselves.
For the sin which we have committed by tolerating violence against children,
And for the sin which we have committed by showing contempt and impatience for the old.
For the sin which we have committed by not campaigning for the amelioration of rights for the disabled,
And for the sin which we have committed by thinking that only those of able mind or body can play a part in society.

For all these sins, O God of forgiveness; forgive us, pardon us, grant us atonement.

For the sin which we have committed by failing to express outrage at the abuse of our planet,

And for the sin which we have committed by not taking positive action to punish those organizations and nations guilty of such abuse.
For the sin which we have committed by using the environment for our own ends,
And for the sin which we have committed by not thinking about the implications of our own irresponsibility.

For the sin which we have committed by behaving as if natural resources were limitless,
And for the sin which we have committed by failing to constrain our voracity to consume.
For the sin which we have committed by accepting dirty streets and parks,
And for the sin which we have committed by thoughtlessly adding to their squalor.
For the sin which we have committed by fostering the delusion that **we** are the crown of creation,
And for the sin which we have committed by not acknowledging the worth of other creatures.
For the sin which we have committed by not campaigning for the preservation of endangered species,
And for the sin which we have committed by ignoring the fact that we will be judged as human beings by the way that we treat defenseless animals.

For all these sins, O God of forgiveness; forgive us, pardon us, grant us atonement.

For the sin which we have committed by failing to recognize the truth about ourselves,
And for the sin which we have committed by denigrating or misusing the talents we possess.
For the sin which we have committed by loving too much,
And for the sin which we have committed by loving too little.

For the sin which we have committed by taking advantage of those closest to us,
And for the sin which we have committed by shutting our eyes and ears to **their** needs.
For the sin which we have committed by thinking with our bodies,
And for the sin which we have committed by ignoring the call of our minds.
For the sin which we have committed by being self-obsessed and arrogant,
And for the sin which we have committed by being so much less than we knew we could be.

V'al kulam, elo'ah s'lichot, s'lach lanu, m'chal lanu, kaper lanu.
For all these sins, O God of forgiveness; forgive us, pardon us, grant us atonement.

"Our Sins? They're Not All Mine!"

Rabbi David A. Teutsch, PhD

The confession of transgressions is at the heart of Yom Kippur because it is a prerequisite for the reconciliation with God that is the day's purpose. That reconciliation requires acknowledgment of the causes of alienation, followed by contrition, apology, and the commitment not to repeat the confessed moral errors. This is the process of *t'shuvah*. It starts with confession.

Jewish tradition holds that reconciliation with God must be preceded by reconciliation with other people. The month of Elul and the period from Rosh Hashanah to Yom Kippur are designated as a time to accomplish that task, which requires not only apology but also a concerted effort to repair the damage to others that has resulted from the transgressions. Then Yom Kippur focuses on the relationships between people and God. *Ashamnu* and *Al Chet* repeated, traditionally, ten times over Yom Kippur need to be understood in that context.

If the confession is the individual's effort to return to God, why does it repeatedly say "we" rather than "I"? There are several answers to this question, and they are not mutually exclusive. One answer is that if

---

Rabbi David A. Teutsch, PhD, is the Wiener Professor of Contemporary Jewish Civilization and director of the Center for Jewish Ethics at the Reconstructionist Rabbinical College, where he served as president for nearly a decade. He was editor in chief of the seven-volume *Kol Haneshamah* prayer book series. His book *A Guide to Jewish Practice: Everyday Living* (RRC Press) won the National Jewish Book Award for Contemporary Jewish Life and Practice. He is also author of *Spiritual Community: The Power to Restore Hope, Commitment and Joy* (Jewish Lights) and several other books. He contributed to *Who by Fire, Who by Water—Un'taneh Tokef* and *All These Vows—Kol Nidre* (both Jewish Lights).

the confession used "I," most people could not in honesty recite most of it. Indeed, it would encourage avoidance rather than facing our conduct. A related answer is that reciting the confession as part of the "we" of the community allows us to consider the transgressions before dismissing them. Since some of them are subtle (sins committed through lack of knowledge, for instance) and others are a matter of degree (gluttony, for example), such probing has value. This all takes time and thoughtfulness. Owning up personally to what one has done may not occur until several repetitions of the confessions have already gone by.

A more traditional rationale for using the plural holds that every member of a community is culpable for the transgressions of every other member. But isn't that unfair? I don't think so. The culture of a group shapes its members' values and behavior. Some group cultures do little to inculcate good values or regulate moral behavior. In such a group, everyone is responsible for the resulting transgressions unless they have been fighting to change the culture.

One of the ways that people find out they have acted improperly is that others tell them so. As Leviticus says, *Hokhe'ach tokhi'ach et amitekha*, "You shall surely reprove your neighbor" (Leviticus 19:17). While offering reproof effectively has never been easy, in our time it is even harder. Mottos like "Do your own thing" promote the notion that what others do is not our concern unless it affects us directly. The "we" of the confession reminds us that if we have not been offering reproof when we see wrongdoing, we share culpability for the wrongs that follow. Third parties may well see us when we do not comment or intervene. They can easily take our silence for consent and commit similar transgressions themselves. *Kol yisrael arevim zeh lazeh*, "All Israel are responsible for each other," proclaims the Talmud (Sh'vuot 39a). We confess in the plural to remind us that we are partly responsible for the transgressions of everyone with whom we share community.

Sometimes, sins are not simply between one person and another; they entail complicity across an entire community. Normally that is not so—normally, that is, we simply harm another person and then make up for our transgressions by apologizing to the party we have wronged and repairing the damage. The apology for transgressions of *hokhe'ach tokhi'ach* (the duty to reprove would-be sinners), however, is not so straightforward. On the one hand, we could apologize to the people we did not reprove—they have sinned in part because we did not warn them in a timely fashion. On the other hand, we could apologize to the third party who was indirectly damaged by our silence. But neither person sees us as responsible. It does not make sense to apologize to either party for this particular kind of sin of omission. Furthermore, quite often it is an entire community that witnesses a sinful act and says nothing. And it is the whole community that suffers when we do not have the moral courage to do *tokh'chah*. A communal confession allows for the possibility that any single wrong may well have occurred in part because of invisible sins of silence when *tokh'chah* should have been offered. In such cases, communal confession is singularly appropriate for people who could have known or actually did know that the crime would occur, but did nothing to stop it.

Another function of communal confession is its emphatic statement of behaviors the community considers unacceptable. We can understand this as a general form of admonition (of *tokh'chah*), by which the community proclaims its expectations to its members. "We" affirm the standards of our community together.

Yet another answer to the question "Why we?" is that if people had to confess only their own sins aloud before the congregation in the "I" form, everyone would hear what the sins were. That would be a form of *halbanat panim*, "personal humiliation," a sin in itself, since Judaism asks us not to shame people publicly. Our worship should reflect the same values we live by.

Most Jews would probably be unwilling, in any case, to confess their most serious sins aloud in the hearing of the congregation, and if they did, they would not only be engaging in a kind of self-humiliation that Jewish ethics of speech forbids, but they would also be an interesting example of self-reflective *motzi shem ra*, "besmirching someone's reputation," by revealing unsavory conduct or character flaws (in this case, their own) to others. By confessing together, we protect the privacy of each individual's statements before God. Therefore the liturgy says "we."

Why two forms of confession? Wouldn't the longer *Al Chet* be sufficient? The two confessions differ both in form and in function. *Al Chet* is a long list of sins on which we can meditate individually as we consider our own culpability. The much shorter *Ashamnu* is a formulaic summary of sin that is usually sung in unison. Through recitation of *Ashamnu*, the community acknowledges the simple fact that transgression within the community has occurred and that everyone shares part of the responsibility for that. We first draw strength from acknowledging collective wrongdoing; only then do we turn to our individual confession.

The first words of the *Al Chet* are "*Al chet shechatanu.*" They are usually translated in contemporary *machzorim* in one of the following ways: "We have sinned," "For the wrong we have done," "For the sin we have committed," or "For the wrong we did." The 1999 JPS *Tanakh* translates *chet* as "guilt." When people commit crimes, they are guilty. They don't just feel guilty. They are guilty. When they disobey God, they are sinning. When they do wrong, they are unethical.

The difference in translations carries a significant difference in meaning. Translating *chet* as "sin," rather than as "wrong," has certain consequences.

To speak of sin is to invoke a God whose will has been violated. Jews who use that language often believe that God's will is embodied in the Torah, its Rabbinic interpretations, and halakhah (Jewish law). But liberal Jews who refer to *chet* as "sin" normally don't believe in the divine authority of the halakhah or the infallibility of Torah. I think they often do believe, however, that the divine will is evident in the world and that violating that will is sinful.

Using "wrong" instead of "sin" suggests this-worldly moral error. Doing wrong is a violation of ethical standards confirmed by the culture or community within which it occurs. Some of those ethical standards are considered to be universal—an idea the Rabbis capture in their claim that God made covenants with every people, not just Jews (the Noahide laws, which are binding on everyone). Other standards apply only in the community that accepts them. Both kinds of standards are reflected in *Al Chet.* By declaring some actions are wrong, it states norms of conduct—about forty of them in traditional *machzorim*; the exact number and words vary according to the local custom from which each version comes.

Some Jews believe that the divine is infused in the world and in the laws of nature through which God's creation is made manifest. People who hold that belief understand ethics to involve our living in harmony with that divine presence. Understood that way, Jewish tradition reflects the Jewish search for the path of harmony and holiness. Translating *chet* as "wrong" certainly indicates that it involves moral transgression, but also, for some, disharmony with the divine will. From the latter perspective, doing wrong might also be considered sinful.

Committing sins involves alienation from the divine within us. Confessing sin initiates a return to harmony with self, community, and God. From that perspective, *Ashamnu* and *Al Chet* are opportunities to uncover and confess our collective and individual transgressions. Thus the path back to harmony is walked together by the community of worshipers. If the Yom Kippur process works, the worshipers will acknowledge their transgressions, experience contrition, and make a commitment not to repeat their wrongdoing. By the end of the concluding confession of the last *Ashamnu* in *N'ilah*, the community has also reinforced its norms by reciting them during each part of the Yom Kippur service. Making a shared commitment to living better helps restore the harmony that is a wellspring of holiness in our lives.

It is part of the human condition that we make moral errors. We sin, and Yom Kippur provides the opportunity to return to God, to do *t'shuvah*, to become whole once again. We sin, we do wrong. And when we confess it, we are on the path to reconciliation.

Part IV
Ashamnu and *Al Chet*
Interpretations for Today

We Are All Unrepentant Humanists

Rabbi Tony Bayfield, CBE, DD

For quite some years it has been my privilege to preach on Yom Kippur at the compellingly named North Western Reform Synagogue, Alyth Gardens, in London. Last year, I reflected to myself that I was in a relatively small minority of the two thousand people looking up at me with expressions ranging from eager anticipation to bored resignation. I am a traditional theist—traditional, that is, in my dissatisfaction with post-Kaplan naturalism. I am not a secularist, someone whose view of the world has no religious or metaphysical dimension—unlike the majority of my countrymen and women.

Yes, a majority. By a majority that our elected officials (whether in the United Kingdom or any other democracy) could only dream of, this country would self-categorize as secular. I am certain that many at Alyth would have said that they, too, are secular. Admittedly this is the UK, not the United States, but American observers too have commented on the degree to which Jews especially have become secularized.[1] In any event, here in England the phenomenon is everywhere.

By a similar majority, however, the congregation would also accept the label "humanist," subscribing to fundamental Jewish teachings about the significance of the human being and the values that should govern behavior *ben adam lachavero*, "between human beings." "Humanism" is what unites so many of us, whether we define ourselves as religious or secular. We are Jewish humanists who recognize that at the spiritual and ethical heart of Yom Kippur lies the *Vidui*, the confession of sins.

Rabbi Tony Bayfield, CBE, DD (Lambeth), is president of the Movement for Reform Judaism in the United Kingdom. He teaches personal theology at the Leo Baeck College in London. He contributed to *Who by Fire, Who by Water—Un'taneh Tokef* and *All These Vows—Kol Nidre* (both Jewish Lights).

I remember, years ago, an interview with Edward Heath, one of Britain's least attractive prime ministers, whom even a male Meryl Streep could not make sympathetic.[2] Heath was asked what he regarded as his greatest failing. He paused for what seemed an interminable length of time and then said, "A tendency to work too hard." That's it? He worked too hard? Most of us in the daylong service have a greater sense of our own moral fallibility than that!

Both *Ashamnu* and *Al Chet* are composed in alphabetic acrostics, which are merely formulaic. As formulas, they are only suggestive of the dozens of small, highly personal pebbles[3] that make up most of our individual aggregate[4] of sin. I am, therefore, grateful for the courage of the British Reform Movement's more detailed and specified *Al Chet*,[5] which regularly strikes a painful chord and points me down the murky path of my most personal failures of love and responsibility. More importantly still, *Ashamnu* and *Al Chet* suggest collective responsibility for the public and the private, the intentional and the unintentional—the entire comprehensive and appalling range of human folly and evil. As we humanists, whether religious or not, would have it, we really are responsible for what we do.

Let me remind you of a simply astounding Talmudic text:

> Rabbi Chanina bar Papa expounded: The name of the angel appointed over conception is Night. He takes a drop of seed, lays it before the Holy One, blessed be God, and says: "Ruler of the universe, what is this seed to become—strong or weak, wise or stupid, rich or poor?" He does not say "wicked or righteous." This is in accordance with Rabbi Chanina's teaching, for Rabbi Chanina said: Everything is in the hands of heaven, except the fear of heaven.[6]

There are many things that are largely predetermined, either by our genetic inheritance or by our social situation, but *not* our ethical behavior, said Rabbi Chanina seventeen hundred years ago. Much is beyond our control but not—to a significant extent—our moral choices![7]

That is the conviction that lies at the very heart of the Jewish sensibility. A non-negotiable belief in an omniscient God forced us into a paradox: "Everything is foreseen and everything is laid bare; everything is in accordance with human will."[8] Similarly, "Everything is foreseen and free will is given; the world is judged according to goodness, and everything is in accordance with the amount of work."[9] Whatever we believe or do not believe about God today, the conviction that moral choice, ethical behavior, is our responsibility remains the focus of the Yom Kippur service.

There lies the contemporary battle line with dominant secularity. It has been drawn by a school of neuroscientists, British and American, Jews as well as non-Jews, who claim that the capacity we call "mind" (with all its moral and spiritual dimensions) is just a material brain and that what goes on in the brain is largely determined by genetics and by mechanically conditioned behavior after that. We may think that we make choices, but that is pure illusion. Being determined or conditioned, we have no moral competence to do anything other than what we in fact do. There can be no sin, therefore, nothing for which one ought to feel guilty.

One of the sources for this assertion lies in the work of Benjamin Libet, a Jewish American psychologist from Chicago. Back in the 1980s, he observed:

> The brain "decides" to initiate, or, at least, prepares to initiate the act at a time before there is any reportable subjective awareness that such a decision has taken place.... Cerebral initiation, even of a spontaneous voluntary act, can and usually does begin *unconsciously*.[10]

Many of Libet's conclusions have been shown to be wide of the mark, but that has not stopped a significant number of neuroscientists repeating them and pressing on with the claim that we are simply brain activity, "waves of physical and chemical excitation passing along a neuron,"[11] hardwired by evolution and conditioning rather than initiated by conscious reflection. The influential philosopher Daniel Dennett sums up this portrait:

> There is only one sort of stuff, namely matter—the physical stuff of physics, chemistry, and physiology—and the mind is somehow nothing but a physical phenomenon. In short, the mind is the brain ... we can (in principle!) account for every mental phenomenon using the same physical principles, laws, and raw materials that suffice to explain radioactivity, continental drift, photosynthesis, reproduction, nutrition, and growth.[12]

We are, if you like, just a computer in a machine.

Although this attack on the humanity of human beings is directed by scientists, it is hardly mounted with the dispassion that we think of as sober science. Indeed, one can only be amazed at the extent to which it is driven by "passionate intensity."[13] In a brilliant book, *Aping Mankind*, the British neuroscientist Raymond Tallis dismantles the arguments one by one. At best, the "neuromaniacs," as Tallis calls them, are working in a single dimension, that of brain function. The human being, like life itself, is multilayered, complex, incapable of reduction to a single, flat perspective.[14]

Typical of these attackers is John N. Gray, actually not a scientist at all but a widely known professor of European thought at London University, who writes:

> Human beings are simply animals … a result of blind evolutionary drift … assemblies of genes interacting at random with each other and their shifting environment.… Humanity does not exist.… Human beings think they are free, conscious beings—when in truth they are deluded animals who never cease trying to escape from what they imagine themselves to be.… Their religions are attempts to be rid of a freedom they never possessed.… Morality is a sickness peculiar to humans. Personal autonomy is the work of our imagination.… We are hardwired for the illusion of self.[15]

This is extraordinary stuff but not as extraordinary as the fact that Gray's book, *Straw Dogs*, was named as either *a* or *the* book of the year in virtually every British national newspaper. Gray was acclaimed by a variety of international figures, ranging from novelist J. G. Ballard to financier George Soros.

I find the attitudes exhibited by Gray and the neuroscientists on whom he draws deeply shocking but hardly surprising. The Shoah lies at the heartlessness of a catastrophic eruption of inhuman behavior—the gulags, Hiroshima—from which nothing was learned. Mao, Pol Pot, Rwanda, and Bosnia followed. For many, faith in human goodness and human progress has been destroyed. The consequence is widespread despair expressed in the reassertion of mechanical determinism and the denial of our humanity. We fall back on an old alibi couched in new terms.

The people most justified in despairing (since we suffered uniquely as Hitler's intended victims) and the most secularized as well are us, the Jews. But we have a long tradition of saying *davka*,[16] "precisely." *Precisely* because the evidence for human inhumanity is so strong, we are *not* going to give way to despair. We know, deep in the recesses of the minds that Gray and the neuromaniacs deny, that we are multilayered creatures and our behavior is infinitely complex. We know all about instinctual, unconscious, and conscious drives—but we also know that Rabbi Chanina was astoundingly prescient and right on the mark. "Everything is in the hands of heaven, except the fear of heaven." We can and do make moral choices; we can and do bear responsibility for our own deeds and for those of our community and society.

I look out from the pulpit and observe two thousand upturned faces—some attentive and approving, others pained or bewildered, some just glazed over. Theists and nontheists, religious humanists and secular humanists, we are united in our defiant declaration: *Ashamnu*, "We have sinned."

Forgiving God

Rabbi Will Berkovitz

Once, on the eve of the Yom Kippur, the tzaddik Rabbi Elimelech of Lizensk said to his disciples, "If you want to know what a Jew should do on the eve of the Day of Atonement, go to the tailor who lives at the end of town."

And so the Hasidim went to the tailor's house and stood outside the window. They watched the tailor and his children recite the afternoon prayers. Then they put on their best clothes, lit the holiday candles, and ate the pre-fast meal. After services that evening, when the house was quiet, the tailor went to the closet and took out a ledger.

"Master of the universe," he said, "now the time has come for You and me to reckon up our sins for this past year." At once he began to list the sins he had committed, all of which were written down in the notebook. Then he went back to the closet, took out a thicker, heavier notebook, and said, "Lord, first I listed my sins, and now I will list yours." And with that he began to enumerate all the suffering, sorrow, illnesses, and tragedies that he and his community had endured during the year. When he was finished, he said, "Master of the universe, to tell you the truth, You owe me more than I owe You. You know what, though? I'd just as soon not keep strict accounts with You. We are commanded to forgive the wrongs that have been done to us. Why don't I just forgive You and You forgive me?"

So much of what we do during Yom Kippur is a recounting of our sins—great and small. The tradition teaches: For transgressions between individuals and God, Yom Kippur atones. We ask God for forgiveness. But often I feel like the tailor in that story. I feel that we are not the only ones who need forgiveness.

Rabbi Will Berkovitz is the senior vice president of Repair the World, a national organization that seeks to make service a defining element of American Jewish life.

I have lost friends and family to cancer, and I feel outraged at God. Regularly I am sickened by the cascade of images from natural disasters across the planet. And when I read these stories of thousands dead here, hundreds dead there, a sister swept away, a child buried, I feel like washing my hands of this abusive relationship.

My wife is a pediatrician, and when I hear her stories of the suffering of children, I want to scream—to scream into the whirlwind, the void I was sure God once filled. I want to scream, "I don't believe in You. We are alone in the universe. There is no master plan. There is no power or creator." That's how I feel when I look back on the horrible tragedies that punctuate each year. What are we doing asking God to forgive us?

We are not the only ones needing forgiveness. When people I love, children, suffer the terror of cancer, God is the One who needs forgiveness. When a father wakes up to find his newborn daughter has stopped breathing, God is the One who needs forgiveness. When a tsunami kills hundreds of thousands of people, God is the One who needs forgiveness. I fight against all of my instincts. I rage and I struggle and often, against all reason, I try to forgive God.

God may not ask for my forgiveness. God certainly does not need my forgiveness. I may be a heretic. But I feel a need in my soul to struggle to forgive God for all God's sins against humanity. If I do not forgive God, how can I believe in God?

When we recite *Kol Nidre*—the annulment of vows—I often wonder, does God annul God's vows with us on *Kol Nidre*? Is there a divine rescinding of agreements, to match the human one? Have all the promises with our ancestors been stamped null and void? Is all of this some withering vestige of a dying myth? That is often how I feel.

When AIDS orphans thousands of children in sub-Saharan Africa I find it very difficult to stand here, bow, and recite the *Bar'khu*—a praise of God. What brings a mother to stand and recite the *Kaddish* over her deceased daughter? The *Kaddish*? A declaration of God's greatness? Yes, I believe in the great and small miracles that surround us every day. And I believe God is present everywhere if we only look. But that does not absolve God.

And I do not accept trite religious apologetics. That God only tests those who are strongest. Or a hurricane or an earthquake is some divine retribution. Or the reason children are orphaned in Israel is because their parents did not have a mezuzah on their front door. Or God "needs them more in heaven." God needs them more in heaven? Retribution? A mezuzah? That is not my theology. That is not my God.

I do not understand God's ways. And many of God's ways are most certainly not my ways. The only honest answers we should dare give in response to human suffering is, "I do not understand what this means." And, "I cannot explain the reason for your pain. But I am here. And you are not alone. Your pain is not going unnoticed. I am a witness to your suffering. I am a witness. And you are not alone."

I want to hold God responsible. After I have listed all the places where I was not my highest self. The places where I fell. After that hard uncompromising look into my soul. After I ask for forgiveness, I leave a silence and then I list God's sins against humanity. The places where God has tested the limits of my faith. Those crevasses filled with doubt, anger, and disappointment. The vast wasteland of uncertainty and frustration.

And I reject any position that claims we should never be angry with God. Of course be angry with God. I recall religious school teachers when I was younger warning me not to question God's perfection. Never to doubt that God is all-powerful. Of course I doubt God's perfection and the idea that God is all-powerful. God cannot give me common sense and then expect me not to use it.

My religious life feels like one epic struggle to believe there is some higher order in the universe. That somehow all of this matters. And I believe that whatever God is or is not, God is certainly strong enough to endure my doubts. The God I believe in is not so fragile as to not understand our confusion.

When I am standing in a place of prayer, I bring my confusion and my doubts. I have no choice. That is who I am. But I ultimately strive to believe God is *el elyon*, God on high. When I stand for the *Amidah*, I may at times feel like I am talking to myself, but I struggle to believe I am standing before *ribono shel olam*—the master of the universe. If I am standing, leading a community in prayer, a servant of God, I want to believe there is a God to serve. And on Yom Kippur I believe that God needs forgiveness. If not for God's sake, then for my own.

By forgiving God, I make God relevant in my life. By forgiving God, I can allow room for my doubts, my struggles, my confusion. By forgiving God, I maintain my relationship and a connection with God—no matter how tenuous it may be at times.

It is not easy to forgive God. It takes huge effort. It is painful, contradictory, and maddening. The human suffering that surrounds us feels utterly unforgivable. But I will forgive God because I do not want to write off the relationship. Because I feel there is too much to be lost by simply walking away. Because I want my children to develop their own relationships and come to their own conclusions. Because, despite the pain, sorrow, and suffering, I want my universe full of miracles, not void of them. Because I do not want to be one more angry, old cynic in the world. I want to believe a voice still calls out from Sinai, from heaven. That is why I will forgive God.

I want to engage in the eternal conversations with the ancestors and sages. Despite it all, I want to live my life in praise and awe—in wonder and hope. Even if I am wrong. Even if at the end there is nothing but darkness.

Despite it all, I want to surround myself with the people of Jacob, of Israel, with those who struggle with God. Who sing a portion of that song. Who stand above eternity—a nation of priests and priestesses. A holy people.

For whatever reason, I know I am a better person because of that relationship with God. I want to believe there is a maker of peace in the heavens and here on earth. I want to be able to say amen and mean it. I want to equally feel that at *N'ilah*, when we stand before the open ark, and when the final shofar blasts and the gates of heaven close, that I am forgiven by God. I have faith in the power of that two-way forgiveness.

By forgiving God, God becomes a force in the world. Not some dusty ancient relic, the focus of Hasidic parables. By forgiving God, God reigns. And God regains some exalted place in the universe and in my life. Despite everything. Despite everything. Despite disease that steals parents from their children, and children from their parents. Despite the hurricanes, earthquakes, and tsunamis. Despite my desire, my overwhelming desire to walk the other way. Despite it all, I will strive to forgive.

Despite not having been asked for forgiveness, I take the lead and forgive God. I shout forgiveness into the whirlwind. And beg, please God. Please God, forgive us. Please God, forgive me. Forgive me.

For the Sin of …
Poor Leadership

Dr. Erica Brown

> Though the silenced opinion may be in error, it may and very commonly does, contain a portion of truth. It is only by the collision of adverse opinions that the remainder of the truth has any chance of being supplied.
>
> **John Stuart Mill**

"For the sin we have committed against You through callously hardening the heart."

There are so many ways that we harden our hearts. We turn aside when someone is in need. We pretend we did not hear a conversation that might burden us with additional responsibility. We know that we should give more charity—but don't. We allow distraction to divert us from looking at someone face-to-face in conversation.

Leaders, too, run the risk of hardening their hearts, with the additional consequence of disappointing people who count on them. They are impatient; they cannot manage their overwhelming to-do list; or they

---

Dr. Erica Brown is a writer and an educator who works as the scholar-in-residence for the Jewish Federation of Greater Washington and consults for the Jewish Agency and other Jewish nonprofits. She is an Avi Chai Fellow and the recipient of the Covenant Award. She is author of *Inspired Jewish Leadership: Practical Approaches to Building Strong Communities*, a National Jewish Book Award finalist; *Spiritual Boredom: Rediscovering the Wonder of Judaism; Confronting Scandal: How Jews Can Respond When Jews Do Bad Things* (all Jewish Lights); and *In the Narrow Places*; and coauthor of *The Case for Jewish Peoplehood: Can We Be One?* (Jewish Lights). She contributed to *Who by Fire, Who by Water—Un'taneh Tokef* and *All These Vows—Kol Nidre* (both Jewish Lights). Her articles have appeared on the *Newsweek/Washington Post* website "On Faith."

lack good management skills. Over the years of working with Jewish leaders, I've noticed an especially grievous leadership transgression, however: the closing down of conversation. For this sin alone, Jewish leaders should say this *Al Chet* with particular care.

We've all sat in meetings where the group leader allows a conversation to be closed to the point where it becomes unsafe to share new ideas, and participants keep their thoughts to themselves. Such leaders diminish the conversation, lose credibility, damage group relationships, and squander the support and brainpower that are generated when good minds share creative space. These leaders usually intend no harm; they just lack the self-awareness to see what they are doing.

Imagine, for example, a board member with a fertile mind, trying to speak up at a meeting. Preoccupied with other matters, the leader doesn't fully listen while the person speaks. Realizing that the leader is distracted or checking his e-mail, the board member loses the wind in his sails. His last words trail to a close. Despite prodding from colleagues to continue, he makes some excuse and leaves. On his way out the door, he wonders why he came. His first thought as he hits the parking lot is to renege on his board commitment. He does not have enough hours in a day to volunteer for a cause where he is, at best, a rubber stamp.

I teach leaders. Every year, as Yom Kippur rolls around, I ask classes to write down three *Al chets* specifically related to their leadership—two that are personal and one that is collective (in antiquity, we offered guilt and sin sacrifices both personally and collectively). I have collected many of these over the years and make a point of posting them on my website. Those who share theirs are always met with knowing nods of recognition. This honest soul-searching is a remarkable and often painful exercise in self-reflection. By comparison, it makes the remote language of most prayer books pale with irrelevance.

Often the leaders I teach confess to this hardening of the heart through the closing of conversations. They may suffer from an "I can do everything better" complex. They may fail to delegate. They may not respond to e-mails. They may lack patience to entertain ideas not their own. Driven to distraction by full agendas, electronic devices, and the many pulls on their time, they sacrifice *panim el panim*, "face-to-face," communication. So I ask people to pair up in chairs that are arranged to face each other, almost knee-to-knee, and experience the mouth-to-mouth communication that God describes as the highest level of intimacy that humans can achieve

(Numbers 12:8). Even then, few people speak easily or naturally to each other about their leadership sins. Too vulnerable from past experiences, they prefer the safety of closures and boundaries. When the heart is hardened for a long time, it cannot soften easily or quickly.

The arsenal of a leader's hard heart includes a multitude of ways to cut off conversation:

- Having a scripted answer
- Using electronic devices while others are talking
- Not validating comments that others make
- Moving the conversation in a totally new direction
- Failing to listen with your eyes
- Ending a conversation prematurely
- Embarrassing someone who disagrees with you
- Using sarcasm in retort to a comment
- Disagreeing publicly and vehemently
- Using body language that suggests closure or disagreement
- Not allowing sufficient time to discuss an issue thoroughly or comprehensively
- Dealing with a topic that is too large or demanding for the current setting—and thus trivializing it
- Not participating in group activities or brainstorming, suggesting to others that it is beneath you
- Overriding a conversation—especially when you are in a position of power over the person speaking
- Interrupting someone mid-sentence
- Name-calling
- Redirecting a conversation due to fear of change

Leaders should open up conversation. Business management experts Tom Peters and Nancy Austin coach leaders to "encourage, excite, teach, listen, facilitate … [to] say people are special and [to] treat them that way—always."[1] Good leaders "grow" people. Leadership coach Liz Wiseman, author of *Multipliers: How the Best Leaders Make Everyone Smarter*, contrasts growing people with diminishing them by dismissing their ideas, hoarding compliments, and seeking all the credit. We all know leaders like this. They have perfected the art of hardening the heart.

How do you soften a leader's callous heart?

Get Feedback

Most leaders never know what people think because they don't create an honest feedback loop. The higher you rise in an organization, the less people tell you what you might not want to hear.

Redefine Leadership

If you think leadership means having the authority to make decisions solo, then think again. We joke about "executive decisions," but those should be made rarely and with a full sense of accountability. Open leadership encourages transparency, bringing everyone's talents and opinions into a public forum for debate.

Balance Power with Humility

You can have a great idea and want to run with it but, in your enthusiasm, not realize that you have run other people over. You have not listened. You have not created space for another opinion. Leaders often get unstated permission to take up all the space, but they have to monitor their exercise of power within that space, lest their need for control blind them to the desires and needs of others. Martin Heifetz and Ronald Linsky, authors of *Leadership on the Line*, remind us, "The person who has a disproportionate need for control, who is too hungry for power, is susceptible to losing sight of the work."[2] Be wary of the leader who frequently says, "I have the situation under control."

Ask Questions

One of the best techniques for opening conversation is asking questions. I watched a one-man play where the actor wanted to demonstrate a time of confusion and ambiguity. Slowly his body morphed into the shape of a question mark, his back humped into the arc of the question. "Questions create energy and vitality in the group by triggering the need to listen, to seek a common truth." Instead of monologues, they "generate a dialogue in which everyone begins to leave their individual limitations to find a new wholeness."[3]

Listen for Understanding

Too often we listen to others as a mere formality, waiting it out until it's our turn. What we really seek is an opening to get others to listen to us. That is entirely different from listening for understanding, without which conversations close and future discussion vanishes. Leadership development consultant Chalmers Brothers differentiates listening with the *intent to respond* from listening with the *intent to understand.* "How many of us, while we're listening to someone else, are also constructing and readying our response?... The first step to begin listening with the intent to understand is to notice—notice the automaticness with which we begin to create stories, and then quiet the voice."[4]

Brothers also warns us against the tendency to listen just to find a way to prove the speaker wrong. "Here, the listener is poised, ready and waiting for the chance to pounce on the speaker and make the speaker wrong." When we do that, we "miss a great deal of what's said, as so much of the internal conversation is busy elsewhere."[5]

People who feel they are not being heard may repeat themselves or speak louder and more emphatically at first, but they will eventually give up altogether.

Listen with Your Eyes

Make sure your body language says, "I am fully present with you in this moment. I am not distracted. In this moment, you have all my attention."

Toward the close of Deuteronomy, we find a very curious use of language related to the heart. "Adonai will open up your heart and the hearts of your offspring to love Adonai your God with all your heart and soul that you may live" (30:6). The Hebrew verb that we translate as "open up" is *mal,* "to circumcise." Circumcision is used in the Bible in the sense of correcting a fault. Abraham is not "whole" (*tamim*) until he is circumcised. So here, in Deuteronomy, an uncircumcised heart is a heart that is calloused and will not function correctly. Without actively creating an opening, our hearts will not properly love God or each other. It is as if a layer of callous tissue must be removed for the heart to function well. Only then will we be open to others in a way that true love presupposes.

Without an open heart we cannot lead. We cannot change. We cannot listen. We cannot love.

We Can't Really Be That Evil!

Rabbi Lawrence A. Englander, DHL

I have a vivid childhood memory of attending High Holy Day services at our local Talmud Torah. With my father standing on one side of me and my great-grandfather on the other, I ran my finger over each line of the *machzor* in an attempt to keep up with the pace of davening. Eventually we came to the *Vidui*, which included the recitation of *Al Chet*, the long list of sins that we confess before God. At one point, I received a jab in the ribs and a mischievous wink from my Zaide Joe. It was during the line that reads, "For the sin we have committed against You by disrespect for parents and teachers." I got the message; what nine-year-old kid can claim innocence of that offense?

But as I grew older, there was something about the *Vidui* that gave me pause. I was not bothered by the usual problem: the phrasing of *Al Chet* in the plural. I understood that it did not imply that any one person is guilty of every sin on the list, but simply that we are all responsible for one another. What did disturb me was the statement that appears between *Ashamnu* and *Al Chet*:

> We have veered from your commandments and from your good laws and we are worthless. You have been righteous throughout all that has happened to us, for You have done justly with us and we are the ones who did evil.

This statement implied a relationship with God that I no longer accepted: a perfect, omnipotent God who constantly finds fault with us sadly

---

Rabbi Lawrence A. Englander, DHL, has been rabbi of Solel Congregation of Mississauga, Ontario, since its inception in 1973. He is author of *The Mystical Study of Ruth* and is former editor of the *CCAR Journal*.

inadequate humans. I wondered: can we really be that evil? No matter what our shortcomings may be, should we not also take pride in our moral accomplishments over the past year—the kind words that brightened someone's day, the extra effort we made on another's behalf, the time and energy spent on helping to make a better world? Where do we find an acknowledgment of our *better* selves in the *Vidui*?

When I first struggled against this doctrine, I felt like a heretic rejecting "the" accepted Jewish view of God. But as I read further, guided by wise and understanding teachers, I came to realize that this "classical" view is only one of several Jewish understandings of God. I learned that the notion of divine omnipotence and human inadequacy, championed by Moses Maimonides and other medieval philosophers, reflected an era when society was organized hierarchically: emperors or sultans at the top, governors beneath them, and the lowly populace at the bottom of the pyramid. Early scientific perspectives, too, supported this one-sided imbalance between a perfect God and imperfect human beings: the universe operated like a well-oiled machine; human errors and misdeeds tended to gum up the works; and it was up to God, the flawless Designer, to make the necessary repairs. This classical theology was promoted so successfully that, to this day, most Jews identify it as the normative Jewish view.

I think I spoke for many, therefore, when I expressed a disconnect between this classical outlook and the world we live in today. Our society—at least the democratic model that most Jews now (thankfully) inhabit—is based on egalitarianism and inclusiveness; it stresses the ability of *human* (not just *divine*) initiative to shape our destiny. And ever since the advent of quantum physics, scientific inquiry has shed its deterministic worldview. Ian Barbour, a scientist and devout Christian, explains that "science arises from the interplay between nature and ourselves; we have no access to things as they would be apart from our investigation. No clear separation of subject and object is possible."[1] Rather than giving facts, scientific observation generally yields probabilities—and those probabilities are influenced by the observers themselves.

Emboldened by this knowledge, I began to explore a divine-human relationship that is based more on partnership and mutual responsibility—albeit with God as the senior partner. I did not have to look very far. Centuries before Maimonides, the Rabbis of the Midrash had already perceived a crucial role for humanity in the evolution of the universe:

> Rabbi Judah bar Simon said in the name of Rabbi Levi ben Parta: So long as Israel acts according to the will of heaven, they add power to God's strength, as Scripture states, "In God we shall make power" (Psalm 60:14); and if not, it is as if "they have gone without strength before the pursuer" (Lamentations 1:6). (*Pesikta D'rav Kahana* 26:166a–b)

This midrash teaches that God has a real stake in our behavior, for it is we who add strength to God. The classical theology, by contrast, maintains that God works independently of us. The end of history will come through a divine "fix"—in both senses of the word: first, God will fix (i.e., set) the time when the messianic redemption will arrive; and second, God will then fix (i.e., repair) all the fragmentation and evil in the world. The above midrash, however, takes human free will seriously; our actions *during* the course of history can either complete the process of creation or destroy it.

The Jewish mystical tradition takes this notion even further. In the *Zohar*, the thirteenth-century kabbalistic text, I read the following teaching:

> "If you walk in my statutes, and keep my commandments and do them" (Leviticus 26:3). Why is it written "and do them" afterward? The answer is: Whoever performs the commandments of the Torah and walks in its ways is regarded as if they make the One above. The Holy Blessed One says, "as if they had made Me." (*Zohar* 3:113a, trans. Moshe Idel)

According to the mystics, we humans hold not only the fate of the universe in our hands, but the fate of God as well.

I was overjoyed to find such a profound text for human empowerment, especially coming from an era when Jews had more limited choices than we do today.

But if we take the *Zohar* too literally, might we risk attributing too much to ourselves? After all, ours is a generation with a greater sense of entitlement than we sometimes deserve. Perhaps, I thought, we need some balance between the divine attributes of power and vulnerability and between the human capacity for mending the world and destroying it.

My search brought me, this time, to a thinker of more recent vintage. Rabbi Henry Slonimsky (1884–1970) was a towering figure in the history of the Hebrew Union College–Jewish Institute of Religion in New York. He served as its dean and then taught Midrash and philosophy there almost to the day he died. His study of Rabbinic literature brought him to a new understanding of God's power:

> Maybe it is our task as human beings to be helpers and co-creators with a God who is still in process of gradual realization, who needs our strength to carry out His [*sic*] designs as we need His strength to hearten us. Maybe God and perfection are at the end and not at the beginning. Maybe it is a growing world and a growing mankind and a growing God, and perfection is to be achieved, and not something to start with.[2]

This leads Slonimsky to the following understanding of the divine-human relationship in prayer:

> But what is true prayer?... It is a prayer which God Himself puts into our hearts to give back to Him enriched by our fervor, our power.... And if in the supremely tragic case in which it happens that man [*sic*] prays, and God gives, and still both together go down in apparent defeat, that defeat is ... itself a spiritual victory, because it is an heroic effort, which ... adds stature to God and man.[3]

Taking the wisdom of all these texts, I now propose what I call an "evolutionary" perspective of the divine-human relationship. Our understanding of God and Torah will change as we mature through history. Therefore, when we read our Jewish texts, we should see them as earlier manifestations of larger truths that later generations will express differently. Our task is to reinterpret the wisdom of our ancestors into insights that reflect our contemporary worldview.

If this is the case, how can we interpret the readings cited earlier? We begin with our current scientific perspective that the only constant in our universe is change. Thus, when the Midrash says that our deeds add to God's power, and when the *Zohar* claims that we play a role in "making God," we may understand this to mean that God, too, changes and evolves through time. I perceive God as the vector who points us in the direction of goodness and completion; but we, too, play a role in charting the course. Every deed that we perform, every insight that we discover, adds to God's knowledge. And by combining the wisdom of our ancestors with our current understanding of the world, we truly become *m'shutafim im Hakadosh Barukh Hu*, "partners with the Holy Blessed One," in furthering the evolution of creation, of ourselves—and of God.[4]

This approach becomes especially important in reading our High Holy Day liturgy. I find two symbols, in particular, in the *machzor* that we need to reinterpret for our time:

1. In the *Un'taneh Tokef*,[5] God is depicted as a shepherd who counts each sheep and determines its fate for life or death. From the perspective of my "evolutionary" view, I perceive a shepherd as more than a sheepmaster. A shepherd epitomizes the larger role of guiding the way into the future, like the "vector toward goodness" outlined above. When I pray, I strive to understand the direction God is pointing out to me and to steer my own life's path along that course.
2. In the High Holy Day *Amidah*, we beseech God to inscribe us in the Book of Life for the coming year. In the evolutionary view, each of us has our own book that we write—and that God reads—during the course of our life. During the Days of Awe, I imagine God holding up that book for us to read what we have written thus far. God then turns to a new and blank page, urging us to plan our next chapter with care.

Therefore, on the High Holy Days I shall continue to say *Al Chet.* Afterward, however, I will construct my own silent list in which each item will begin: *Al tikkun shetikanti l'fanekha*. The word *tikkun* is difficult to translate, since it has several meanings, but this is the general idea: "For all my efforts, in your presence, to work toward completion—of my life, of the world in which I live, and of You—may these all be recorded for blessing in my Book of Life for the coming year."

We Have Sinned

T'shuvah in a Globalized World

Lisa Exler and Ruth Messinger

Yom Kippur is about seeking forgiveness, making things right, and starting the year with a clean slate. And yet, the confessional prayers that form the basis of the liturgy on the day itself seem disconnected from this goal. The litany of sins that we repeat so many times does not reflect our specific misdeeds and has little practical impact on rectifying our transgressions or repairing our broken relationships. It seems strange that on a day when we aim to examine ourselves truthfully and change for the better, we repeat a list that is far from personal.

Instead, we stand under the anonymous cover of the whole congregation, expressing collective regret for a range of possible sins committed against a nameless group of unspecified victims. Together, we intone: "*We* have sinned ...; For the sin *we* have committed before You ...; Forgive *us*." We admit all manner of possible transgressions, yet never in the liturgy do we pause to name specific individuals or pledge to confront the victims of these misdeeds and ask for their forgiveness.

This stands in stark contrast to the process of repentance that our tradition encourages us to undertake in the days and weeks leading up to Yom Kippur: examining our actions and the harm that we have done,

---

Lisa Exler is a senior program officer in the education and community engagement department at American Jewish World Service (AJWS).

Ruth Messinger is the president of American Jewish World Service. She contributed to *Who by Fire, Who by Water—Un'taneh Tokef* and *All These Vows—Kol Nidre* (both Jewish Lights).

intentionally or unintentionally, to our friends, family, neighbors, and colleagues—and approaching those people to apologize and commit to doing better.

Our *t'shuvah* process echoes Maimonides's prescription for seeking forgiveness, which focuses on repairing interpersonal relationships. According to Maimonides, the first step is to take personal responsibility for having committed a sin by verbally confessing it, a confession phrased in the singular: "*I* sinned, *I* erred, *I* transgressed...."[1] The second step—making restitution and asking the victim of the sin for forgiveness—is an intimate interaction between two individuals. And the final step is a personal pledge not to commit the sin again. According to Maimonides—and probably many of us—repentance and forgiveness are personal matters; relationships are mended at the individual level.

Given that this individualized repentance process seems much better suited to actually righting our wrongs than the collective confessional of the Yom Kippur service, what is the purpose of the liturgy?

While the litany of collective sins against nameless victims may not advance our personal processes of repentance, it dictates a radical view of our responsibility for each other. By implicating ourselves in this long list of sins inflicted by our fellow humans—including hardening our hearts, denying and lying, sins in commerce, haughty eyes—we remind ourselves that we play a role in the injustices taking place around the world that likely don't make our list of individual sins. But the liturgy forces us to remember that by association in the global community, and through our actions and inactions, we too are guilty of causing the poverty, hunger, and disease, the inequality, prejudice, and cruelty in the world.

This reminder is especially necessary for injustices that occur far from our view, such as those that affect people living in the developing world. As individuals, we do not take money or resources from people facing poverty in developing countries. We are not directly employing them and paying unfair wages or fueling wars that inhibit their development. But we are not blameless.

As the Yom Kippur service reminds us, again and again, ***we** have sinned.* We participate in the global economic and political systems that lead to many people's poverty. We buy clothes produced in sweatshops in which they work. We drink the coffee they grow. Our government, through legislators whom we elect, enacts trade policies that undermine their ability to grow and sell their produce. Corporations in which we invest appropriate their land for factories and limit their access to life-saving medications. The confessional prayers on Yom Kippur—in their collective formulation—force us to confront our obligations to others in a global context and to reflect on how we can make amends if we have failed to meet those obligations.

So rather than being irrelevant for our personal *t'shuvah* process, it seems that the Yom Kippur liturgy just urges us to broaden it. But how to go about doing so—especially within the framework suggested by Maimonides—is a challenge. Although we may be able to name and confess the ways in which we have contributed to the oppression of people in developing countries, the role we play is complex and indirect; we do not know specifically whom we have harmed, nor could we find them in order to ask for forgiveness. And if we were to pledge never to commit these sins again, we would have to opt out of the global economy and go off the grid—a prospect that, for most of us, is impossible. So where does this leave us?

While we may not be able to complete this *t'shuvah* process, we can at least begin—vowing to act in ways that mitigate harm to the world's most marginalized people. As individuals, we can invest in socially responsible funds, purchase goods that were produced by workers who were paid fairly, and give *tz'dakah* to support organizations and initiatives working to improve the lives of people in developing countries.

And as a community, we can take action to pursue more widespread change. Peruvian theologian Gustavo Gutierrez suggests that just as our sins against people facing poverty are collective sins of our society, our response must be collective action as well:

> The poor person does not exist as an inescapable fact of destiny. His or her existence is not politically neutral, and it is not ethically innocent. The poor are a by-product of the system in which we live and for which we are responsible. They are marginalized by our social and cultural world.... Hence the poverty of the poor is not a call to generous relief action, but a demand that we go and build a different social order.[2]

We can take up Gutierrez's call to build a different social order by recognizing and leveraging our collective power as citizens and consumers to build a more just world. As Gutierrez recognizes, this requires finding solutions to poverty that move beyond offering short-term relief and instead empowering people to improve their own lives. On a practical level, we can engage in community-wide *tz'dakah* campaigns to provide our financial support to communities and organizations in developing countries that work for greater justice and equality. We can organize ourselves as investors and consumers to pressure corporations to carry out their business more ethically. Finally, we can marshal our collective power as citizens by lobbying our elected officials to enact policies that strengthen—rather than undermine—the self-sufficiency of people facing poverty.

And regarding those we have wronged: while we can't complete the *t'shuvah* process by asking individuals for forgiveness, we can instead use the Yom Kippur confessional liturgy as a substitute. As we recite the list of sins that "we" have committed, we can name and own these sins and, through our prayers, seek the forgiveness of those whom we will never meet, but who suffer because of us.

As we pray this Yom Kippur, let us pledge to pursue a global *t'shuvah*: to work collectively—not only to alleviate poverty and mitigate the negative effects of our global economic and political systems, but also to build a new social order in which poverty and oppression are replaced by equality and justice.

The Power of Words

Radical Creation, Radical Atonement

Rabbi Shoshana Boyd Gelfand

Reciting a Yom Kippur confessional has become so commonplace that we sometimes forget how radical an innovation it was when it began. As we know from both the Torah reading on Yom Kippur morning and the *Avodah* service during *Musaf*, Yom Kippur in the Bible was a service of sacrifice, not of words. It consisted of the high priest transferring the sins of himself, his household, and the entire Israelite community onto a scapegoat, which was then released into the wilderness. An additional goat was then sacrificed with a relatively modest verbal recitation that accompanied the main "event"—physical sacrifice and the sprinkling of the victim's blood.

In the Bible, then, we find a Temple ceremony conducted by a single individual who atoned for himself but also for others. Those "others" (if they were present at all) just witnessed the event as silent spectators, waiting expectantly for forgiveness to arrive—rather than active participants whose own behavior (entailing a *t'shuvah* process) influenced the outcome.

The Temple ritual, while including a verbal element, was fundamentally not about words but about blood: the blood of an animal that

---

Rabbi Shoshana Boyd Gelfand received her rabbinic ordination in 1993 at The Jewish Theological Seminary in New York. She has served as chief executive of the United Kingdom Movement for Reform Judaism and prior to that was vice president of the Wexner Heritage Foundation in New York. Currently she is director of JHub, an operating program of the London-based Pears Foundation. She contributed to *All These Views—Kol Nidre* (Jewish Lights).

substituted and atoned for human sin. In contrast, today the atonement process is all about words, as a crucial step in the larger process of self-reflection and making amends that we call *t'shuvah.*

This transformation from sacrificial to verbal atonement and from intermediary to direct confession remains one of the most radical innovations of Judaism. I often wonder how the Rabbis found within themselves the necessary creativity and courage to even suggest such a thing. Where did this inspiration come from? The Talmudic tradition is somewhat self-reflective about the general shift from sacrifice to prayer (it even has a midrashic tradition that claims that each recitation of the *Amidah* replaced one of the Temple services). But I remain in awe of the courage it took to make such a claim; what a remarkable act of leadership! At the moment of crisis when the Temple was destroyed, the Rabbis dared to replace sacrifice (which was no longer possible) with words (which were). How could they have known that words would suffice, when it had always been sacrifice that God had requested of Israel? In particular, what convinced them that the *Avodah* service of the high priest alone could be replaced by the congregational recitation of a confessional alphabetical acrostic?

While (to my knowledge) the Rabbis never say so explicitly, I like to imagine that they derived their confidence from the very first words of the Torah—which demonstrate that words indeed have immense power. Surely, if words can *create* the world, then they can also *re*-create and even *repair* the world. Thus, if God's words have formed the universe, then surely our words, modeled on God's, can reverse whatever damage to the world our sins have caused. It was, then, I like to think, the account of creation in Genesis that inspired the Rabbis to replace the primal power of sacrifice with the (perhaps even more) primal power of words.

For the genius of Genesis is its insistence on God creating the world with words and nothing else—a revolutionary departure from other creation myths of antiquity, where the world arises from conflict (e.g., the earth is formed from the dead body of a god defeated in battle with another god).

Not only is Genesis a radical text in that we meet a divine being who can create something out of nothing using only words, but there is also yet another astounding breakthrough in the Jewish description of creation. As if it were not revolutionary enough for the Torah to tell of a God who creates through speech instead of violence, Genesis also describes how at each and every act of creation, God stops to reflect on the *moral* nature of the component that has just come into being.

Thus, from the first words of the Torah, speech is intertwined with *creation* and *evaluation*, the two central themes of the High Holy Days: Rosh Hashanah focuses on the first; Yom Kippur, on the second. I would like to suggest that the appearance of these two themes in both the creation story and our High Holy Day liturgy is not coincidental, but that the Rabbis who wrote the liturgy purposefully utilized these themes (whether consciously or unconsciously I do not know).

The creation story thus prefigures our High Holy Day liturgy, just as the High Holy Day liturgy recapitulates the creation narrative. In Genesis, language *forms* reality; at the High Holy Days, it *trans-forms* it. In Genesis, language *creates*; in our liturgy, it *re-creates*. Through divine words, God reflects and evaluates divine behavior; through our human words (of confession), we reflect and evaluate our own human behavior. Genesis itself should therefore give us confidence (as it did the Rabbis) to declare that prayer in general and the Yom Kippur service in particular are adequate replacements for the sacrificial system of the Temple.

If that were not enough of a justification, however, Genesis offers us additional reasons to trust the atoning power of words. Following the repeated reflection and evaluation present in Genesis, chapter 1, where almost every element of creation is dubbed *ki tov* ("it was good"), we reach chapter 2, the first instance in the world where something is declared *lo tov* ("not good"). That something is loneliness: "It is not good for man to be alone," God declares (Genesis 2:18). All is good in the world until loneliness emerges. The instance in question is Adam's solitude and the subsequent need to create Eve, but the rest of Genesis can be seen as God's own search for a partner so that *God* too will not be alone. God's choice of Abraham and the covenant with the Jewish People reflect this divine desire to be in relationship with human beings.

In other words, loneliness is not good; it is painful; it is not the way things are supposed to be. Therefore, God (and the Torah) become obsessed with relationship. The relationship between human beings and God and the relationship between human beings and each other are the focus of the rest of the Torah. Along the way, we see other key relationships that sustain or root the fundamental two: the relationship between the Jewish People and the Land of Israel, for example, and the relationship between human beings and the natural world. But all of the laws of Torah explicitly or implicitly support one of the two core relationships that guard against the Jewish "original sin" of isolation. The clear message of the Torah is that human beings are meant to seek and treasure relationship, with each other and with God.

Thus, from Genesis 1 we get language as a tool for creation and evaluation; from Genesis 2 we get the imperative to restore relationship as the primary guard against loneliness and the means to make the world good, not bad. Taken together, we get the philosophical groundwork for the Yom Kippur confessional.

Interestingly enough, however, even though words were sufficient to create the universe, they required action as well to create relationships. Think of how God creates Eve. God doesn't just speak Eve into existence the way God created people in Genesis 1; God works at creating her out of Adam's side. That must be because language alone cannot repair relationships. While divine language alone may be capable of creating something from nothing, when it comes to relationships, action too is necessary.

On Yom Kippur, we imitate God: we use language to create ourselves anew and to reflect and evaluate on what is good and not good about our lives. But to conquer loneliness, we turn to relationships, and there we commit ourselves to action beyond our words. We can recite the entire alphabet and reflect on each sin ad naseum, but until we actually act to repair what we have done to damage our relationships—with God, with others, and with the world at large—we have not fulfilled the requirements of Yom Kippur. So in the long run, we do not altogether depart from the Temple ritual of the high priest. He too took action: he released the scapegoat. We no longer have the scapegoat—we have words instead—but we still must take action to complete our work of restoration on Yom Kippur.

Perhaps in the final assessment, therefore, the Rabbis were not as radical as they seem at first glance. In truth, all they did was return to the source of all inspiration, to the divine words and action of Genesis. What an appropriate way to respond to the crisis of the destruction of the Temple—they did literal *t'shuvah*, "returning" to the creation story to discover a new method for restoring and repairing our relationships with each other and with God.

What We Learn from Having So Many Sins

Dr. Joel M. Hoffman

The details of *Al Chet* jump off the page and prompt questions: How is insolence different from arrogance? When does lying turn into deceit? And isn't mendacity the same thing? In typical Jewish fashion, the questions don't yield answers but more questions: Is there a pattern to the list? Why are some sins (murder, say) missing? If we created a list from scratch, what would it look like?

Amid all of these nuances and minutiae, it's easy to miss two crucial assumptions without which the list wouldn't even be possible.

The first is that some things are wrong. This basic tenet of Judaism, so obvious to those who already know it, is neither intuitive nor universal. There are young children who take what they want only because they want it, never asking the deeper, Jewish, question of *Al Chet*: "Is it right to do this?" For them, the world is divided not into right and wrong but, rather, simply into "what I want" and "what I don't want."

Dr. Joel M. Hoffman lectures around the globe on popular and scholarly topics spanning history, Hebrew, prayer, and Jewish continuity. He has served on the faculties of Brandeis University in Waltham, Massachusetts, and Hebrew Union College–Jewish Institute of Religion in New York. He is author of *And God Said: How Translations Conceal the Bible's Original Meaning* and *In the Beginning: A Short History of the Hebrew Language*, and has written for the international *Jerusalem Post*. He contributed to all ten volumes of the *My People's Prayer Book: Traditional Prayers, Modern Commentaries* series, winner of the National Jewish Book Award; to *My People's Passover Haggadah: Traditional Texts, Modern Commentaries*; and to *Who by Fire, Who by Water—Un'taneh Tokef* (all Jewish Lights).

Some of these children grow up to be adults with the same mentality, thugs who kill for a wristwatch because then they have a watch, or corrupt leaders who augment their personal wealth at the expense of those they lead. Their world, like the children's, is one in which actions come in only two varieties: "good for me" and "not good for me," with no sense of anything or anyone else.

It's not just children and sociopaths whose world is devoid of right and wrong. Entire societies and philosophies have rejected these notions. Hedonism, for example, focuses only on the subjective experience of the self: "What's good for me is good." Similar is Nietzsche's categorization of altruism as a "slave mentality" from which higher humans can and should free themselves. According to him, it would be a step forward if we could learn to stop helping the downtrodden.

Modern legal societies are curious in this regard, because they have substituted "illegal" for "wrong." At first glance the two concepts seem similar, and they refer to similar things. Murder is both illegal and wrong. So is theft and, though the details differ, slander. Casual conversation is neither illegal nor wrong. And so forth.

But whereas "right" and "wrong" are statements about actions, "legal" and "illegal" refer to the consequences of those actions. "If you murder, you may be imprisoned or put to death." That's a legal statement, and in essence it establishes a deal. "If you park for two hours in a one-hour parking zone, you may have to pay a fine." That's also a legal statement and also a deal. The second one is really no different from a price for parking. And in the case of the first, the jail term or death sentence is the price to be paid for murder.

But the law doesn't take a stand on whether the deal is a good one or not. While one person may prefer not to murder, so as to stay alive and free, another may prefer the opposite. A man on his deathbed who kills a twenty-four-year-old out of spite may accept the bargain offered by the law. "What are they going to do, kill me?" he may reason. The law dictates the consequences of his actions but doesn't dissuade him from murdering if he finds those consequences acceptable.

By contrast, the statement that "murder is wrong" is about the action itself. Whether or not a potential murderer thinks he will be caught, whether or not he thinks he will be punished, and whether or not he thinks the punishment is a fair price to pay, he still shouldn't do it.

In other words, actions come in two varieties, and it's important to know the difference because we are obliged to avoid one kind. This is where the second implicit assumption of *Al Chet* comes into play, because it is God to whom we are obliged, and it is God who decides which actions fall into which category.

From First Confession to Perfection of Character

Rabbi Walter Homolka, PhD, DHL

I grew up in Lower Bavaria, an area in southern Germany whose population is almost exclusively Roman Catholic; having been raised in a religiously rather than indifferent family I bacame socialized by my Catholic environment until my teens. When I was in the third grade, we were prepared for our first confession, the sacrament of penance—what Jews might call "atonement." This would happen at the huge Baroque St. Mary's Ascension Church in our town in one of the wooden confessionals situated among the various side altars. We would wait our turn at one of those altars, kneeling and contemplating the remains of one of the saints whose skulls and bones (still observable in glass shrines) were held together with gold wire, sometimes dressed up in precious garments.

The priest would be seated in the middle of a freestanding wooden structure, and the penitents would enter the compartments to either side of him. The priest could close off one compartment from another by a sliding screen, so that only one person would be confessing at a time, and curtains concealed penitents and priest from the rest of the church. Kneelers were provided in the compartments, and confessions were whispered.

Rabbi Walter Homolka, PhD, DHL, is rector of the Abraham Geiger College for the training of rabbis, executive director of the Zacharias Frankel European campus of the Ziegler School for Rabbinic Studies, and a professor of Jewish studies at Potsdam University in Germany. He is author of many books, including *The Gate to Perfection: The Idea of Peace in Jewish Thought*, and coauthor of *How to Do Good & Avoid Evil: A Global Ethic from the Sources of Judaism* (SkyLight Paths).

I had often seen the faithful outside these booths waiting to make their regular confession in preparation for the Mass, or Eucharist—the primary worship of the church. A green light above the priest's side indicated that the priest was present and ready to hear confession. When somebody entered the penitent's side and knelt on the kneeler, a red light appeared above that area to show that the confessional was occupied and confession under way. One could not help but think of traffic lights. Somehow, there was always a lot of traffic to regulate in front of these mysterious booths, where people waited in line to slip behind the curtain as soon as the red light went out and then make contact with the kneeler to ignite another red light in its place.

How tempting it was to imagine stealing into the church and tiptoeing close to one of the confessionals. What would one hear? The rule was to cover one's ear with one's hand in order to show respect for the sanctity of the seal of confession. This was pious practice even when passing an empty confessional. The conversation with God in this box was obviously a great secret.

Theologically speaking, confession is the Catholic way for reconciliation with God. I remember, though, that for my school pals and me, there was little that was reconciliatory about the prospect of entering this secret box. Most school kids felt rather frightened at the prospect of confessing for the first time. It was not God whom they feared to meet so much as it was the priest, who was a very distant dignitary and much respected for studying in Rome itself before taking holy orders. And then what to say?

The beginning was fairly straightforward—a ritual exchange of conversation with the priest, indicating purpose and intent. It seemed rather obvious to me, but was something one had to learn by heart:

> O my God, I am heartily sorry for having offended You and I detest all my trespasses, because I dread the loss of heaven and the pains of hell. But most of all because I have offended You, my God, who is all good and deserving of all my love. I firmly resolve with the help of your grace, to confess my sins, to do penance and to amend my life. Amen.

This alone led to theater jitters for many who simply couldn't remember the right phrases, however long they rehearsed. But at least it was a given, nothing one had to make up.

Not so the confession itself. What kind of sins could a nine-year-old come up with in the examination of conscience? To help us along, our religious-education teacher would explain the act of repentance. A simple equation really:

Penance = contrition + rejection + amendment + resolution for the better

Then he would go through the various categories of sins: mortal sins, capital sins, cardinal sins, venial sins, peccadilloes. One had to reiterate the right definitions, such as the following:

> Mortal sin is a deadly offense against God, so horrible that it destroys the life of grace in the soul. Three simultaneous conditions must be fulfilled for a mortal sin: (1) the act must be something very serious; (2) the person must have sufficient understanding of what is being done; (3) the person must have sufficient freedom of the will.

Nine-year-olds brooded about such things as the contrite heart and the freedom of will (on one hand) versus original sin (on the other). The rule was, "In order to make a good confession, the faithful must confess all mortal sins, according to kind and number." So we had to start with the ones that were most difficult to say. Here we were, sin-born, but just when we needed it, the memory of applicable sins was likely to go totally blank; so before any first confession, our rural primary school became a real hotbed of sins to which we might plead guilty when the proper time came. Lists were secretly drawn up, surreptitiously passed along under the desk from neighbor to neighbor and, later, in the schoolyard, categorized for use in confessional without too much embarrassment.

Luckily, the manual of confession helped. Like a mail-order catalogue, it provided the possibilities from which we could choose whatever seemed applicable. Gradually a whole script appeared: a crib, or cheating aid, that would get us safely through the whole matter. The sins could not be too heavy—the kind that kids in our age and circumstance were unlikely to have committed; and they could not be too shameful, since we would regularly bump into the priest later on in the street. Looking back on all of this, I can see how truly fascinating first confession was.

How much time we spent preparing for the ritual! How much energy went into memorizing the typology of sins and the theology of sin and forgiveness! But at the same time, I now realize, how little thought went into preparing us nine-year-olds for the real task of facing God with our trespasses in mind. Confession was so awe-inspiring, but for more immanent reasons of facing the priest and mastering the rite, not transcendent ones of being alone with God.

Judaism has its own confession, and now, as an adult who chose to be Jewish as a teenager, I can't help making comparisons with my early youth. The confession manual we encounter in Jewish liturgy is *Al Chet*. It is reminiscent of my growing up in that it too is a catalogue of sins—some familiar to me and others that I personally have never even contemplated, let alone committed. There is, however, no priest as intermediary, and I feel relieved that I do not have to choose a light potpourri of digestible sins in order to avoid horrifying him. I may simply approach God directly. Ten times I recite the *Al Chet* manual of forty-four sins, and while I do this publicly with the rest of the congregation, I also acknowledge within myself my own personal share of sins omitted and committed. I do both: I recognize my personal share of sinfulness and at the same time realize our common responsibility as human beings and as God's holy people for the sinfulness of the world.

As a little Catholic boy, I knew that I would be making confession regularly. That was part of Talmudic Judaism, too—the Rabbis insisted that we say our own private prayer daily, "even as much as a confession" as the Rabbis put it. For centuries, daily confession was part of the silent prayer after the *Amidah*; it is still a daily staple in some places; in others, we have the *Tachanun*, itself something of a confession that is said privately. Reform and Progressive Jews in most of the world have done away with both. But I sometimes wish we hadn't. I feel we Jews would be better off if we were to deal daily with the issues of a contrite heart, correction, and amendment. There is something to be said for more regular examinations of conscience as spiritual checkups for our daily ride on the road of betterment. I think the Rabbis of antiquity and the Catholics of my youth got that right.

I think the Rabbis also got right our "direct line" to God without a priest as intermediary, and that part remains true of all Jewish practice, my Progressive version as well as the various kinds of Judaism practiced anywhere in the world. I cherish the intimacy with which we may approach God as Jews. I like also Judaism's insistence on maintaining a powerful public confession that we recite together at the gates of repentance, where God offers us all the forgiveness we need, because we all have responsibility for each other.

The details of our catalogued list of sins in *Al Chet* are many. But they all boil down to a single overriding intent, something we all should desire regardless of what particular sins we have been guilty of: perfection of character.

Judaism is my route to perfection of character. I may never get there, but I seek it out. Yom Kippur's insistence on *Al Chet* reminds me of this search.

The Jewish "ABC Song"

Rabbi Delphine Horvilleur

A B C D E F G H I J K L M N O P Q R S T U V W X Y Z …
Now I know my ABCs, next time won't you sing with me?

It all begins with a nursery rhyme, maybe the most famous nursery rhyme of all—every child in the world knows some version of it. From generation to generation, it is repeated, passed down, taught and transmitted as a sacred mantra, a holy childhood liturgy.

The alphabet song is like a passport to kindergarten, one of the few tunes kids share on their very first days of socialization. They learn it long before they even consider what a letter is and what an A, B, or C might even mean or be used for. Yet, parents or caregivers insistently impart this twenty-six-digit code, convinced that these mysterious elements hold a key to every child's future. The song is an alphabetic shorthand to a sort of *olam haba*, a post-childhood "world to come," not yet accessible, to be sure, but brimming with promise. It guarantees knowledge, connection to ancestors, and dialogue with their cultural world through books that may some day be entered and mastered. Think of the nursery-rhyme text midrashically:

Rabbi Delphine Horvilleur is the rabbi of congregation MJLF (Mouvement Juif Libéral de France) in Paris. She was ordained at Hebrew Union College–Jewish Institute of Religion in New York in 2008 and became the third woman rabbi in France. She is the creative director of Le Café Biblique, a pluralistic group of Jewish study, and chief editor of *Tenou'a*, a French magazine of Jewish thought. She contributed to *Who by Fire, Who by Water—Un'taneh Tokef* and *All These Vows—Kol Nidre* (both Jewish Lights).

"Next time": That is, in your future.

"Won't you sing with me?": Won't you come to live, at least temporarily, in my culture, in my books, in the written record of the people you will someday recognize as your ancestors?

The midrashic subtext of the song is the collective promise of a gateway to a shared worldview. It ties the knots of a common identity across time and space.

The Jewish parallel is not just an "*alef-bet* song," although we do have that as well. No, the Jewish equivalent is, of all things, two confessions, *Ashamnu* and *Al Chet*. They too are powerful generators of collective belonging, an invitation for the individual to join the Jewish People in its feeling of shared destiny.

Every year, on the holiest days of the Jewish calendar, the days we call *Yamim Nora'im*, no less, "the Days of Awe," we Jews reunite in synagogues, to pray, read, and sing a liturgy, at whose core is the "Jewish ABC":

> *"Ashamnu, Bagadnu, Gazalnu, Dibarnu Dofi ..."*
> *Alef, Bet, Gimel, Dalet ...*

This melodious enunciation of our sins coincides elegantly with the letters of the Hebrew alphabet, from *alef* to *tav*. It is an A-to-Z list of our misdeeds, our faults, and our mis-achievements. Not just mine and not just yours, but *ours*. The *Yamim Nora'im* are all about *us*, as a group. We attend a yearly sinners' reunion, a getting together of wrongdoers who recapitulate alphabetically what they collectively might have misdone.

The alphabet reminds us that the list of confessions must be complete, an A-to-Z symbolic recognition of all possible transgressions and all potential transgressors, which means whoever sits in the room. If you know your ABCs, you probably belong.

Some congregations and prayer books offer translations of the *Ashamnu* that preserve the alphabetical order of the sins enumerated: "I sinned abjectly, boldly, cruelly, dramatically ..."; "I assaulted, brutalized, coerced...." The list is reiterated again and again, so that by the time the gates finally close at *N'ilah*, everyone in the room can indeed "sing with me."

Ashamnu, not just *alef, bet, gimel*, as in ABC—an alphabet song about sin is more powerful than an ABC song with nothing but an alphabet to memorize. To begin with, the ordinary ABC requires no specific move or physical position, whereas the confessions do. *Ashamnu* and *Al Chet* come outfitted with liturgical choreography.

As they hear the first notes of *Ashamnu*, worshipers immediately stand, wrapped in their *tallitot*. They beat out the rhythm of each passing Hebrew word, with fists clenched against their chests. *Alef* to *tav*—twenty-two letters, twenty-two sins, twenty-two knocks. The choreography is simple but incredibly powerful. Knock knock knocking on sinners' door.

This is the closest we Jews come to a mantra dance. We repeat the motion in a shared space, a simultaneous performance of a collective experience that leaves no one untouched. For sure, no single one of us, even the worst transgressor we can imagine, could possibly be guilty of all the enunciated crimes. Our liturgy asks us, however, to endorse a collective responsibility that blurs individual frontiers. The skin that separates us is literally beaten, as if ripped apart. We are connected, in a heartbeat. *Ashamnu*, like many other liturgical pieces of the High Holy Days, is perceived as the verbalization of an undifferentiated "guilt trip."

One cannot help asking, however, as we do elsewhere in the High Holy Day liturgical drama, from *Un'taneh Tokef* to the martyrology: Do we really believe what we say? Do Jews seriously mean what they are rushing to synagogues to say and to hear on that day? Are we essentially and collectively guilty?

What I often tell congregants is that the Days of Awe are probably the most paradoxical days of the Jewish calendar. They are a collective rendezvous with the synagogue—for many, the only rendezvous with the synagogue that they will have, the only annual occasion to witness the face of a Judaism they do not visit very often.

Yet, in many ways, those very same Days of Awe are the least Jewish of all days in the year. In my mind, what our synagogue's liturgy and choreography convey then is almost a contradiction to the normative message of the Judaism we teach all year long. The once-a-year visitors actually get a kind of anti-model to what Judaism is about the rest of the year. Let me give a few examples.

All year long, we teach that God is our partner, who created us in God's image and empowered humanity to act in the world. On the Days of Awe, we use only metaphors of a powerless humanity, judged by a distant and elevated sovereign. We keep calling God "king," "master," and "father," images we do not often use in our liturgical discourse all year long.

On the High Holy Days, we call upon God's mercy, *ki ein banu ma'asim*, "because we are empty of good deeds." But the rest of the year, don't we feel comfortable enough with our deeds to pray in the vertical position, standing proudly in a face-to-face dialogue before our creator? All year long, we do not prostrate, but on Rosh Hashanah and Yom Kippur, we do—for God then appears as a shepherd and a father to the servants, kids, and flocks that we suddenly become.

Nowhere else in the year is Judaism defined as an ascetic religion, but on Yom Kippur our deaths are rehearsed: we mortify ourselves as if we are leaving the land of the living.

People who come to synagogue only once a year might easily confuse the exception with the rule. They are likely to conclude that Judaism is a permanent guilt trip, a constant chest-beating and *oy-vey* lament about past misdeeds. Yet in reality, Judaism knows no original sin, as it knows no permanent failure. No one need be born to (or remain in) a condition of guilt. Guilt exists only to be cured and surpassed, as the idea of *t'shuvah* demonstrates. We are never indelibly marked by mistakes. We may always find redemption, a "going back" to where we were before we erred. Guilt is a temporary station, not a destination.

Therefore, Judaism envisions a number of rehabilitation processes that are carefully narrated or even played out on the High Holy Days. One of them is telling the story of how we offered sacrifices when a Temple still stood—how the worshiper brought an animal of his belonging and watched it being killed and dismembered, broken into pieces in front of his eyes. Witnessing brokenness is a necessary prelude to envisioning repair. Witnessing shattered reality may be prologue to becoming one and whole again.

In a word, Judaism's once-a-year guilt trip is not supposed to imprison us in this feeling of unworthiness but to lead us out of it. An entire day spent in High Holy Day confession is indeed an anomaly, but a necessary one if we are to appreciate the Jewish ideal whereby failure is temporary and wholeness the norm.

On Yom Kippur, we play the role of collectively being broken because we are *l'lo ma'asim*, "empty of good deeds." As individuals and as a group, we experience being utterly demolished, completely shattered—from bottom up, from inside out: from A to Z, that is! We declare to God, who judges us, "Here we are, totally 'unwholly,' and facing your holiness."

We admit our brokenness verbally and even effect it physically with our beating movement, hoping to rebuild a sense of wholeness by *N'ilah*, by the time "the gates are closed."

Our choreographed confession is like a collective self-destruction on our way to reconstructive surgery.

Liturgical pieces are like popular songs that we carry through life and become part of our very being. We return to them at moments of transition, associating them with seasons of our journey through life. Worship is like a travel in time.

On the Days of Awe, we revert to childhood: we are like children, adults still merely in the making, who have yet to become and to belong. This might be why these days, and no others, open the Jewish year; annual time, like biographical time, begins with childhood. We reexperience nursery rhymes and this feeling of being yet nothing, being yet "unbuilt" and "un-grown." We call out to God, as a parent who will care. We need songs that guide us toward another future.

Every new year thus catapults us back into childhood and a sacred appointment with beginning. When *N'ilah* ends, we will be adults again.

Aval Chatanu ("But / In Truth, We Have Sinned")

A Literary Investigation

Rabbi Elie Kaunfer

Confession is one of the most central aspects of Yom Kippur. What does it mean to really confess?

The Babylonian Talmud (Yoma 87b) offers an answer to this question through the action of Samuel, one of the most influential teachers of the Rabbinic age. Samuel's student, Bar Hamdudi, reports of his teacher: "I was standing before Samuel, and he was seated. When the prayer leader arrived at the phrase 'But we have sinned' [*Aval chatanu*][1] Samuel stood up. We learn that this is the essence of confession."

In fact, Mar Zutra, a later authority, reports that if one says only "But we have sinned," one need confess no further.

So what is so significant about the words *aval* ("but") *chatanu* ("we have sinned")? The announcement that *chatanu*, "we have sinned," makes sense. But what about *aval*, "but"? Why *aval*? Couldn't we do with *chatanu* alone?

I think the many meanings behind the word *aval* reveal a deeper comprehension of what confession is all about.

Rabbi Elie Kaunfer is cofounder and executive director of Mechon Hadar (www.mechonhadar.org). He is an Avi Chai Fellow, the author of *Empowered Judaism: What Independent Minyanim Can Teach Us about Building Vibrant Jewish Communities*, and a contributor to *Who by Fire, Who by Water—Un'taneh Tokef* and *All These Vows—Kol Nidre* (all Jewish Lights). *Newsweek* named him one of fifty top rabbis in America.

Aval as Turning Point

In the *Vidui* of most communities today, these two words, *aval chatanu*, appear in the larger context of saying, "We are not so arrogant and insolent as to say before You, Adonai our God and our ancestors' God, we are righteous and have not sinned. But we have sinned." But in many versions this reads, "We *are* arrogant and obstinate ... we *say* before You that we are righteous and have not sinned. But we have sinned."[2]

In this formulation, the word *aval* is not just a rhetorical addition. It is a radical disjuncture in the penitent's thought process, a psychological turning point. Consciously or subconsciously, we spend so much time living the lie that we are blameless, that we are righteous, that we have not sinned. The turning point comes only when we say the word *aval*, "but." We like to say we haven't sinned, but, in fact, we have.

Confession is only useful once we set aside our rationalized self-deception and confront the reality of our actions. It is not enough to say, "We have sinned." We must also (at least implicitly) concede that we prefer imagining we have not, hence the all-important "but." We pretend to be someone blameless. But we are not the person we pretend to be.

Aval as Accepting Responsibility

Although very common in Modern Hebrew, the word *aval* occurs only eleven times in the Bible, and only twice in the Torah, both of them in Genesis. The first time, Genesis 17:19, is when Abraham cannot believe that God is going to give Sarah a son. When Abraham laughs at this prediction, God responds: *Aval Sarah isht'kha yoledet 'vkha ben*, "*Aval* Sarah your wife will give birth to a son for you."

What does *aval* mean in this context? Both Rashi and Onkelos make it clear: *aval* means "in truth."[3] Although conceptually related to "but," "in truth" has a different valence. It is a statement of the actual reality, not the apparent reality.

Rashi connects this verse to the other time *aval* appears in Torah: Genesis 42:21. Here the context is very different. Joseph and his brothers are encountering each other for the first time since the brothers sold Joseph into slavery. The brothers (who do not recognize Joseph) are starving from famine, while Joseph (who does recognize his brothers) commands a whole storehouse of food.

Joseph accuses the brothers of being spies and demands that they return with Benjamin, after which the brothers say among themselves: *Aval ashemim anachnu*, "*Aval* we are guilty on account of our brother [Joseph], because we looked at his anguish, but we did not listen. Therefore this trouble has come upon us" (Genesis 42:21).

Here too, Rashi and Onkelos translate *aval* as "in truth."[4] This is a moment of truth for the brothers, an experience of facing up to the reality of their sin from so many years ago. Their guilt runs very deep. And they only start to confront it by recognizing the truth, introduced by *aval*.

Ironically, the brothers admit their guilt to each other, assuming Joseph, in their eyes an Egyptian prince, can't understand them. But, the Torah makes clear, Joseph does understand. In a twist, Joseph listens to their conversation, whereas the brothers hadn't listened to Joseph when, as the child they were casting away, he had pleaded directly with them.

This story serves as intertextual backdrop to the *aval* in our liturgical confession. Indeed, recall that the most Talmud manuscripts do not have the word *anachnu* in the anecdote about Samuel; they say just *aval chatanu*. Our liturgy, however, has added *anachnu*, so we now have *aval anachnu chatanu*. This addition may be a deliberate reflection of the Genesis prototype. That Genesis model may even explain the choice of *ashamnu* as the *alef* word in the alphabetical acrostic that follows—an echo of the brothers' realization, *ashemim anachnu*.

Yom Kippur liturgy	*aval*	*anachnu*	*chatanu*
Genesis 42:21	*aval*	*ashemim*	*anachnu*

The sin of Joseph's brothers becomes paradigmatic for Jews. Midrashim and *piyyutim* (poems) explain the death of the ten Rabbinic martyrs following the second-century Bar Kokhba revolt as recompense for the fact that the ten brothers of Joseph had not been punished for their sin. We include such a *piyyut* in *Musaf* of Yom Kippur; its lesson stands behind the Yom Kippur confession of sin: namely, *aval anachnu chatanu* = *aval ashemim anachnu*.

In light of this literary parallel, what does confession mean? Confession means dredging up sins that were buried long ago. Confession means beginning to take responsibility for our actions. Confession means recognizing how people plead with us while we refuse to hear them. Ultimately, confession means recognizing the ugly truth and stating it out loud.

Aval as Relationship after Sin

The early morning section of our regular weekday liturgy (the Morning Blessings, or *Birkhot Hashachar*) also contains a confession.[5] It mirrors Rabbi Yochanan's confession in Yoma 87b: "Master of all worlds, not because of our righteousness do we lay our pleas before You, but because of your great compassion." This, in turn, is followed by Samuel's recommendation for the text of *N'ilah* (also Yoma 87b): "What are we? What are our lives?" In the daily prayers, this defeated cry ends with, "The advantage of man over the animals is nothing, for all is vanity/vapor" (quoting Ecclesiastes 3:19). This text is also recited in our current *N'ilah* confession.

But in the daily prayers, this otherwise hopeless ending turns a corner: *Aval anachnu amkha*, "But we are your people, the children of your covenant, the children of Abraham, your beloved."

Siddur commentators connect this to a set of midrashim that elaborate on the meaning of Exodus 15:18, from the Song of the Sea: "Adonai will reign forever and ever."[6] "Rabbi Yose Hagelili said: If Israel had said: God reigns forever [cf. Psalm 10:16], then no foreign power would ever have ruled over them. But they said: God *will* reign forever—in the future."[7]

The midrash recounts a core sin of Israel. Following the splitting of the sea, Israel had the opportunity to be redeemed eternally. But instead of crowning God as king currently, they hedged their bets and called God king only in the future. At the time of momentary redemption, ultimate redemption was lost.

The midrash continues, however: "But we are your people [*aval anachnu amkha*], your flock of sheep that You tend, the children of Abraham who loves You, the children of Isaac your only one, your chosen one...." The language mirrors the passage from the daily liturgy.

Here the word *aval* introduces neither an admission of sin nor an acceptance of responsibility. Instead, it highlights a relationship. It is as if the children of Israel miss their chance for ultimate redemption but highlight their ongoing relationship with God, despite this missed opportunity. Yes, the moment has been lost, but we are still your flock, whom You tend.

This is the reality of our ongoing connection to a forgiving God. As human beings, we will often miss the moment to vault toward true redemption. But we are not alone or abandoned as a result. We remain in deep relationship, and that is the *aval*, the "in truth," the "however," that allows us to keep moving through the day or the year.

Samuel indicated through standing up that *aval chatanu* is the essence of confession. Indeed, if we can recite those two words alone, with all of the implied meanings of the word *aval*, we will have attained an experience of confession that will allow us to move forward to the next chapter in our relationship with God.

Confession and Its Discontents

Rabbi Reuven Kimelman, PhD

Nothing shakes up the kishkas as much as the confessions of Yom Kippur.[1] So intrinsic are they to Yom Kippur that they are supposed to appear in every service[2]—ten times in all, which is thought to correspond to the ten times the high priest invoked the tetragrammaton in confessing for himself, his household, and the whole people on Yom Kippur. According to Leviticus 16:21, the order of the sins in the high priest's confession is *chet*, *avon*, and *pesha*, a model that the liturgy follows, thereby structuring our sins in ascending order of gravity: *chatanu*, *avinu*, *pashanu*, "*We* acted carelessly, we acted perversely, we acted spitefully." The first is not willful, the second is not only willful but also seeks to advance our interests, and the third not only willfully seeks to advance our interests but also defiantly seeks to displace divine authority with our own.

The individual confession follows the model of the high priest. What was once solely his prerogative became the lot of all. Some even say that the multiple full bowings while reciting the high priest's confession during the *Avodah* service is like "playing high priest" ourselves. By making available the high priesthood once a year, we remember once again that we are "a kingdom of priests and a holy nation" (Exodus 19:6). This is more than the democratization of Judaism; this is the aristocratization of Jewry.[3]

Rabbi Reuven Kimelman, PhD, is professor of classical Judaica at Brandeis University in Waltham, Massachusetts. He is the author of *The Mystical Meaning of Lekha Dodi and Kabbalat Shabbat* and of the audio books *The Moral Meaning of the Bible* and *The Hidden Poetry of the Jewish Prayerbook*. He contributed to *Who by Fire, Who by Water—Un'taneh Tokef* and *All These Vows—Kol Nidre* (both Jewish Lights).

Still, the high priestly model is problematic in that the Temple cult left little room for individuality, innovation, and internalization. By contrast, confession needs to be personal and heartfelt. The verb for "confession" is *hitvadah*, which originally meant "to reveal oneself," the opposite of concealment. Through confession (*vidui*), we expose our sins. Without coming clean, there is no purging. Only sins exposed to the light of day can be wiped away.

Initially, there was no fixed confession at all. The Talmud (Yoma 87b) records five alternatives. There are also two positions on its implementation. Rabbi Yehudah ben Beterah required the sin to be specified; Rabbi Akiva did not.[4]

The liturgy adopted some of these alternatives and developed two forms of the confession—one following Rabbi Akiva, the other Rabbi Yehudah. The first is called the Short Confession (*Vidui Zuta*); the other, the Long Confession (*Vidui Rabbah*). The first, following the twenty-two letters of the Hebrew alphabet, is nonspecific. The second, also alphabetical, spells out each sin. The first has an entry for each letter of the alphabet but three for the last, totaling twenty-five. The second, according to the Sephardi tradition, has one sin per letter, totaling twenty-two; and according to the Ashkenazi liturgy, two per letter, totaling forty-four.

The two modes of confession reflect two psychological realities. The Long Confession (following Rabbi Yehudah) assumes that forgiveness is in particular, not in general. Specifying the sin hones in on the wrongness of the act, inducing regret (and possibly shame), thereby reducing the chance for recidivism. The first step in repair is pinpointing what is broken, because healing requires a correct diagnosis, and admitting a mistake can prompt its amending. True, a wrong confessed is not yet a wrong forsaken, but it is a first step.

Because our moral decline so often begins with words, its rectification starts with words. In any case, it is our wrongs we confess, not our faults. Deeds can be disowned; traits make up our nature. Still, altering behavior can induce changes of character. After all, what are traits if not crystallizations of patterns of behavior?

The downside of specifying sins is that, perversely, it can sometimes solidify adherence to sin. The risk of public shame can tempt us to avoid the truth or to concoct less embarrassing crimes than the ones we actually committed. We may even confess minor crimes to cover up larger ones, hoping that our focus on peccadilloes will deflect detection of real felonies. Worse still, we may apologize to pave the way for an encore performance of the same sin, viewing facile apologies of offenses as preliminary to their repetition. The opposite is possible, too: some people gloat over the opportunity to rehearse their misdeeds to all within earshot.

Cognizant of these problems, the liturgy mandates that our confessions be recited silently in the *Amidah*, not just out loud in the repetition that follows. Yes, there is a time to specify and a time not to specify; a time to go public and a time to remain private. While private confessions may be conducted in the first person singular, public confessions require the first person plural.

On the verse "Blessed is the man to whom Adonai imputes no iniquity, and in whose spirit there is no guile" (Psalm 32:2), the midrash comments:

> Rabbi Eliezer ben Jacob said: The sins that a man confesses one year, he may not confess the next year; unless he repeats his sins, in which case he must, of course, confess them again the next year. If he does not repeat them, yet confesses them the next year, Scripture says of him, "A fool who repeats his folly is like a dog that returns to its vomit" (Proverbs 26:11). But the Rabbis said: Even someone who does not repeat the sins that he confesses one year should confess them again the next year, thereby fulfilling the verse "I acknowledge my transgressions; and my sin is ever before me" (Psalm 51:5).... Rabbi Phinehas said in the name of Rabbi Abba bar Papa: When you say you have nothing new to confess, you disdain the command of your Maker [who tells us], "Let the lips that lie to the Righteous One be stilled [meaning lips that] in pride and disdain speak [only] of old [sins]" (Psalm 31:19), for you boast that this year you have no sins.[5]

This midrash deals with guile in confession. One can err by over- or by under-confessing.

Over-confessing entails confessing last year's sins. Those opposed argue that over-confessing keeps you mired in sin. Because confession is like vomiting, it is sheer folly to go back to it. Those in favor hold that repeated confessions are not for the purpose of visiting past wrongs; rather, they forestall future ones by expressing continued regret. Confessions function to forewarn us.

Under-confessing entails repeating last year's confession without anything new or not confessing at all and thereby boasting (in effect) that you are free of sin. The latter is an impossibility, for Scripture long ago observed that "there is no one who does not sin" (1 Kings 8:46). "Indeed there is no one on earth so righteous as to do good without ever sinning" (Ecclesiastes 7:20). Thus, the need for confessing is part and parcel of the human condition.

It is important to understand the nature of the sins catalogued. Tellingly, the list contains no cardinal sins of Judaism: murder, adultery/incest, and idolatry. Nor does it mention the sixth, seventh, and eighth of the Decalogue ("Thou shalt not murder, thou shalt not commit adultery, thou shalt not steal"). The closest the Short Confession comes to stealing is the entry for the letter *gimel*, *gazalnu* ("we defrauded"), implying the more subtle crime of pocketing ill-gotten gain, but not the blatant *ganavnu* ("we outright stole"). In the Long Confession, the closest is the taking of bribes. The Short Confession makes no reference to killing or adultery at all. The closest the Long Confession comes to adultery/incest is the general expression for sexual impropriety (*gilui arayot*) and forbidden trysts (*v'idat z'nut*) of the first section.

The sins that characterize the Long Confession are hard to litigate, difficult to detect, and almost impossible to deny. The questions "Did you murder, commit adultery, or steal?" easily elicit, for most, a resounding "No." The questions "Did you ever contemplate or commit a sexual impropriety, disrespect your parents or teachers, engage in shady business practices?" at most eke out a hesitant "No."

Most prominent are the sins of the tongue. True, the hardened heart, the supercilious and begrudging eye, the obdurate brow, the stiff and haughty neck, the violent and misplaced hand, the running legs to evil, and the light head all get their due, but there are ten references to the sins of the mouth, including vain utterances, gossipy tongue, slanderous speech, false words, deceptive promises, insolent tone, cynical asides, foul language, idle words, and lip-alone confessions.

The Short Confession also focuses on difficult-to-deny sins such as lying, jeering, and acting wickedly, obdurately, or violently. Twenty-one of the twenty-five offenses are formulated as a single verb. The other four consist of two words, of which three deal with speech. *Dibarnu dofi* can refer to duplicitous speech,[6] *tafalnu sheker* to deceitful speech, and *ya'atznu ra* to misleading speech such as rendering self-serving advice, which transgresses "Do not place a stumbling block before the blind" (Leviticus 19:14).[7]

Both confessions deal with everyday sins, some of them so quotidian that it takes the Yom Kippur confession to shock us out of our complacency into awareness of their wrongness—the first step in their correction.

On Hitting Yourself

Rabbi Lawrence Kushner

Instead of directly commenting on the liturgy of *Ashamnu* and *Al Chet*, I want to examine a simple—and still widely practiced—ritual performed during the recitation of sins and propose a slight modification.

The current Conservative liturgy, *Mahzor Lev Shalem*, notes, "It is customary to strike one's heart when we say the words *al chet shechatanu*," and "Customarily, we each strike our heart as we recite every phrase of this [*Ashamnu*] confession."[1]

The gesture, naturally, has many variations. Some hold the *tzitzit* of their *tallitot* in a fist and beat their breasts. Others softly pat their chests with their open palms. And some, I notice, simply leave their hand over their heart as if they were reciting the Pledge of Allegiance! But, for all, the intent is identical: I've been bad; I must symbolically punish myself. The closest, contemporary analogue I can find is the "Stupid me!" we whisper (or think) when we've done something egregiously dumb and then mime hitting ourselves on the forehead with the heel of our palm.

Rabbi Lawrence Kushner is the Emanu-El Scholar at Congregation Emanu-El of San Francisco and the author of many books on Jewish spirituality and mysticism, including *I'm God; You're Not: Observations on Religion and Other Disguises of the Ego; The Way Into Jewish Mystical Tradition; Honey from the Rock; The Book of Letters: A Mystical Alef-bait* (all Jewish Lights); and his novel, *Kabbalah: A Love Story*. He contributed to all volumes of the *My People's Prayer Book: Traditional Prayers, Modern Commentaries* series, winner of the National Jewish Book Award; as well as to *My People's Passover Haggadah: Traditional Texts, Modern Commentaries*, a finalist for the National Jewish Book Award; *Who by Fire, Who by Water—Un'taneh Tokef*; and *All These Vows—Kol Nidre* (all Jewish Lights).

Punch and Judy

Self-punishment requires two players or one split personality: a bad part that needs to be punished and a good part to do the punishing. We run little "Punch and Judy" shows in our heads where we play both roles. This lets us repudiate the evil we have done (or believe lurks in our hearts) while simultaneously continuing to call ourselves good. Or, to put it another way, "It's not really me; it's only the *bad* part of me. The rest of me is still good." In a gesture of placating some internalized parent, we punish ourselves. "See what a good kid I am. When I mess up, you don't even have to hit me; I hit myself!"

Then we feel better.

The primitive logic is that if I hit myself, maybe God won't. But hitting ourselves during prayer? Self-flagellation? What's going on?

Despair

At issue here, of course, is our view of the human psyche. Are we essentially good or essentially evil? Such asceticism and self-flagellation testify to a gloomy view of human nature and correspond to psychologist Lawrence Kohlberg's lowest stage of ethical development. They inevitably lead to an expectation of punishment, strict chastisement, and the resultant need for an external source of grace. And, while such a worldview has had ample representation throughout Jewish history, in our generation it is, happily, in decline.

For a more sanguine view of the psyche, we can turn to much of classical Hasidic thought, which is predicated on the innate goodness of people. Here, the enemy is not some bad part of ourselves, but despair. This is because when we feel hopeless—no damned good—we are debilitated, "confined to bed," incapable of serving God. And, when we are unable to serve God, we lose our hold on meaning.

The Baal Shem Tov taught:

> Sometimes the evil instinct leads a person astray, telling him that he has committed a grave transgression, even though it was only a simple mistake—no transgression at all. This is because the evil instinct wants a person to be depressed by such thought. For, once depressed, a person then leaves off the service of ... God. Rather one must

> seek to serve God in joy.... One should guard oneself from depression as much as possible.[2]

To despair means that you have forgotten you are the child of God or, what is worse, you believe that God has forgotten you.

But there is more. Our feeling toward ourselves predetermines how we find God—and ourselves.

God and Self

Professor Alexander Altman, *z"l*, observed:

> Finding God ... is but another way of saying that we have found our Self. For every act of submission to God unifies our being, and means a birth. Thus [a person] is spiritually reborn in God, and God is, as it were, reborn in [each person].... God is in the Self but the Self is not god. The Self is transparently grounded in the greater and all-encompassing reality of God, both lost and preserved in Him.[3]

This would mean that God must somehow also be in the perverse things we plan and do! In the words of Rabbi Tzadok Hakohen of Lublin, "God is present even in our sins."[4]

And rejecting any part of us, even the part that committed sins, only postpones the task of healing and unification.

To Raise and to Sweeten

Professor Daniel Matt cites Yaakov Yosef of Polnoye:

> One must believe that "the whole world is filled with God's presence" [Isaiah 6:3] and that "there is no place empty of [God]" [*Tikkunei Zohar*]. All human thoughts have within them the reality of God.... When a strange or evil thought arises in a person's mind while he is engaged in prayer, it is coming to that person to be repaired and elevated.... It is necessary to find the root of love in evil so as to sweeten evil and turn it into love.[5]

Perhaps that is the underlying dynamic: On Yom Kippur we reexamine the evil we have intended or done, not to excise it as an alien growth but to discover its deepest motivation—the holy spark within it. And, once we have done that, we are to receive it, embrace it, raise it, sweeten it, to take it back into ourselves—to redeem it.

We lose our temper because we want things to be better right away. We gaze with lust because we have forgotten how to love the ones we want to love. We hoard material possessions because we imagine they will secure us in life and happiness. We turn a deaf ear because we fear the pain of listening might damage us. We live on the Internet because we have forgotten how to maintain living relationships. We cheat a little because we fear it is the only way to survive in a corrupt society. At the bottom of them all is something holy, something divine.

Yaakov Yosef of Polnoye:

> The essence of the finest *t'shuvah* is that deliberate sins are transformed into merits, for one turns evil into good, as I heard from my teacher [the Baal Shem Tov], who interpreted the verse [Psalm 34:15] "Turn aside from evil and do good" to mean "Turn the evil into good."[6]

Holding Oneself

Phrased in this way, the goal becomes clear: to own, to take responsibility for what we have done. But now we realize that it wasn't some bad or rogue part of us behaving shamefully and independently; it was the good part, because *there is only one part*. You. All of you. We say: "I acted that way because, at the time, I meant to. I am not proud of that; I wish I had never done it. Indeed, it hurts to even recount it. But I did it. And, since it will remain forever a part of me, I accept it; I own it; it, too, is me."

The confession of sins is not about self-rejection or self-flagellation but the healing that can only come from regret and, then, self-acceptance. This does not mean we are proud of what we did, but it does mean that we have taken what we did back into ourselves—acknowledged it as an eternal part of our psyches. Now, however, we have uncovered its original motive, realized how it became disfigured beyond recognition, made an apology, and done our best to repair the damage.

Such a confession of sins accepts our evils as our own deliberate creations—long-banished children taken home again at last. And that, of course, is the only way to truly transform them. A whole human being remembers all of his or her past and accepts everything that he or she has done. And, for this reason, when we recite the *Al Chet* or *Ashamnu*, we don't hit ourselves; we *hold* ourselves and cry.

What We Do Not Know

Rabbi Noa Kushner

I am troubled by this verse in *Al Chet*: *Al chet shechatanu l'fanekha b'yodim uv'lo yodim*, "For the sin we have committed against You through things we know and do not know."

I am troubled because the value in ritual confession seems to lie in its potential for tangible behavioral modification. In other words, it's only if the confession leads me to change my ways—to make *t'shuvah* (a spiritual "turn")—that the confession takes on value. Right?

I could also stretch the point and say that a confession need not actually produce a behavioral change as long as it reinforces a good change that has already taken place. Perhaps the confession supports a turn away from an action I have already left behind, a bad habit. In this case, even though the confession does not *initiate* any *new* action, it helps maintain a change I've already made for the better.

I might even say that ritual confession still has worth even if it only raises the *possibility* of goodness or virtue or justice. Even through the act of naming negative behavior as limiting, confession allows me to explore the possibility of behaving differently—to reimagine a behavior that once seemed inevitable. Here, too, while there are no demonstrable results, we can see the value in introducing an idea that could inspire positive change in the long run.

By these measures, then, confession should (1) bring about behavioral change, (2) support change that is already under way, or (3) inculcate a new mind-set that is likely to produce change in the future. But

---

Rabbi Noa Kushner is founding rabbi of The Kitchen, which is one part indie Shabbat community, one part San Francisco experiment, and one part tool kit for DIY Jewish practice. The Kitchen works to build a connected, spiritually alive Jewish generation and a new resonant approach to religious life. She contributed to *Who by Fire, Who by Water—Un'taneh Tokef* and *All These Vows—Kol Nidre* (both Jewish Lights).

in all three scenarios, of course, we require conscious knowledge of the negative behavior that is at stake.

What, then, is the use of confessing to something we do not even know we have done and likely will not ever know that we did? How could such a confession lead to change?

Note, too, that this specific confession is different from our admitting to those things we know we did unwillingly or by accident. In those cases, even though the action was inadvertent, at least we know we are the ones responsible for it. As well, unintentional wrongs are included elsewhere in *Al Chet*. What I do not understand is why we would confess to wrongs we know nothing about and, therefore, can never hope to do anything about. What is the purpose of confessing to something we do not know (and will never know) that we did?

Given that tangible results are impossible, the value of this kind of confession must lie in our admission that we are not the sole arbiters of our own behavior, because we do not know, and never will know, everything about ourselves. We cannot even rely completely on what we learn about ourselves from the people around us. The purpose of confessing to the very sins that we do not know is to admit that there are limits, not only in our own ability to behave justly (that much is obvious), but also in our self-perception and understanding of how to be just altogether.

I believe that these human limitations lie at the heart of the confessions of Yom Kippur. In confessing to what I do not know, I express humility—not just humility regarding my ability to act with justice, but also humility in my self-understanding. And if I cannot fully know even myself, how much less can I be certain that I understand the whole balance of the world? By confessing to the limits of my understanding, I allow for possibility beyond my imagining.

Admitting to what I do not know cannot possibly be for the purpose of amending those specific wrongs, because the point is that I would not even know what to fix. I am, however, acknowledging that I am not the center of all that is and not even the sole determiner of who and what I am. I am, instead, a small part of something bigger, not an independent whole. I recognize now that even seeking to justify the confession in terms I can fully understand and quantify puts me at the center of the universe, a place where, upon reflection, I am not at all comfortable.

This line of *Al Chet* reminds me of an Aramaic passage that we say right before Passover, the evening before the first night's seder. After we have cleaned our homes of *chametz* (anything leavened), in our annual switch over to matzah, we burn the last bits of bread and say:

> *Kol chamira* ...
> All *chametz* in my possession
> *Whether I have seen it or not* and
> Whether I have removed it or not
> Shall be nullified and ownerless as
> The dust of the earth.

Here is another case of acknowledging a sin of which we are unaware: having in our possession *chametz* that we do not see and therefore could not know of, crumbs hiding beyond the limits of our perception. In practice, this can be a welcome moment, a moment where we have cleaned as best we can and may now let go of that which we are not aware. The same sentiment may be welcome on Yom Kippur, when we overturn every emotional stone to uncover where we have gone wrong. In both places, Jewish ritual provides the opportunity to stop searching and move on.

But in both places, the liturgy is not meant only to soothe. Were that the case, our search (whether for sins or for *chametz*) would be just one more exercise in feeling better, in narcissism. Rather, the liturgy introduces a different truth—that we do not have the *ability* to see everything; this is not our role. For whether in cleaning the soul or in cleaning the house, if we are the final arbiters, then not only does the search have no end, but our perspective also becomes ultimate.

By the same token, once we admit that we do not know the whereabouts of all the *chametz*, once we admit that we do not even know all our own sins, then we may be more willing to give ourselves over to the idea that there is One who does.

So every year we ask for forgiveness for these hidden things, the crumbs and the sins; we declare both of them null and void as a reminder that as much as we imagine we can keep track of our own faults, there remain some that are forever unknowable. There is much that we do not know. And in return, we hope for humility and to be a part of a greater whole, one that is beyond us and beyond our understanding.

Vidui and Its Halakhic Contexts

Rabbi Daniel Landes

Vidui (confession) has a number of halakhic contexts:

1. *Vidui* over the various sin offerings brought by individuals who have sinned
2. *Vidui* of the high priest three times on Yom Kippur
3. *Vidui* as part of *t'shuvah* (repentance)
4. *Vidui* as part of *t'fillah* (prayer)

Vidui over Sin Offerings

Vidui of a sin offering is offered only for sins performed inadvertently (*shogeg*) and requires *s'mikhah*, the act of pushing both hands forcibly down upon the animal's head between its two horns, touching the animal directly, as if to signify that the sacrifice should actually be of himself—as if to say, "There, but for the grace of God, go I."[1] At that moment the *Vidui* is recited:

Rabbi Daniel Landes is the director and *rosh hayeshivah* of the Pardes Institute of Jewish Studies in Jerusalem. Pardes brings together men and women of all backgrounds to study classical Jewish texts and contemporary Jewish issues in a rigorous, challenging, and open-minded environment. Rabbi Landes is also a contributor to the *My People's Prayer Book: Traditional Prayers, Modern Commentaries* series, winner of the National Jewish Book Award; *My People's Passover Haggadah: Traditional Texts, Modern Commentaries*, a finalist for the National Jewish Book Award; *Who by Fire, Who by Water—Un'taneh Tokef*; and *All These Vows—Kol Nidre* (all Jewish Lights).

> How does he confess? He says: *chatati, aviti, pashati*—"I have sinned, transgressed, and committed iniquity, and I have done such and such. I am returning in repentance before You, and this is my atonement."[2]

This confession has three parts:

1. Listing the standard categorization of sin: *chatati* ("I have sinned inadvertently"); *aviti* ("I have sinned knowingly"); *pashati* ("I have sinned rebelliously"). Using the example of the classic ritual prohibition of mixing meat and milk, this would be: *chatati*—"I didn't know it was a cheeseburger (I thought it was soy!)"; *aviti*—"I knew it was a cheeseburger, but it smelled so good"; *pashati*—"I don't like cheeseburgers, but I wanted to violate the law!"
2. Specifying the sin in question, the proximate cause of the sacrifice that is being brought, known halakhically as *perut hachet*, "specifying the sin." This is a crucial element, for it links confession to the specific sin and appropriate sacrifice.
3. Connecting the three items of *s'mikhah*, *vidui*, and *perut hachet* with the desire for *kaparah* ("atonement") in the context of *t'shuvah* ("repentance") (more on this later).

Part 1 is purely ritualistic; part 2 adds specificity, the individual moral component; part 3 raises the issue of spiritual cleansing. *Vidui* is, therefore, the normative response to sin, combining the three bases of religious life: ritual, moral, and spiritual.

Vidui in the Sacrificial Cult

From the mundane to the dramatic: all eyes are upon the *kohen gadol*, the high priest on Yom Kippur. An essential element within the *avodah*, the sacrificial cult of old, is the *Vidui*. The biblical source is the verse: "And he shall atone for himself, for his household, and for the entire congregation of Israel" (Leviticus 16:17). Maimonides interprets this verse:

> From the oral tradition we have learned that this [i.e., "atone"] means verbal confession (*Vidui d'varim*). The verse continues: "On that day, he makes three confessions:

> the first, for himself; the second, for himself and for the rest of the priests. Both are recited over his bull sin offering. The third is for all of Israel and is recited over the scapegoat. He includes the name of God in each of these three confessions. What does he say? 'Please, God [*Ana hashem*; literally, "the Name," implying the use of the ineffable name that we no longer pronounce]—I have sinned, transgressed, and committed iniquity in front of You. Please God, pardon the sins, transgressions, and iniquities that I have committed,' as it says: 'For on that day, He shall pardon you, to purify you from all your sins; before God you shall be purified' (Leviticus 16:30). He thus pronounces the name within each *vidui*."[3]

The sacrificial *Vidui* of Yom Kippur differs from the one that accompanies the normal sin offering in several ways:

1. It is recited in successive circles of concern on behalf of everyone.
2. It is read by one person only, the high priest, who vicariously represents everyone else.
3. As pointed out by Rabbi Joseph B. Soloveitchik, each of its two requests—to be heard by God, and to be forgiven by God—is preceded by a prayer: *Ana hashem*, "Please, God...." The regular sacrificial *Vidui* has no such prayer for atonement.
4. The holy name of God (*hashem*) is invoked. The Mishnah informs us that it had such a pronounced effect upon all present that they would prostrate themselves and respond, *Barukh shem k'vod malkhuto l'olam va'ed*, a phrase we now insert into our congregational *Sh'ma*, usually translated as "Blessed be the name of his glorious kingdom forever and ever." Rabbi Lawrence A. Hoffman, PhD, suggests that since it followed the experience of hearing God's ineffable name, it may originally have meant "Blessed is the name [*Barukh shem*]; the glory of his kingdom is forever and ever" [*k'vod malkhuto l'olam va'ed*].
5. The high priest then concludes the Leviticus verse with the one word, *titharu*—"You shall be purified."[4]

This sacrificial *Vidui* of Yom Kippur was, therefore, part of a larger atonement ritual that included *s'mikhah* upon the bull and goat, a prayer for atonement, the evocation of God's presence through the rare utterance of the ineffable name, religious awe that prompted those present to prostrate themselves, and the oracular voice confirming, "You shall be purified!"—all together, a complete, transformative event.

Vidui as Part of *T'shuvah*

Up to now we have presented *Vidui* as part of the sacrificial mechanism for attaining atonement. But *Vidui* is essentially part of the system of seeking *t'shuvah*, literally, "return" or "repentance"; although originally accompanying sacrifices, *t'shuvah* is independent of them. As Maimonides comments, "Now that the Temple does not exist and we have no altar of atonement, there is only *t'shuvah*,"[5] and thus *Vidui* is the key act of the *t'shuvah* process. Maimonides's very first statement in his Laws of Repentance reads, "Regarding all the commandments in the Torah, whether positive or negative, if a person transgresses on any of them, whether intentionally or accidentally, when he does *t'shuvah*, and turns away from his sin, he is obligated to confess before God."[6]

Vidui even without sacrifice continues to demand *perut hachet*; generalities are insufficient, according to Maimonides. One confesses to having done (or not done) something in particular. And this *Vidui* requires two other things: "regret" (*charatah*) and "resolve" regarding the future (*kabbalah al he'atid*). These are accomplished by saying, "Indeed I regret and am shamed by my deeds. I shall never return to this [ugly] thing."[7] *Vidui* demands a loathing of the sin in which one has been enmeshed and a resolve to avoid that sin in the future. It is a transformative act of the deepest personal change—freeing us from the domination of sin.

But even though in theory *t'shuvah* demands specifying the sin intended (*perut hachet*), regret (*charatah*), and resolve (*kabalah al he'atid*), practice may fall short of the ideal, in which case the whole edifice of *t'shuvah* falls. "Verbalizing a *vidui*, without the internal commitment to leave [the sin behind], is like immersing in a *mikveh* ['a ritual purifying bath'] with [dead] vermin in hand. The immersion is not effective until the vermin is cast away."[8] Halakhah demands complete sincerity about ridding oneself of that "verminous" sin (even though despite all intention, one may indeed sin again anyway).

Vidui as Liturgy

We have seen that *Vidui* incorporates prayer in the *Ana hashem* of the everyday sacrificial confession and in the high priest's Yom Kippur request that God listen and grant atonement. But it is also part and parcel of our Yom Kippur liturgy—not just the standard confessions (*Ashamnu* and *Al Chet*) that are the topic of this book, but the entire *Avodah* service of Yom Kippur afternoon, where the *Vidui* of the ancient Temple cult is replayed as if it were happening in real time. In traditional services, participants shout out the "Blessed be the name ..." and fall on their faces as the prayer leader evokes the memory of God's ineffable name being called out. To be sure, the actual name is no longer pronounced—it is now hidden, a consequence of Temple times. "When cynics increased, the high priest would recite it in a low voice, swallowing it in a sweet murmur until even his fellow priests could not recognize it."[9] But the evocation of antiquity is everything; the Temple service is *as if* renewed, and at its public performative heart is the *Vidui*.

Still, the dominant occurrence of the confession is the *Ashamnu* and the *Al Chet* that we say in connection with the *Amidah*. These two confessional formulas immediately follow the silent *Amidah*, while we remain standing without moving our feet; they are then repeated aloud by the prayer leader within the *Amidah*, such that the final penitential prayers (called *s'lichot*) come afterward. The whole is experienced as if the confessions are intrinsically a part of the *Amidah*—tellingly called, Rabbinically, *Hat'fillah*, "*The* prayer par excellence," for it is the paradigmatic expression of all prayer, a continuation of the sacrificial service now denied us. *T'shuvah* was the pinnacle of that service, and *Vidui* was the core of *t'shuvah*. So, now, *Vidui* is the core of the *Amidah*, which has taken the place of the sacrifices. Consider also the classic understanding of *l'hitpalel*, "to pray," as, literally, "to self-judge." The self-critical *Vidui* becomes the ultimate form of halakhic prayer.

The Liturgical *Vidui* as a Halakhic Institution

The liturgical *Vidui* of our Yom Kippur service is a halakhic "success story," for it preserves the crucial elements of *Vidui* that were at the center of the cult itself. As the high priest included all Israel in his *Vidui*, so does our *Vidui* include us all: it is formulated in the plural and is recited publicly in the *Avodah* and in the *Amidah*, both of them reflections of actual sacrificial practice when the Temple still stood. At the same time, it has a pronounced individual and personal meaning as well, for the practice of accompanying the words by symbolically beating on our heart places the onus on the individual—no less than *s'mikhah*, laying on of priestly hands, specified the particular animal being offered as a sin offering at the time.

People sometimes complain that the confessions are pro forma, mere alphabetical listings of sins. But this poetic vehicle actually fulfills the need for *perut hachet*. The long listing makes the recitation feel exhaustive, as if all categories have been covered, allowing individuals ample opportunity to consider their sins under the various categories included in the text.

But do *Ashamnu* and *Al Chet* accomplish what they intend? Do they remove us from our sins? This is not a simple issue to answer. But I am encouraged by the anomaly of the music that accompanies them. The refrain of *Al Chet* and the entirety of *Ashamnu* are sung to an unforgettably uplifting and optimistic melody. An old European tradition, from the school of the Hafetz Hayim (Rabbi Yisrael Meir Hakohen Kagan, of Radom, Poland, d. 1933), has an explanation. He considers the case of workers who come to clean a dirty and neglected mansion. The normal reaction would be to sigh, complain, and curse during the arduous work. But good workers attack the job with promise, slowly and steadily cleaning the house, and humming a melody that matches their spirits. So, too, when we clean our souls, as dusty, dirty, and neglected as they are, we could sigh and complain. But instead, we sing optimistically, as, bit by bit, we clean ourselves until the *ba'al habayit*—the divine owner of the house—declares: *Titharu*, "You shall be purified!"

Putting the Performance of the *Vidui* in Its Context

Rabbi Ruth Langer, PhD

The language of Jewish liturgical confession is intensely communal, but never more so than on Yom Kippur. The expectation of this day is that we enter the communal space of the synagogue and join in its prayers having already made amends for our personal sins, preferably immediately after their commission throughout the year. Then, on Yom Kippur, we stand as a community before God, all responsible for one another (Talmud, Sh'vuot 39a). In this, there is inherent tension and a great sense of vulnerability. I confess not only my personal sins, but those of my community as well, just as the high priest did in the Temple, as described in Leviticus 16 and, after it and in more detail, in Mishnah Yoma. As our liturgy has emerged, we cast up to God entire alphabets of transgressions. At some level, this is saying to God, "We mortals lack the skills to verbalize fully what we want to confess. Here are our inchoate attempts. Please take these letters and formulate more appropriate words for us!" At another level, we can look at this as the *performance* of the *act* of confession, where it is the intent behind the words that matters more than the precise words.

Rabbi Ruth Langer, PhD, is professor of Jewish studies in the Theology Department at Boston College, where she also serves as associate director of its Center for Christian-Jewish Learning. She received her PhD in Jewish liturgy and her rabbinic ordination from Hebrew Union College–Jewish Institute of Religion. She contributed to *Who by Fire, Who by Water—Un'taneh Tokef* (Jewish Lights).

This performed act of confession happens over and over throughout the day on Yom Kippur, twice at each of the five services (in traditional practice), abbreviated only at *N'ilah*. Poetic selections (*piyyutim*)[1] introduce the confession, during the repetition of the *Amidah*—most elaborately at *Kol Nidre* and at *N'ilah* (in today's Ashkenazi practice, other services have abbreviated this). These then lead up to recitations of God's thirteen attributes of mercy (Exodus 34:6–7a). Taken together, the *piyyutim* and the thirteen attributes have a dual purpose: they bring the gathered *human* community to full repentance, and they petition *God* to favor the divine attribute of mercy over that of judgment. It is in these passages that the real work of Yom Kippur occurs, thus setting the stage for the high point of the performance of the actual *Vidui*, this meeting of humans and God. Not only must we the human community achieve the correct *kavvanah* (intentionality) for our confessions, but, somehow, so too must God for receiving them. This *kavvanah* is well expressed in the rousing and joyful hymn that precedes *Ashamnu*, the first and shorter confession—a hymn that proclaims supreme confidence in our ability to enter this moment of intimate relationship with God, "For we are your people and You are our God...."

How do we create this dynamic? The human elements, at least, are theoretically in our control, however much we may fall away from the ideal state. But how can we be so certain about God? Prayers of various genres address this dilemma and seek to overcome it, some reminding God of human frailty and dependence upon divine mercy, some petitioning God outright,[2] but others calling on God to remember promises and relationships established with Israel in the past. All of these are worthy of their own discussion, but here I would like to focus on the last, for these frame the entire *Vidui* and have become part of the fixed traditional prayers.

In the Orthodox synagogues I have attended for the past quarter century, the passages calling on God to remember are generally mumbled at breakneck speed. Perhaps this is why non-Orthodox *machzorim* omit them. But they are fundamental to setting the scene for the *Vidui* that follows. Following the last recitation of God's Thirteen Attributes of mercy, we find a composition that contains a series of propositions, each of which is then supported by a biblical citation that echoes and sometimes expands upon and explains the language of the proposition.[3] These propositions are as follows:

1. Remember for us the patriarchal covenant (Leviticus 26:42).
2. Remember for us the covenant of the "first ones" [whom You brought out of Egypt] (Leviticus 26:45).
3. Do for us as You promised us [to be true to the covenant even when we are in exile] (Leviticus 26:44).
4. Be merciful to us, do not destroy us, and do not forget the covenant with us (Deuteronomy 4:31).
5. Circumcise our hearts to love and revere your name (Deuteronomy 30:6).
6. End our exile and have mercy on us (Deuteronomy 30:3).
7. Ingather our exiles (Deuteronomy 30:4).
8. Be accessible to our petitions (Deuteronomy 4:29).
9. Wipe away our sins [and do not remember them] (Isaiah 43:25).
10. Wipe away our sins like a cloud or mist (Isaiah 44:22).
11. Make white our sins like snow or wool (Isaiah 1:18).
12. Cast upon us purifying water and purify us (Ezekiel 36:25).
13. Atone for our sins on this day and purify us (Leviticus 16:30).
14. Bring us to your holy mountain and let us rejoice in your house of prayer (Isaiah 56:7).

On the one hand, it is easy to understand why non-Orthodox Jews excised this prayer, as significant elements of it contradict modern liberal Jewish theologies. The theme of exile from Jerusalem runs deep in the prayer (lines 2, 3, 6, 7, and 14),[4] suggesting that its origins lie among Jews who understand themselves to be in exile from the Jerusalem Temple and its worship and who find this distance from biblically mandated liturgy to cause deep concern about the efficacy of the day's prayers. The existence of the modern State of Israel, even without a rebuilt Temple, makes the exilic focus of this prayer seem even more dated. Jews who simply reject prayers for the rebuilding of the Temple would need at least to edit this.

However, there are themes here that deserve attention. This prayer juxtaposes biblical verses, as a way of overcoming human insecurity before God. The divine nature of these words gives them extra binding force. God, the prayer says, You yourself made these promises—as is evident in these texts—and now we call upon You to fulfill them. We who stand before You on this day are the heirs to the covenants You made with the most significant of our ancestors, (1) the patriarchs and (2) the Israelites who stood at Sinai. Therefore, we have a claim on your mercy.

Remember us on this day when we are most vulnerable! Of what will this divine remembering consist? It certainly includes God's being true to the divine side of the covenantal promises (3, 4), but in lines 8–13, it extends to the themes of the day, to God's forgiving and purifying us of our sins, even before the messianic restoration of the Jerusalem Temple and its worship (14). Subtly present is another theme that cannot be accidental: many of these verses discussing God's blessings come from biblical contexts that otherwise delineate divine curses (Leviticus 26; Deuteronomy 4, 30). The composition's choice of verses itself is thus emphatically a petition for blessings and not curses.

This use of biblical precedents to ensure divine attention to the human confessions of the day continues in even more obvious form after the conclusion of *Al Chet* (the second and longer confession), where the traditional liturgy lists a series of biblical precedents of confessional prayers to which God did indeed listen. Implied or explicit in each is a petition by contemporary worshipers that God should do the same now:

1. David's prayer that God would purify him from unintentional and unknown sins (Psalm 19:13), reinforced by Ezekiel's assertion that God will do just that (36:25)
2. Micah's assertion that God will forgive sins to the point of forgetting them (7:18–20)
3. Daniel's plea that God speedily take note of the destroyed Jerusalem, not for our sake, but because of God's mercy (9:18–19)
4. Ezra's admissions of enormous sins, yet petitioning God to forgive Israel (9:6)[5]

Mahzor Lev Shalem accompanies this prayer with a comment by Nina Beth Cardin, who points out that through it, "we subtly imply that since we are their children, we have inherited their spiritual legacy. In placing our own prayer in the context of theirs, perhaps what is implied as well is that we seek to live our lives in accordance with that which gave them honor."[6] This, of course, could be stated in more abstract terms about the prayer preceding the *Vidui* as well. It points to the degree to which this passage, though different in its specific referents, acts as an *inclusio* to the performance of the *Vidui*—that is, it echoes and restates the themes of the earlier prayer, thus giving a sense of conclusion to the entire confessional liturgy. It reminds us that we can have some confidence in the efficacy of standing as a community before God on this day because we participate in the relationship that God established with our ancestors. A series of litanies reinforces this. The first goes through an alphabetical listing of God's names, thereby calling on God (who is merciful) to act positively toward us for the sake of this alphabetical listing of God's own characteristics. The second petitions God to answer us for the sake of a chronological list of biblical heroes whom God did answer.

Although all this may be muttered at breakneck speed in the many synagogues that include it in their liturgy at all, these prayers establish the context for the performance of the *Vidui*. We do not stand alone in our confessions of sins and our expectations of divine forgiveness. We stand in the presence of God, among an extended set of friends and family that goes beyond those gathered in our particular synagogue and even those gathered at this time around the world: it encompasses those alive today and those who preceded us throughout time. Although our individual *kavvanah* is important, it is part of this transtemporal coming together of humans and God, past and present.

Back to Zero

Catherine Madsen

Converting to Judaism in midlife means living with many other influences already knocking around in one's mind. The echo chamber of experience, which accommodates one's reading as well as one's life, resounds with inappropriate vibrations. On Yom Kippur I sing *Al chet shechatanu l'fanekha* with full concentration; sitting at my desk and wondering what to say about the *Al chet,* I think of the Anglican *Book of Common Prayer.* "We do earnestly repent, and are heartily sorry for these our misdoings; the remembrance of them is grievous unto us; the burden of them is intolerable." "We have left undone those things which we ought to have done; and we have done those things which we ought not to have done; and there is no health in us." I think of the English mystic Julian of Norwich, who said in her *Revelations of Divine Love* that "sin is behovely"—somehow necessary in the scheme of things—"but all shall be well, and all shall be well, and all manner of thing shall be well." I think of *Cosmopolitan* editor Helen Gurley Brown: "Good girls go to heaven. Bad girls go everywhere."

I think of Dante, who himself went everywhere. After working his way through hell and purgatory, he arrives at the Garden of Eden, the jumping-off place to heaven, where he passes through two rivers. The first (which he borrowed from Greek myth) is Lethe, the river of forgetfulness, which washes away the memory of one's sins; the second (which he invented) is Eunoë, the river of "good memory," which restores the memory of one's good deeds. Penitent sinners who have worked off their

---

Catherine Madsen is the author of *The Bones Reassemble: Reconstituting Liturgical Speech; In Medias Res: Liturgy for the Estranged*; and a novel, *A Portable Egypt.* She is librettist for Robert Stern's oratorio "Shofar," recently released on the CD *Awakenings* (Navona Records NV5878), and bibliographer at the National Yiddish Book Center. She contributed to *Who by Fire, Who by Water—Un'taneh Tokef* and *All These Vows—Kol Nidre* (both Jewish Lights).

punishment retain only a general sense of the nature of their sins, with the temptation and the shame—and apparently the details—subtracted. It is hard to imagine what that would be like.

To some extent, the structure even of Dante's heaven is determined—or its inhabitants' range circumscribed—by their earthly sins. Sometimes these are not even volitional: the little Piccarda de' Donati, whose brother removed her forcibly from a convent to marry her off, is placed in the heaven of the moon (the lowest) with those who "neglected" their vows. Piccarda assures Dante that she does not long for a higher heaven, that everyone in paradise is happy with their station, that "in His will is our peace" (*Paradiso*, Canto 3, 85). A few cantos later, in the sphere of Venus, the once-notorious Cunizza explains that she is placed there "because this planet's radiance conquered me" (Canto 9, 33). Bad girls go only to the third heaven, not all the way to the tenth. "But," adds Cunizza,

> in myself I pardon happily
> the reason for my fate; I do not grieve—
> and vulgar minds may find this hard to see. (34–36)

The Provençal poet Folco, also in the sphere of Venus, recounts how passionately he "burned" with lust in his youth, but adds:

> Yet one does not repent here; here one smiles—
> Not for the fault, which we do not recall,
> but for the Power that fashioned and foresaw. (103–5)

In Dante's imagination, operating within the Christian schema, this is what forgiveness is like. Having made their apologies to God, Cunizza and Folco need make them to no one else, not even themselves. They matter-of-factly accept their own constitutions; their former promiscuity is even a sort of evidence of the capacity to love. (Cunizza, in real life, had four husbands and two lovers, and spent her old age—she lived to be over eighty—doing works of mercy, including freeing the family slaves.) I think of Edith Piaf's defiant assertion: "*Non, je ne regrette rien, / Ni le bien / Qu'on m'a fait, / Ni le mal, / Tout ça me bien égal.*" "No, I regret nothing—neither the good I've done nor the bad, to me it's all the same."

It's not all the same: moral life is a harvest of regrets. You do damage out of malice and out of ignorance. You try to do good and botch it shamefully. You look back at intervals on your deeds (and your lack of deeds) and repent for new reasons, seeing for the first time what, if you had known how to do it, you would have done. Yet according to Dante, the phenomenon Piaf sang about is real.

Where do we go with all this in the Jewish schema? The Christian confessional formulas create a sense of sin, a generalized emotional pressure; the Christian remedy is a general deliverance, one man's expiation of the sins of the whole world. Individuals are encouraged to accept the deliverance as a means of relieving the pressure. The Jewish confessions, by contrast, are long lists of specifics: the serious damages and the simple daily irritants that we and our fellow Jews have inflicted on other people. The remedy is not to accept God's forgiveness or even to relieve the pressure, but to stop inflicting the harms. We are encouraged to think not of what we do to our own souls, but of what we do to other people's bodies, to their prospects, to their standing in the community.

Most of us know—some of us are—people who ricochet from self-loathing to self-exculpation without knowing how to stop at responsibility. Although the alphabetical lists of sins on Yom Kippur may seem to compound the enormity and weight of our errors each time they are repeated, in another sense they break those errors down into manageable units. If *chet* literally means missing the mark, as in aiming incompetently, *t'shuvah* amounts to taking better aim.

How do we learn responsibility? By having responsibility: by having practical tasks that will not get accomplished unless we accomplish them. The Jewish schema lays out these tasks all year in the system of *mitzvot*, and concentrates the particular tasks of *t'shuvah* in the month of Elul and the Days of Awe: making amends to the people we have hurt and asking their pardon and God's. I think of Emmanuel Levinas, who locates the source of our moral life in the face of the human Other. Levinas says little or nothing about sin or forgiveness, but he speaks of responsibility in the strongest possible terms. His concern is not for the past but for the present act of response.

Levinas was from Kovno, the birthplace of the Musar movement: the austere nineteenth-century introspective ethical movement that aimed at transforming the self for the sake of the Other. Chaim Grade's novel *The Yeshiva* gives an unappetizing portrayal of the early twentieth-century

Musar movement in practice: moral introspection and moral critique of the Other run amok, like an encounter group in *tsitsis*. For Grade's characters the struggle becomes exhausting; their consciousness of their sins is oppressive and immobilizing. Levinas, with the simple and crucial shift of focus to the face, avoids the paralysis of self-loathing. The relentless vigilance of the attempt to transform the self is not always the most useful effort: vigilance still focuses on the self. The face of the Other breaks this obsessive concentration on one's own flaws, and calls forth spontaneous moral effort. That shift of focus is all the transformation we need. The Other is not a stepping-stone to your own moral self-improvement but a person you can be good to, simply and directly.

Can sins be forgiven? Between oneself and another person, apology makes sense; even forgiveness, if you don't look too closely at it, makes sense at a rough-and-ready human level. We have to be able to live together. But what can God's forgiveness mean? The book of life cannot be rewritten. Whatever our good intentions for the future, the past is the only past we have; God knows it and cannot alter it. The *Ashamnu* and the *Al Chet* essentially verify that at a certain point—being made in the image of God—we simply are what we are. They confirm the moral necessity of knowing what we are and going on. *Je repars a zero.*

Even Piaf returns to zero by casting off everything that has gone before: a sort of *tashlich* that enables her (as we discover at the end of the song) to start afresh with a new lover. To have the next task—to see it before you in the face of the Other—is, in a sense, to be washed clean; your sins are not erased, but are no longer obstacles. What the Other needs may be something you know how to do.

In the end, the exhaustive specificity of the Jewish confessions puts some distance between us and our sins. As in the story of Elijah (1 Kings 19:12) God was not in the wind or the earthquake or the fire but in the still small voice that followed, we are not in our past or in our sins or in our failures and oversights, but in the deeds that follow them. The vast and damaging natural disasters are God's handiwork, but not God's presence; your own damage, though it cannot all be repaired, is not your living self. *Aujourd'hui*—today—*hayom*—we begin again.

Secrets and Silence

The Hidden Power of the Un-confessional *Vidui*

Rabbi Jay Henry Moses

In the seemingly endless liturgy of the *Yamim Nora'im*, certain passages have achieved iconic status. Our two confessions are prime examples: *Ashamnu*, because of the incongruously upbeat melody common in Ashkenazi congregations; *Al Chet*, because of the rhythmic repetition with which each line begins, its pounding refrain (*v'al kulam* ...), and its exhausting (if not quite exhaustive) list of sins.

But the subtlest and most profound sentiments in the *Vidui* come from the "connective tissue" between *Ashamnu* and *Al Chet*. These snippets of liturgical poetry—"What can we say to You ..." (*Mah nomar l'fanekha*) and "You know the secrets of the universe ..." (*Atah yode'a razei olam*)—are less universally recognizable, but provide a theological context into which the jarring lists of sins might land with a bit more softness. They also articulate a more personal, inward-focused plea, directed at God yet holding up a mirror to provide the self-awareness that makes *t'shuvah* and change possible.

> *Mah nomar l'fanekha?*
> What can we say to You, the One who sits on high?

Rabbi Jay Henry Moses is director of the Wexner Heritage Program at The Wexner Foundation. Previously, he served for five years as associate rabbi at Temple Sholom of Chicago. Rabbi Moses has taught at Hebrew Union College–Jewish Institute of Religion, the Jewish Community Center in Manhattan and its Makom: Center for Mindfulness, and in many other adult education settings.

And what can we tell You, the One who dwells in the heavens?
For you know that which is concealed and that which is revealed.

Atah yode'a razei olam
You know the secrets of the universe,
and the hidden enigmas of all that lives.
You scrutinize and examine every detail of our organs.
Nothing is hidden from You,
And nothing is enigmatic to You.
So let it be your will, Adonai our God and our ancestors' God,
That You forgive all our sins,
pardon all our iniquities,
and absolve all our missteps.

The liturgy of the *Vidui* shares with classical sources of the Jewish mystical tradition an abiding interest in secrets or mysteries. The *Zohar*, Jewish mysticism's crowning literary achievement, is replete with allusions to the secret and hidden meanings of the Torah, which, in turn, reveal the mysteries of God's reality and how we mortals can connect to the Infinite.[1]

These Zoharic references include *raza d'shabbat* ("the secret of the Sabbath"), an extended metaphor on the unification that happens on Shabbat within the divine realm itself and, by extension, between the divine and human realms as well (2:135a–b). *Raza d'razin* ("the secret of secrets") refers to a person's inmost character, which can be discerned by studying his facial features and other physical characteristics (2:70a–75a). And *raza d'mehemnuta* ("the secret of faith") is a common trope in the *Zohar*. It has many nuances, but in essence *raza d'mehemnuta* denotes the flow of energy within the divine realm and the need to balance its tensions and polarities: the male and female, for instance, but more important for our purposes, the realms of good and evil, which include both acts of righteousness and the sins for which we atone on Yom Kippur.

The *Zohar* so reveres the dimension of the secret because its author knows that to be human is to risk deception on all three channels by which we obtain understanding. To begin with, (1) science itself demonstrates that our limited *senses* deceive us routinely. Similarly, (2) our finite *minds* inevitably leave us unable to grasp the fullness and truth of ideas. And finally, (3) we deceive ourselves *morally* by rationalizing our own weaknesses, faults, and sins. If the search for truth is so impaired by our faulty tools, then the deepest level of reality must be hidden, accessible only through other channels; hence the obsession with secrets and mysteries.

Of the three systems of human cognition mentioned above—sensory, intellectual, and moral—the moral one is especially flawed. Our senses are just too limited to grasp the reality behind appearances; our minds fall short of comprehending the fullness of the universe. But our moral compass is not just incomplete; it is skewed from within by our ego needs and petty grievances.

In each case, the "secret" or ultimate truths that elude normal consciousness are known to God. God makes these secrets available to humanity, but only esoterically, in lessons buried deeply within Torah. The same is true of the *machzor*. It too holds keys to unlock God's mysteries—in this case, the mysteries relevant to the High Holy Days, namely *t'shuvah* ("repentance") and *m'chilah* ("pardon"). These keys are found in the very words of our confessions.

The *Zohar* acknowledges that it is quintessentially human to "know evil." But the "secret of faith" is that even though we necessarily inhabit the flawed and corrupt realm of mortals, the deepest ripples of our actions influence the vital energy of the cosmos. Awareness of the cosmic impact of our actions, even our sinful ones, is the deeper realization that only a mystical understanding of our confessions can provide.

To arrive at that understanding, the mystics revel in taking fundamental biblical metaphors and casting them in the starkest and most dramatic of poetic imagery. If we are made in the image of God, for example, it must follow that any secrets that belong to God must belong somehow to us as well. We must already know the moral truths that we have buried within our psyche. They remain hidden only because of the blocking or unbalancing of the flow of energy between our world and God's. Confession is an opportunity to restore the balance we have thrown off or to free up the flow we have blocked up. The process starts by acknowledging that our secrets must already be revealed to the One who knows all—and, therefore, must be somehow accessible even to us, if we dig deeply enough within.

Yet these two passages that link *Ashamnu* to *Al Chet* highlight the obvious contradiction of the *Vidui*: if God knows all of our secrets already, why do we confess? *Mah nomar l'fanekha*, indeed? "What can we say" to the One who knows the secrets of the universe? What do we expect will be the impact upon God, or the outcome, of uttering these words?

Yes, God does know all of our secrets. But they are buried so deeply within *us* that *we* are not aware of them. In reciting the *Vidui*, then, God becomes the divine sounding board, the One who allows us to reveal our most painful and shameful inner secrets to ourselves. *Mah nomar l'fanekha* is like a knowing wink offered by our dramatic Yom Kippur script toward God: *These confessions aren't what they appear to be. You know it all already anyway. But we do not know it yet. You neither need nor desire our words, but we need them for ourselves.*

The *Vidui* is meant to awaken the recognition that somewhere among the tangle of our actions, motivations, and words are the secrets we are keeping from ourselves. This is the point of the comprehensive acrostics, the *alef*-to-*tav* listing of sins in both *Ashamnu* and *Al Chet*, an effort, apparently, to capture every nuance of transgression. Here am I, we are saying, a faint image of God, part of a species that falls short of our potential in innumerable ways. Let me enumerate them anyway, and in so doing construct a mirror, a sounding board that may reflect back to me a faint echo of my own deepest and most hidden flaws. I turn to You, knower of secrets, revealer of secrets, that by opening my heart to You I may come to know the depths of my own being.

But *mah nomar l'fanekha* hints at something deeper yet. Poised as it is between two long lists of words, the question "What can we say to You?" has an obvious answer that we too often overlook: *nothing*. By this we mean not merely that our words are wasted because God knows them already, but something deeper: that the truest, most authentic spiritual posture of the mortal toward the Infinite is silence, as the psalmist says, "To You, silence is praise" (Psalm 65:2). The silence is sandwiched by words, lists of words, but true *vidui* is achieved simply by heightening our awareness that God permeates all, "knows" all, "reveals" all. The lists are for us. The silence is for God. This is the great secret.

The Remembrance of Things Past (and Future), Private (and Public)

Rabbi Aaron D. Panken, PhD

I

It was the recent tragic death of two megastars, Michael Jackson and Whitney Houston, that first alerted me to it. In our postmodern, media-driven world, the very instant famous people die, all available forms of contemporary communication converge on their memory and commence paying simultaneous tribute. Television and radio stations, Internet sites, Twitter, Facebook, Tumblr, blogs—you name it—begin showcasing their stories and their music in a memorializing frenzy. Just minutes after hearing of Houston's death, one major station abandoned its entire regular schedule to dedicate the evening just to her.

This practice jump-starts a lovely element in the communal process of mourning. By sharing the creative contributions of an artist's life, the media invite all manner of fans into a virtual community sharing memories. The intense moments following death thus launch a communal pattern of recognition and remembrance, allowing those touched to feel a heightened sense of gratitude and of loss.

What is disconcerting about this process, however, is this: the very moment when the living voice of an artist is stilled becomes, paradoxically,

---

Rabbi Aaron D. Panken, PhD, teaches Rabbinic and Second Temple literature at Hebrew Union College–Jewish Institute of Religion in New York. He is author of *The Rhetoric of Innovation*, and contributed to *Who by Fire, Who by Water—Un'taneh Tokef* and *All These Vows—Kol Nidre* (both Jewish Lights).

the moment when you hear that voice the most. That is to say, just when eternal silence settles over them, they suddenly make more noise than ever. Such a paroxysm of sound in the midst of death is altogether new to our time; what has happened to the former sad stillness of recent death is disquieting, in every sense of the word.

A personal version of this phenomenon came to me last year in the form of a minor subgenre of our modern media: the voice mail message.

My mother-in-law had passed away, but not before leaving a small oeuvre of voice mails scattered over various family voice mail boxes and answering machines. Nothing stunning or relationship bending, mind you, simply the regular remnants of routine communication among loving family members going about their business. During the eleven months of mourning, we thus found ourselves reencountering her voice from time to time. It was oddly comforting to hear her familiar cadence; to catch the occasional unique expression she used to deliver "live" with such inimitable intonation; to be reminded in that quotidian way of what she had meant to us when she was alive and what she still represented at a far deeper level in her death. The stunning combination of her virtual presence with her actual absence regularly caught us off guard.

As the disembodied sound of her voice sporadically broke the silence of our mourning, we were forced to reevaluate again and again the mysterious boundary between death and life and reconsider our place in an odd world that gives us transitory life on the one hand but enduring connectivity to the dead on the other. Such recordings rekindled facets of our relationship—her hopes and dreams for us, her guidance and advice, her helpful and loving critique. Even beyond the temporal boundaries of her life, her short declarations influenced us as we lived on without her.

II

Talmud scholar Saul Lieberman was the first to notice an interesting fact in the history behind the Hebrew word *vidui*, the term we now use for prayers of confession, especially the well-known *Ashamnu* and *Al Chet*. Lieberman pointed out that the original meaning of *vidui* was not "confession," but "declaration."[1] Joseph Tabory, professor of Talmud at Bar-Ilan University, and others have linked this idea of declaration to an obligation from the Torah: the commandment to confess the specific violation one had committed as one performed a sacrificial sin offering to atone for it.[2] The quite logical idea was that penitents making an atonement sacrifice ought to declare the sin for which it atoned. The declaration—an early form of prayer—could not effect atonement on its own. It was secondary to the sacrifice it accompanied, but necessary nonetheless to direct attention to the intent behind the sacrifice.

Sometime after the destruction of the Second Temple in 70 CE, when the sacrificial system no longer obtained, prayer fully replaced sacrifice, at which time our current understanding of confessional prayer as efficacious on its own appears to have gained wide acceptance. It was in this context, probably during the Tannaitic period (70–c. 200 CE), that declarations over sin offerings gave way to Yom Kippur confessional prayers in the *Amidah*. While these prayers were surely not of uniform structure or wording at this early stage, the core act of stating aloud that one was a sinner and then listing one's particular sins became normative, as it still is today. Such prayers have developed extensively since then, but at their core, they remain essentially the same.

The *Shulchan Arukh* (by Joseph Caro, sixteenth century) addresses this core concept when it says:

> One does not need to detail the sin; but if one wants to detail the sin, one is permitted [to do so]. And if one confessed quietly, it is correct to detail the sin.
>
> [Rabbi Moses Isserles (the *R'ma*), author of the *Mappah*, a commentary built upon the *Shulchan Arukh*, adds:]
>
> But if one is praying aloud, or one is leading the service and repeating the *Amidah*, one does not detail the sin; saying *Al Chet* as an acrostic does not constitute detailing it, since that [the acrostic] is just the customary nature of the prayer.[3]

This vision of confessional prayer highlights just how far Judaism has come from the time of an individual's verbal declaration of sin over a sacrifice. Jews have moved from enumerating aloud our own personally relevant sins to reciting fixed lists of sins as part of a communal liturgy and only then adding the personal details quietly, and thus privately.

The benefits inherent in this transition are legion. First off, because no one hears the specific confessions of others, individuals may pray without fear of shame, anger, or reprisal. Second, the seemingly endless collection of sins recited is sure to include sins one has committed and forgotten, holding up a critical mirror that reminds us to search ourselves carefully for those sins that might easily slip our minds. In the public listing of sins, strangely enough, there is companionship for sinners and privacy for penitents. If *all* of us sin and *all* of us recite these lists, then *all* of us are part of one common community seeking repentance. We confess as part of that community, but not, thankfully, at the cost of exposing details of our own exacting (and embarrassing) list of sins. The Yom Kippur confessions operate within this liminal space between public and private.

III

Proclaimed publicly, yet considered privately, our confessions act upon us much like the recorded declarations of those now lost to us—whether our late relatives we knew privately or the famous personalities we knew publicly. Like the sound of their recorded voices, the sound of our own confessions invites us to the boundary of here and not here—in this case, the "not here" of our own recent past, which is dead to us but still addresses us in the memories of sins we have committed. The confessions point us, with some sadness, backward toward the losses we have sustained as we left the path of righteousness, and forward toward the potential cost of persisting in our failures. They point us also toward the private pain of failure, set amidst the public commonality of imperfection that we share with our fellow community members, who, like us, have much to improve within themselves.

The sounds of communal confession, like the voices of those now gone, jolt us with just enough pain from the past to wake us up. But embedded in that sad past is a hint of an imminent and brighter future, if we will only listen carefully. In the remembrance of things public, we find private meaning; in the remembrance of things past, we find the possibility of better things yet to come.

Can "Sin" Be Redeemed?

New Metaphors for an Old Problem

Rabbi Jeffrey K. Salkin, DMin

> Mrs. Hall: How do you plan to spend the holidays, Mrs. Singer?
> Mrs. Singer: We fast.
> Mr. Hall: Fast?
> Mr. Singer: No food. You know, to atone for our sins.
> Mrs. Hall: What sins? I don't understand.
> Mr. Singer: To tell you the truth, neither do we.
>
> —Woody Allen, *Annie Hall*

And, to tell you the truth, neither do we.

I cannot be the only contemporary Jew who has a problem with "sin." The problem is not with the reality of human sin; it is with the word "sin" itself.

Like "repentance," "redemption" and *olam haba* (or its baptismal name, "heaven"), "sin talk" seems Christian. Say the word, and it conjures up Catholic school or an evangelical preacher channeling the early

---

Rabbi Jeffrey K. Salkin, DMin, is a noted author whose work has appeared in many publications, including the *Wall Street Journal, Reader's Digest,* and *The Forward.* He is editor of *The Modern Men's Torah Commentary: New Insights from Jewish Men on the 54 Weekly Torah Portions* and *Text Messages: A Torah Commentary for Teens*; and author of *Being God's Partner: How to Find the Hidden Link Between Spirituality and Your Work*, the bestseller *Putting God on the Guest List: How to Reclaim the Spiritual Meaning of Your Child's Bar or Bat Mitzvah*, and *Righteous Gentiles in the Hebrew Bible: Ancient Role Models for Sacred Relationships* (all Jewish Lights), among other books.

American preacher Jonathan Edwards delivering his famous, fiery sermon "Sinners in the Hands of an Angry God."

I sense that there are many Jews today who would like to find a different translation and definition of *chet*, the Days of Awe's most prominent term for "sin." We have been quick to relate *chet* to its original connotation of "to miss the mark," as when an archer misses the target. This explanation might still work—if more people played with bows and arrows.

How, then, should we now understand "sin"?

In *Sin: A History*, Gary Anderson paraphrases George Lakoff, Mark Johnson, and Paul Ricoeur in noting that the most effective way to understand how a culture imagines sin is through the metaphors that it uses for such an act, as well as the act of forgiveness.[1] Throughout their history, Jews have had a treasure trove of such metaphors, including "stain," "debt," and "burden."

In particular, sin as "burden" gets top billing on Yom Kippur. Its traditional morning Torah reading (Leviticus 16) depicts the high priest symbolically transferring the people's sins to a goat and sending that goat out into the wilderness, which was under the domain of the desert-demon Azazel. For the ancient Israelites, the transfer of sin was no mere metaphor; it was a reality. The ancient Israelites *carried* their sins (*nosei avon*), and the scapegoat was a veritable beast of burden.

How do we find a new—or perhaps, old—metaphor for sin?

We start not with a *text*, but with a *gesture*—the rhythmic beating on the chest during the *Al Chet* confessional on Yom Kippur.

The question is, why do Jews do this?

Let's assume that the chest beating is, in reality, heart beating. Biblically speaking, the heart is the seat of the intellect. When Exodus speaks of Pharaoh's "hardening of the heart," it means neither a surplus of cholesterol nor a numbing of the emotions. It means the failure of the intellect to guide the individual in making the right decisions. So, a ritualized beating of the heart is the "freeing up" of the hardened heart and the act of forcing it to "jump-start" its potential for moral introspection.

But the heart is also the seat of the passions. By beating upon the heart, we are attacking the very organ that is the source of sin (*Ecclesiastes Rabbah* on Ecclesiastes 7:2).

Or, perhaps we are not *beating* on the heart. Rather, we are *knocking* upon the heart as we would knock upon the gates of heaven. In the words of Joseph Soloveitchik:

> God is referred to as "He [*sic*] Who opens the gate for those who come knocking in repentance" ... unless one knocks on the gates loudly and continuously, repentance and confession are impossible. The entire liturgy for Yom Kippur, from beginning to end, is geared to this one goal: knocking upon the gates, again and again, crying out over and over again: "Oh, I beseech Thee!"[2]

Or, perhaps beating on the heart is a way of symbolically breaking the heart and preparing it to be an offering to God. In the words of theologian Louis Jacobs: "The beating of the breast denotes that God accepts the broken heart and the heart responsive to the cry of the oppressed and the unfortunate."[3] Others might say that beating on the heart is simply a Jewish version of self-flagellation, akin to what we find in the Christian Bible: "But the [tax collector] stood at a distance. He would not even look up to heaven, but beat his breast and said, 'God, have mercy on me, a sinner'" (Luke 18:13). From there, the practice migrates into the Mass of the traditional Christian liturgy, in the Roman and Eastern rites, in which the penitent beats on the breast three times: "Lamb of God, you take away the sins of the world, have mercy on us"—*mea culpa, mea maxima culpa.*

We even find the practice in American literature's understanding of New England Protestantism. In *The Scarlet Letter*, Nathaniel Hawthorne presents the reader with the image of the guilty and tormented Reverend Dimmesdale secretly flagellating himself as, mysteriously, the scarlet letter A appears on his chest.

But, in fact, the beating on the chest/heart might be even more powerful, and more suggestive, than we had once thought. Beating on the chest appears to have been an outward manifestation of mourning. The Sages (*Genesis Rabbah* 96; Talmud, Shabbat 148b, Megillah 3b, and elsewhere) refer to beating on a chest at a funeral as a sign of mourning. When Rabbi Eliezer died, Rabbi Akiva beat his breast until it bled (Talmud, Sanhedrin 68a).

So, it is fair to say that the ritualized beating on the chest during the *Al Chet* confession symbolizes that someone has died.

Who has died?

The worshiper.

How do we have the audacity to imagine sin as a miniature death?

It is hardly far-fetched. In fact, if we look at only the scriptural readings for the Days of Awe, we discover that their overarching theme is *death* and *resurrection.*

On the first day of Rosh Hashanah in the traditional synagogue, we read the story of how Sarah prevails upon Abraham to expel the handmaiden Hagar and her son, Ishmael, into the wilderness (Genesis 21). Abraham does so, giving them only a skin of water for the journey. Hagar stumbles through the desert with her son. Unable to "look on as the child dies," she casts the lad under a thornbush (Genesis 21:16). At that precise moment, an angel of God opens Hagar's eyes to the presence of a well of water. Ishmael drinks from the water and survives.

The haftarah that accompanies that portion features the barren Hannah, praying for a child (1 Samuel 1). God hears her prayer, and she becomes pregnant. Barrenness is itself a miniature death; pregnancy and subsequent childbirth are a resurrection.

On the second day of Rosh Hashanah, Abraham brings his beloved, long-awaited son Isaac to what should have been a certain sacrificial death on Mount Moriah (Genesis 22). In a "repeat performance" of the scriptural reading from the first day of Rosh Hashanah, an angel stays Abraham's hand. Like Ishmael, Isaac survives.

In the haftarah, the prophet Jeremiah imagines the matriarch Rachel weeping for her lost (that is, dead) children; God says that her children will be restored to her.

The pattern continues on Yom Kippur. As we have seen, in the traditional Torah reading for the morning service, which takes place "after the death of Aaron's sons," one goat is sacrificed, and the other is sent, alive, into the wilderness. Some interpreters have even suggested that the ritual is a mime of the twin stories in Genesis: Ishmael, the "goat" sent out into the wilderness; Isaac, the "goat" who is almost sacrificed. The reading for Yom Kippur morning in the Reform lectionary is Deuteronomy 29 and 30, with its natively Jewish insistence that we "choose life."

And so the pattern continues—all the way to the final scriptural reading of the day (the afternoon haftarah)—in which the reluctant prophet Jonah is thrown into the sea, devoured by a "great fish," and then regurgitated onto dry land to continue his prophetic mission. Again, death and resurrection.

And through it all, we encounter and experience our own death. We wear white, in order to "try on" the burial shrouds in which we will someday be buried. We wear no leather; we fast; we abstain from bathing and sex; in essence, we become our own corpses. In the most physically vulnerable hour of the day, we remember the deaths of loved ones (*Yizkor*), imagining our own mortality and fragility as well.

Finally, at the end of *N'ilah* (the closing service for Yom Kippur), we utter the *Sh'ma*, as if on our collective deathbeds. And then comes the final shofar blast—the cry of the newborn or "born again" infant that is, in reality, each of us.

On a day that is redolent of death, there is every good reason to imagine sin as a miniature death—a death of the spirit. "But if only we make the effort to turn, every force of goodness, within and without, will help us, while we live, to escape that death of the heart which leads to sin."[4]

When we pound on our chests, we are mourning our own inner deaths. And perhaps we might also say that the beating on the chest is not only an act of mourning for ourselves, but also a kind of spiritual CPR.

How, then, would this come out in our prayers? We might choose to translate *Al chet shechatanu*, normally rendered as "For the sin we have committed ...," as "For the death of the spirit that comes from...."

True: it is no literal translation of the Hebrew prayer. But it is a moving metaphorical one. And contemporary liturgists have committed far more adventurous translations.

And, *t'shuvah*, then?

It would be nothing less than a rebirth of the soul. We are no longer dead; we are alive, again, to the possibility of a new moral life.

“Later He Realizes His Guilt”

Rabbi Jonathan P. Slater, DMin

> “Though he has known it, the fact has escaped him, but later he realizes his guilt.”
>
> —Leviticus 5:3

I was a young, innocent, and earnest new rabbi, leading a group of congregants to Israel. I knew next to no one there, so I was dependent on the travel agent to arrange much of the trip. But I did have a cousin, someone I hadn’t seen in well over a decade, who lived in Jerusalem. Trying to be creative and hoping to provide some experience that would connect my people to actual Israelis, I arranged an invitation to attend services and then visit in my cousin’s home for Shabbat lunch. That way we would visit an Israeli synagogue—a “native” community, as it were—and have the opportunity to hear what Israelis were thinking, how they were living.

Now, I knew that my cousin was *frum* (“observant”), but beyond that, I knew nothing of her life. We arrived at her synagogue, and I was somewhat startled. The women’s section was completely outside of the men’s prayer room. I was worried about how the women in my group would manage without English translators—both for the prayers and for the conversation there. Then, I noticed that the men around me were

---

Rabbi Jonathan P. Slater, DMin, was ordained at The Jewish Theological Seminary of America and has a doctor of ministry degree from the Pacific School of Religion. He is the author of *Mindful Jewish Living: Compassionate Practice* and codirector of programs at the Institute for Jewish Spirituality, as well as an instructor in meditation at the JCC in Manhattan and other venues. He contributed to *Who by Fire, Who by Water—Un’taneh Tokef* and *All These Vows—Kol Nidre* (both Jewish Lights).

dressed in what we back home would call "black hat." Orthodox I was expecting, but leaning toward *charedi* (ultra-Orthodox)? That was a possibility I had not considered.

Still, we got through services and then moved upstairs to lunch with my cousin. She was pleasant enough, welcoming and friendly. But soon, the conversation turned to politics: relations with the Palestinians, the possibility of sharing the land in two states, what it means to be a Jew in the Land of Israel. What I heard from my cousin was the type of fundamentalist reading of Scripture I would have expected from Christian televangelists Pat Robertson or Jerry Falwell. Arguing literally from one proof text after another, she advocated exclusive possession of the land, negation of the idea of a "Palestinian" people—even to the extent of identifying them with the biblical Amalek (and a descendant of Haman, therefore), worthy of annihilation. I was outraged.

Despite worries about what my congregants would think about me, the trip unfolded well after that, and we returned home, with no outward negative repercussions from the Shabbat lunch. But inside myself, I remained confused, hurt, shamed, and worried. I wrote my cousin, expressing my embarrassment and abhorrence of her views on the Palestinians. I rejected her expression of Jewish life and (dare I say) prayed that others would prevail in the formation of Jewish life and culture in Israel. That, I thought, was that.

Over a decade later, after significant personal upheaval (divorce) and a time of reflection on my life, my values, and my future, this event returned to consciousness. I replayed the luncheon on that fateful Shabbat day and realized, with shock and dismay, that my cousin had offered me—us—hospitality without expectation of reciprocation. She was friendly and welcoming, fully herself without putting on airs. She was the gracious host, and I was the ingrate—to the point of failing even to have said "Thank you."

I reviewed my letter to her. Who was I, an outsider, a guest, to reprimand or chastise her and her family? What made me think that my response was so obviously correct or even meaningful, given my cousin's life choices? It was certainly inconsiderate. At some distance from the event, geographically, temporally, and psychologically, and feeling more settled, reflective, and open, I looked back more clearly on the fear, anger, and embarrassment that had led me to act so shamefully. I wrote another letter to confess my sin, to ask forgiveness, to acknowledge my wrong.

This is the nature of the consciousness that attends wrongdoing. In the moment of transgression, behavior that should rightfully embarrass us seems perfectly proper—masked, as it is, by the powerful emotions that prompt it: anger, fear, greed, resentment, confusion, and self-righteousness. Only later, when the feeling of threat passes and we settle into a moment of calm and clarity, does our action come once again to mind, so that we may face it, acknowledge it for the mistake it is, and make amends.

This aspect of human nature—our hesitation to admit what would be shameful or a blow to our fragile ego—is at the heart of confession. The first word is *ashamnu*, "we have sinned." The root of this verb appears in the early chapters of Leviticus, regarding the sacrifices brought to atone for an inadvertent, unintentional, or unknown trespass against the domain of the holy.

According to Mishnah Sh'vuot 1:2 and 2:1–2, the sacrifices referred to in Leviticus 5:1–13 apply only when there exists "initial knowledge," "ultimate knowledge," and "lack of notice in the interim." In other words, something originally known was ignored or forgotten and then later recalled. It was at that point that the offender undertook to expiate for his offense.[1]

The event itself—whether entering in impurity into the holy precincts, eating holy food in impurity, failing to fulfill an oath, or misuse of sacred implements—takes place, but the significance is either unknown at the time or is forgotten. When the trespass—once forgotten—comes again to mind, one brings the sacrifice.

Is this not the case with much of our lives? Do we not regularly make mistakes that we choose to ignore, of which we are oblivious, or that we know but are so pained over that we forget? What is it that restores awareness of our mistakes to consciousness? What allows us to face ourselves fully, to acknowledge that we have been wrong, and then to do something about it?

It is my experience that when I allow my mind to settle and my heart to be at ease, I become more open to such awareness. In the event described above, it was in the quiet of the house, in my aloneness, that I began to touch the truth of my life. Divorce was challenging: What was the truth of the relationship now gone sour? Who was really "at fault"? I could stick with my story of innocence, of being wronged, or I could look more deeply to seek the truth. It was in the absence of my partner, before whom I had had to defend my ego, with whom I was unable to be fully present, that I became aware of how guarded, how closed off I had been. I realized how hard it had been to speak the truth of my mistakes. Once I became aware of that truth in my married relationship, I began to see it as well in the rest of my life. However aware I may have been before of my guilt, of my dissembling, of my half-truths, only now was I prepared to fully acknowledge it, confess it, and come clean.

This is the work of Elul and the Days of Awe. While there are specific acts that we may undertake to rectify wrongs during this time, my sense is that we would do well to employ these days to sit quietly, to allow the mind and heart to rest, to allow the habitual narratives that shape our lives to slow down. Perhaps in the quiet, as the stories subside, we will begin to feel our own pain—both at what was done to us and at what we have done to others. Compassion for our own suffering, while seemingly solipsistic, makes it possible to have empathy for others and to face the hard truths about how we have treated them. Meeting our selves, our true selves, our flawed selves, in moments of compassionate calm, informs us as to how deeply others too feel shame, fear, anger, and loss. Knowing our own hearts to have some small measure of ease, we wish only for others to find that as well. So, we are emboldened and heartened to acknowledge our wrongs to others, to confess, and to make amends.

By the time Yom Kippur arrives, we grasp the truth of its signal announcement, *Ashamnu*, "We have sinned." We have, indeed, made mistakes, and are prepared to acknowledge them. But, although awareness has come to us in our inner private practice, we are now challenged to confess in public. Not an easy task! We would rather turn aside, hide, forget again. But, the second word comes along: *Bagadnu*, "We have betrayed"—our true selves, others, God. Who we are at this moment we realize is not who we truly wish to be. Dissembling now, running away now, would truly be a betrayal of all we have learned by paying close attention to our hearts.

Each of the next twenty-two words is helpful, instructive, in turning us more and more to the truth. But, my sense is that the rhythmic chant of the confession, the seemingly unending succession of terms, is meant mostly to keep us connected to the moment, to awareness, to the truth. The confession does not arise from outside—at least not if we have been paying attention, if we have used the preceding period to settle the mind and heart. We are aware of the truth: we have made a mistake. It is time now to make it right.

Rabbi Shimon ben Lakish taught (Talmud, Yoma 86b) that repentance (*t'shuvah*) is so powerful that it can transform intentional sins into mere unintentional mistakes. Yet, he also taught that it can transform intentional sins into merits, as if in performing the deed one had done the right thing. The first applies, says the Talmud, when we turn ourselves around out of fear of punishment, loss of honor, or begrudgingly; the latter is the case when we do *t'shuvah* out of love—of God, ourselves, others. It is in the turning, in our own inner awakening to the truth, that the earlier misdeed impels us to make amends—repairs, actually. In the act of repair, our sin is transformed into merit, the meritorious acts of goodness and of truth.

Several weeks after I sent off my apology to my cousin I received a reply. She wrote that she had no recollection of having received the first letter, and no apology was necessary. She appreciated my taking the time to write to her but hoped I did not feel regret or pain over an incident that had never taken place. She simply looked forward to the next time I would visit. As did I.

Some Are Guilty, All Are Responsible

Dr. Ellen M. Umansky

On Yom Kippur, we recite a long litany of sins for which we ask God to forgive us. We literally beat our breasts with our fists as we publicly confess sins that we have committed intentionally or by mistake. With the exception of profaning God's name, all the sins we mention are thoughts, words, or actions directed toward other human beings: parents, teachers, business clients, friends, and just plain strangers who come our way and are impacted by how we deal with them. Our misdeeds include mockery, gossip, slander, deceit, making empty promises, and outright criminal behavior such as bribery or worse. Some are committed out of pride, others out of anger, stubbornness, narrow-mindedness, or pointless hatred.

These sins do not *define* us, however. As theologian Michael Kogan writes in his *Opening the Covenant: A Jewish Theology of Christianity*, we are *affected* but not *infected* by sin. It is what human beings do, not who we are.[1] In other words, we are not bad or evil by nature, even though what we think, what we say, and how we act often fall short of the requisite standard that has been set for us by God, others, and, perhaps most importantly, ourselves. To confess these sins is a sign of humility, and with it, our humanity, for none of us is God.

Are these sins simply personal failures that with great resolve and effort we can overcome? Conjuring up an image of sin as "missing the mark"—an image that Jews often employ—seems to imply as much. Yet even skilled archers often miss the bull's-eye at which they've aimed their arrows, not

---

Dr. Ellen M. Umansky is the Carl and Dorothy Bennett Professor of Judaic Studies at Fairfield University in Fairfield, Connecticut. She is currently working on a book focusing on Judaism, liberalism, feminism, and God. She contributed to *Who by Fire, Who by Water—Un'taneh Tokef* and *All These Vows—Kol Nidre* (both Jewish Lights).

because they purposely try to miss their target, but because in life there are few guaranteed results. In the case of the archer, his finger might slip just before the arrow has been released, a sudden noise might distract her, or a strong gust of wind might blow the well-aimed arrow in the wrong direction. It is not so simple, then, as to believe that just by paying more attention we can make all our sins go away. We should, try, of course, but despite the familiar dictum, practice makes us better; it does not make us perfect.

The sins enumerated in *Al Chet* may prove instructive as we contemplate the extent to which we can do better. Lying, insolence, corruption, mockery, and deception are not inherent failures or weaknesses of personality, so much as they are instances of willful wrongdoing. I say "willful" because even so-called congenital liars know that they're not telling the truth. Those who are corrupt are well aware that they're breaking the law. Protestations notwithstanding, those who make fun of others are usually not doing so good-humoredly, and they know it. Sinful human beings are not like the archer who aims straight but misses the mark. Rather, out of arrogance, egotism, maliciousness, or greed, they have not aimed straight to begin with. Who are such human beings? As *Ashamnu* implies, it is all of us: "we" have been treacherous, stubborn, gluttonous, and so on. In truth, no single one of us has committed all these failures, yet as Abraham Joshua Heschel once noted, "in a free society, some are guilty and all are responsible."[2] While Heschel spoke these words in 1967 in opposition to the Vietnam War, his words are instructive here, for within the context of community, which is the context in which Jews pray on Yom Kippur, we are responsible for one another.

How often does apathy or indifference prevent us from speaking out against ideas or putting an end to behavior that we know to be wrong? We may not be guilty of harboring certain thoughts or voicing certain sentiments, but we are responsible for creating communities that encourage them. Similarly, tolerating unethical behavior makes us culpable. To paraphrase the Talmud, whoever can stop others within one's community from sinning, but does not, is held responsible for what those others do (Shabbat 54b).

This teaching echoes the words of Moses, who, before the Israelites entered the Land of Israel, spoke to them about what it means to be an *am kadosh* ("holy people"). The blessings and curses that Moses invokes (Deuteronomy 27:15ff.) imply, on the surface, that those who follow God's teachings will prosper, while those who disobey God will be cursed. Yet given the context in which Moses is speaking, his words are not about individual reward or punishment, but rather, the *communal* ramifications of individual words and behavior.

As we know from our own experience, the righteous often suffer, and the "wicked" are often successful. Individuals, in other words, don't always get what they deserve. Communities, however, do. Thus, a community that tolerates or condones sexual immorality, financial dishonesty, family violence, indifference to those in need, a disrespect for the rights of others, and so on will not only be cursed but ultimately will be destroyed, if not by God, then by its members. Indifference breeds indifference, violence breeds violence, and hatred breeds hatred. When we recite the words of *Al Chet*, we ask God to forgive us for sins that we have knowingly committed, individually or communally, recognizing that what we do, and choose not to do, has an impact on others. In the end, how we think, speak, and act shapes not only our life but also the communities and societies of which we are members.

At the same time, however, when I recite the words of *Al Chet*, I cannot help but do so with a sense of what Heschel called "maladjustment," by which he meant the recognition that in some way these words perpetuate a status quo that is not always healthy. We ask God to forgive us for our pride, when some of us suffer from too little sense of self, not too much of it. Not all of us are guilty of gluttony. Some of us, in fact, starve ourselves to death or throw up what we have eaten. We implore God to absolve us from the sin of seeking monetary gain at the expense of others. Yet in so doing, we render invisible those within our communities who are poor or struggling financially to support their families or themselves. Yes, many of us incessantly gossip about or mock others whom we know and perhaps see on a regular basis. Some of us, however, are completely alone.

Some congregations, including my own, seek to rectify these omissions by having people anonymously write down personal or communal sins to be included in their *Al Chet*—these are then spoken aloud by the rabbi from the bimah or by members, standing in their places. It is these sins that move me the most. The honesty with which they are written and the details that they include remind me how important it is to give voice to all of our sins, just as in a different context, at a different time, it is important to give voice to all our achievements.

Al chet shechatanu l'fanekha, "For the sin we have committed against You through silencing ourselves or others." For this sin too, God, we ask your forgiveness.

Sin, Confession, and … Forgiveness?

Rabbi Margaret Moers Wenig, DD

> Repentance and Yom Kippur suffice for forgiveness of sins against God, but *sins against another human being are not forgiven until restitution is made and the injured person is satisfied.* [emphasis added]
>
> **—Mishnah Yoma 8:9**

We know the way it's supposed to work: The offend*ing* party is obliged to make restitution, confess, and ask for forgiveness as part of the process of *t'shuvah* (repentance). And once those steps have been taken, the offend*ed* party is obliged to grant *m'chilah* (forgiveness). But what if those steps are *not* taken? What if one of the parties shirks his or her obligation and no one is satisfied?

I believe that *t'shuvah* and *m'chilah can* wipe away our sins, create in us a new heart, repair a breach, restore a relationship. I believe that *t'shuvah* and *m'chilah* can change not only the future but also the past (because they change our view of the past). I believe that the practice of *t'shuvah* and *m'chilah*, epitomized by Yom Kippur (but not limited to Yom Kippur), can offer us a "new birth." But what if someone with whom we have become embroiled *refuses* to do *t'shuvah* or to offer *m'chilah*?

Rabbi Margaret Moers Wenig, DD, teaches liturgy and homiletics at Hebrew Union College–Jewish Institute of Religion in New York and is rabbi emerita of Beth Am, The People's Temple. She contributed to *Who by Fire, Who by Water—Un'taneh Tokef* and *All These Vows—Kol Nidre* (both Jewish Lights).

For some people, rather than "new birth," there is only the slow death of the soul. "I can't come to Yom Kippur services ever again. They just make me feel bad about myself." "I am sick of hearing rabbi after rabbi, in sermon after sermon, insist that 'repentance and forgiveness are *always* possible.' Repentance and forgiveness take two, and sometimes only one is willing to do the work."

To confess one's sin, to make restitution, and to ask for forgiveness require that we place ourselves in a position of vulnerability: we acknowledge that the party we have offended has power over us. To grant forgiveness to one who has hurt us, confessed to us, offered restitution, and asked us for forgiveness is to surrender power we have over that person. Some people are unwilling to grant that another person has power over them. Some people are unwilling to surrender the power they have over another.

I have known people who have lived most of their adult lives under the thumb of another human being who would not do the work of *t'shuvah* or *m'chilah.* I have known people who felt they simply could no longer live under the burden of guilt they were carrying or with fires of righteous anger burning in their bellies. I have buried people whose spirits were nearly suffocated years before their bodies gave out, suffocated by nooses other people placed around their necks.

If you have a noose around your neck, placed there by someone who will not admit the wrong he or she has done to you, has not offered restitution, and has not asked for forgiveness, or if you have a noose around your neck placed there by someone whom you have wronged who mocks your confession, refuses to accept your offers of restitution, and denies you forgiveness, then I suspect that the promise of "new birth" might ring hollow.

That, suggests our liturgy, is where God comes in.[1]

Consider this conundrum: Given the Mishnah's teaching that Yom Kippur atones only for our sins *against God*, why is it that we spend so much time on Yom Kippur confessing *to God* our sins *against other human beings* and punctuating those long confessions with the refrain: "For all of these, God of forgiveness, forgive us, pardon us, absolve us"?

Perhaps because when we betray another human being, we are also betraying our covenant with God.[2] "When … [a person] commits any wrong toward another, *thus breaking faith with God*, … he shall confess the wrong he has done. He shall make restitution …" (Numbers 5:5–7).

God is an interested party. That also means that God has standing to forgive, even on behalf of others, when those others will not do so.

Confessions made to God, however, are not the same as confessions to another human being. To our fellow, the precise words we use matter. To God they don't. When confessing to another human being, we acknowledge precisely what we have done and accept responsibility for the damage we inflicted. Confessions to God, however, are symbolic. Their very form tells us so: *Ashamnu* is an acrostic. *Al Chet*, too. Are there only two sins that begin with a *gimel*? Sephardi confessions, too, are symbolic. One lists violations of *all* positive commandments, and another, all negative commandments. Some sages say we need recite before God no specific sins at all, for "*atah yode'a razei olam* … You, God, already know … the dark secrets of every living soul."[3]

God "sees" and "takes note of" all our sins, even those we deny or conveniently forget.

We recite these litanies, not for their specifics but, perhaps, as an expression of our vulnerability, our weaknesses, our powerlessness, and our longing to be taken back in love. "We are not so arrogant and insolent as to say before You ... we are righteous and have not sinned. But we ... have sinned [*Aval anachnu chatanu*]." Some authorities say that our confession need consist of those three Hebrew words alone. The details don't matter. The relationship does. On Yom Kippur some long to restore relationships with what- or whomever we conceive of as God from whom failure and shame have estranged us.

We ask God to forgive us for sins we have committed against another person, partly because it is also God whom we have betrayed, and partly because God can do what some human beings cannot. Rabbah Ben Mari warned of this: "Come and see: how different from the character of the Holy One is the character of flesh and blood. If one angers his fellow, there is doubt whether or not a person of flesh and blood will be appeased. But the Holy One will be appeased" (Talmud, Yoma 86b).

And that is precisely what the *machzor* attempts to express. Look at the arch of the liturgy. From *Minchah* before Yom Kippur through *Minchah* on Yom Kippur, the traditional service calls for *Al Chet* nine times—nine symbolic recitations. No less symbolic is it, then, that in *N'ilah* we recite *Al Chet* no more. Its *absence* is, in fact, a central feature of *N'ilah*. In contrast, the presence of the thirteen attributes of divine mercy is a central feature. But this time there are not four recitations, as in *S'lichot* and Yom Kippur Evening. This time there are eight,[4] literally doubling the sense of God's forgiveness. When else does our liturgy give us the very same words eight times in a single service? Imagine how that might sound: the entire congregation reciting these words again and again (except for one recitation reserved for the *chazzan*).[5] Young voices and old, sweet and gravelly, in front of us, behind us, to the left, to the right, swirling around us again and again. Literally, *immersing* us in the sound of those words, "Adonai, Adonai merciful and loving...." *Mah mikveh m'taher et hat'me'im, Hakadosh barukh hu m'taher*, "Just as *mikveh* cleanses those with impurities, so the Holy One cleanses [us from sin]" (Mishnah Yoma 8:9). On the very day we are not permitted to bathe or to drink, the thirteen attributes are our living waters, the *taharah*[6] promised on Yom Kippur evening: *Ki vayom hazeh y'khaper aleikhem l'taher etkhem; mmikol chatoteikham lifnei Adonai titharu*, "On this day atonement shall be made for you, cleansing/purifying you; from all your sins you shall be cleansed before Adonai" (Leviticus 16:30).[7]

In *N'ilah* the recitation of the thirteen attributes increases by 100 percent and the recitation of *Al Chet* decreases by 100 percent. And in place of *Al Chet* is *Atah noten yad*:

> You reach out your hand [not to stone us, not to punish us, not to tie a red rope around our neck as on the goat sent to Azazel]. You extend your right hand to receive us back in love [and to untie the noose from round our necks]. We are not far above beasts [but neither are we scapegoats meant to carry our sins to the grave]. For You singled out humankind from the beginning, and You gave us the power to turn.... *Shene'emar, v'ne'emar....* [as it is said]," continues the prayer

What is God saying to us as the sun is setting and our bodies are weary from fasting and standing? *Lo echpotz b'mot hamet*, "I do not desire [your] death" (Ezekiel 18:32). On Rosh Hashanah and Yom Kippur morning, we say, *Lo tachpotz*, either pleading to God or saying of God (depending on the translation—it can mean both), "May *You* not desire" or "*You* do not desire" our deaths.[8] Now, in *N'ilah*, God speaks to us: God answers our cries of *Sh'ma na, s'lach lanu, p'tach lanu sha'ar*, "Hear ... pardon ... open the gate," with "*I* do not desire [but I cannot prevent your death from natural causes, from accidents, from human cruelty or error, but]

I do not *desire* the death of those whose souls are suffocated by guilt or anger." Rather, *V'hashivu, vich'yu*, "Turn, that your spirits may live." In these words, near the very end of *N'ilah*, comes release from the burden of sin even for those whose *t'shuvah* has not been accepted by flesh and blood. In these words lies the fulfillment of the promise of Yom Kippur.[9]

Percussing the Heart

Dr. Ron Wolfson

A few years ago, my wife Susie and I attended a benefit concert by the Israeli Philharmonic at the fabulous Walt Disney Concert Hall in downtown Los Angeles. Frank Gehry, the famous architect, designed a space-age building shaped with flowing panels of steel that boggles the imagination. Inside the main hall, Gehry situated the orchestra virtually in the center of the space, surrounded by the audience. We scored seats in the section directly behind the orchestra. Not only did we have a direct line of view to Zubin Mehta, the conductor, urging on the musicians, but we were also within touching distance of the percussion section. When the timpani and cymbals were called upon to do their thing, the sound rattled the soul.

"Percussion" is an interesting term. It means, simply, "to tap" or "to beat." Percussionists beat drums to make music. Doctors percuss the lungs and abdomen during physical examinations to assess the condition of underlying organs. Children afflicted with cystic fibrosis must have their lungs percussed to loosen the suffocating mucus.

Jews percuss the heart.

Dr. Ron Wolfson is Fingerhut Professor of Education at American Jewish University in Los Angeles, a cofounder of Synagogue 3000, and a member of Shevet: Jewish Family Education Exchange. He is author of *The Seven Questions You're Asked in Heaven: Reviewing and Renewing Your Life on Earth; God's To-Do List: 103 Ways to Be an Angel and Do God's Work on Earth*; the three volumes *Hanukkah, Passover*, and *Shabbat*, all family guides to spiritual celebrations; *The Spirituality of Welcoming: How to Transform Your Congregation into a Sacred Community; A Time to Mourn, a Time to Comfort: A Guide to Jewish Bereavement; Be Like God: God's To-Do List for Kids*; and, with Rabbi Lawrence A. Hoffman, *What You Will See Inside a Synagogue* (all Jewish Lights). He contributed to *Who by Fire, Who by Water—Un'taneh Tokef* and *All These Vows—Kol Nidre* (both Jewish Lights).

This unusual ritual act of percussion punctuates the dramatic recitation of the Yom Kippur confessions, *Ashamnu* and *Al Chet*. We make a fist and beat our chests in rhythm with the words of the prayer. *Al chet shechatanu l'fanekha*, "For the sin we have committed against You," we pray, pounding our chests on the word *chet*, "sin."

What are we doing? Are we beating ourselves up over the ways we have messed up our lives and the lives of others during the past year? Are we tapping our bodies to assess the condition of our underlying souls? Are we knocking loose our bad habits, so that the prayers of the High Holy Days can renew us and offer us a new beginning?

For me, it is all these things—and it is more.

The High Holy Days are all about forgiveness. Most obviously, given the fact that our prayers are addressed to God, we ask forgiveness from God. We recognize, however, that before approaching God with the request, we must ask forgiveness from those we have wronged—and also grant forgiveness to those who sincerely seek it from us. Less obviously, then, we ask forgiveness from others. One of the high points of my Yom Kippur experience is when our rabbi invites us to turn to our loved ones and say, "I'm sorry"—and only afterward turn to God to say the same.

Yet as moving as this is, it is only a prerequisite to the ultimate confrontation that arrives when I find myself pounding on my chest at *Al Chet*. It is the least obvious but, to me, the most important request for forgiveness that I make.

Beating my chest reminds me that I cannot reach a state of spiritual cleanliness for the new year without experiencing the most difficult forgiveness of all—forgiving myself. I beat my chest as a reminder that I must stop beating myself up over the ways I've missed the mark. I have to recognize my mistakes, my shortcomings, but I must forgive myself before I can ever hope to forgive others. I must forgive myself before I can ask for forgiveness from others—including God.

Percussing the heart is another innovation of the Rabbis to awaken us from our spiritual slumber. Just as the piercing sounds of the shofar are a clarion call to action, the beating of the chest emphasizes the importance, the seriousness, of our confessional prayers. Percussing the heart is the alarm clock for the soul.

Al Chet Shechatanu

Collectively We Own Them All

Rabbi Daniel G. Zemel

We are a society that shies away from the use of the word "sin." We leave the word to such figures as colonialist preacher Jonathan Edwards (1703–1758), whose sermons (such as "Sinners in the Hands of an Angry God") have been made famous by history. We content ourselves instead with "mistakes" and "errors." Even when human lives are lost, families torn apart, and countries destroyed because we went to war over false intelligence, misinformation, and disinformation, we prefer terms like "policy misjudgment" or "misguided decision." No one sins anymore.

No one even thinks about sin—except for one season of the year when we take the *machzor* off the shelf and discover there a litany of sins that indicts and includes each one of us. We rediscover, as if for the first time, that we actually have committed sins—a multitude of them, in fact—all in just the past twelve months; and the list is formidable—arrogance, contempt, deceit, violence, neglect, and lust, to name but a few.

This, according to the *machzor* anyhow, is not just what we do, but who we are, because we never seem to change. Year after year, there we are again, the same list before us. Haven't we learned anything? Have people been like this forever? Despite evolution, history, and eons of education, is this our eternal lot? Is this not a challenge to faith itself? If we are who we are and who we are does not change, what is the point of the entire exercise?

Rabbi Daniel G. Zemel is the senior rabbi of Temple Micah in Washington, D.C. He contributed to *Who by Fire, Who by Water—Un'taneh Tokef* and *All These Vows—Kol Nidre* (both Jewish Lights).

In one of my favorite movies, *Hoosiers*, one of the main characters, Myra Fleener, says admiringly about her home community and what brought her to return to it, "Nothing ever changes. People don't change." In the context of the movie, the words are consoling; they convey the hometown warmth and security that Myra loves. Predictability can be comforting.

Each year as I consider the High Holy Day litany of sins, I find myself thinking about Myra's wisdom and wondering about the extent of their truth. Myra Fleener's words are well worth thinking about.

So, too, is one of the most telling stories in Genesis regarding the human ability to change: the metamorphosis of Jacob into Israel. After twenty years of separation, and on the eve (finally) of reuniting with his twin brother, Esau, the manipulative, scheming Jacob wrestles with an apparition, an angel. As dawn breaks, the angel releases Jacob from his grip and renames him "Israel"—"one who struggles" (Genesis 32:29). But Jacob has been injured and, as Israel now, must leave the scene limping. Change, it seems, is birthed in struggle and hurt. Redemption from sin comes only after time, effort, and pain.

But then my friend Myra Fleener comes back to haunt me. "People don't change," she insists. Indeed, Myra could have gotten this from Torah itself, because no sooner do we turn the page on this very name-changing wrestling match than we see the Torah referring to Jacob again—yes, Jacob, not Israel. This insistence that it is Jacob continues for several chapters; it is no anomaly. Not until Genesis 37:3 does our ancestor reappear as Israel—and only in a mocking, even sarcastic, reference to the very same flawed character we have been reading about since the younger Jacob cheated Esau: "Israel loved Joseph more than all his children." The father in us all wants to shout out to Jacob/Israel, "Haven't you learned anything at all, all these years?"

Call him Jacob—call him Israel. Call him what you like. There has been no change. Jacob/Israel is the same rascal. Just as he manipulated his father Isaac to play favorites, so he now plays favorites himself, giving a gift to his favored son, while the others go off to work in the field.

How can we understand this failure to change even by the patriarch who gives us his name, "Israel"? Isn't Judaism rooted in the fundamental idea that people can change, grow, and become better? Why else have it? If we find ourselves confessing the very same sins every year, how do we avoid the conclusion that we have not grown and cannot grow at all?

But take away the premise that change is possible, and what is left of the entire High Holy Day enterprise?

Perhaps, then, we must insist on change but recognize also that change is even harder than we thought. Like Jacob's wrestling match, it sends us all away limping—but genuine confession is a multiyear process, not a onetime wrestling match. We say these words year after year, throughout our lives, and yes, we change; but not in the course of a single Yom Kippur day, not even in the course of a single year, and (as far as human progress overall is concerned) not in the course of a single life.

Change must be measured cumulatively. What is the impact of confessing our sins not just once but five times every Yom Kippur, and then doing so again, year after year after year? What is the impact on an entire people doing this for centuries? What is the cumulative effect of such a confession on our people's march through history?

Change occurs only over the long haul, and the *machzor* offers not a magic bullet but an invitation for that long haul; and here we come to that pesky but critical reminder that the confession of sins, the *Vidui*, is couched in the plural—"For the sin *we* have sinned." We need the "we" because change occurs cumulatively over the entire chain of people who constitute the centuries; each Yom Kippur, each of us is part of this historical "we," the Jewish People that we call our own, and the human family of which the Jewish People is a part.

We may open the prayer book as individuals, but we read it as part of an eternal people. We should remind ourselves that the very notion of an individual self is a modern one and not entirely accurate. The ancients, our forebears, thought as part of a collective. *I* may have been deceitful and dishonest. *Someone else* was arrogant and devious; *a third* was aggressive and self-serving.

Collectively, we own them all. *Kol yisrael arevim zeh lazeh*, "All Israel is responsible for one another"—we take communal ownership of all our sins.

In his wonderfully challenging book *The Ethics of Memory*, Avishai Margalit distinguishes ethics from morals on the grounds that ethics connotes the responsibility we naturally feel for members of our family or tribe, while morality is our obligation for the world. We feel a particular bond (and with it, a deeper obligation) with those whose memories we share, those whose experiences are our own, but we dare not ignore the universal demands that link us to the world. As a Jew gathered with other

Jews on Yom Kippur, I seek change within my people—that is my ethical obligation. But I know my moral responsibility, too—my part in the moral betterment of all humankind. As descendants of Jacob/Israel, we know how difficult it is to change. We arrange an annual opportunity to try it anyway, knowing that at best we can take but a small step forward in the larger human evolution to being better—some day.

This understanding lifts me up as I prepare to enter the drama of Yom Kippur. I am not here only for myself. I am here for the entire community of those descendants of Israel whose destiny I share. And I am here, through Israel, for the larger human journey of us all. Knowing how hard change is, I join recognition of my failures to the failure of others—the person sitting next to me, perhaps, who cares equally for me. Contrary to popular expectation, change is impossible for me alone. It comes about only through the supporting mutuality of a community. *Tovim hashnayim min ha'echad*, "Two is better than one" (Ecclesiastes 4:9); or in a more contemporary metaphor, "It takes a village."

Hoosier's fictitious Myra Fleener of Hickory, Indiana, was right to say that "people don't change"—not when they live as isolates, and the Hickory that is depicted early in the movie is mean-spirited and vindictive, distrustful of outsiders, ready to pounce on mistakes, and unable to forgive past sins. Redemption in the film arrives through soul searching, public honesty, confession, prayer, and (finally) a town pulling together because they are winners "no matter what the scoreboard says at the end." A very Jewish movie formula.

Throughout his life, Jacob remains Jacob, the name change to Israel notwithstanding. Only at the end of Genesis is his lesson learned, and only by his sons, who finally discover the honesty necessary to reveal their true selves to each other and, in the process, offer support to one another. This is the gift of public confession in community. Overall growth and change may not happen in our own lifetime; meanwhile, we expose our failing publicly and offer support in our wrestling match with history.

Trying to Say Something, Something

Magnolia and Confession

Dr. Wendy Zierler

For several years now, I have been privileged to team-teach a course at Hebrew Union College–Jewish Institute of Religion with Dr. Eugene Borowitz titled "Reel Theology," in which we use film, television, and other popular media as a springboard for Jewish religious and theological conversation. The course utilizes an interpretive method we call "inverted midrash."

Rabbinic midrash often highlights the meaning of a classical text by introducing a parable. The Rabbis explain a verse and then, using the formula *mashal l'mah hadavar domeh?* ("a parable, to what can the saying be likened?"), they elucidate the verse with a secular story or application. Today, however, many Jews are poorly acquainted with the verses of the Bible or the sayings of the Rabbis; introducing a lesson with a classical text is as likely to puzzle them as to inspire them.

"Inverted midrash" reverses the process: it goes from secular story to religious text. Beginning with the serious issues that are raised by

---

Dr. Wendy Zierler is associate professor of modern Jewish literature and feminist studies at Hebrew Union College–Jewish Institute of Religion, New York. She is coeditor with Rabbi Carole Balin of *In My Entering Now: The Selected Writings of Hava Shapiro* (forthcoming). She is also author of *And Rachel Stole the Idols* and the feminist Haggadah commentary featured in *My People's Passover Haggadah: Traditional Texts, Modern Commentaries* (Jewish Lights), a finalist for the National Jewish Book Award. She contributed to *Who by Fire, Who by Water—Un'taneh Tokef* and *All These Vows—Kol Nidre* (both Jewish Lights).

thoughtful books, movies, or television shows, we seek to show what a learned Jew, certainly a member of the clergy, might say about how he or she intersects with Jewish text and practice.[1]

We sometimes address issues of *vidui* ("confession") and *t'shuvah* ("repentance") using the Los Angeles–based film *Magnolia* (1999, written and directed by Paul Thomas Anderson, who garnered an Academy Award nomination for his screenplay).

For some, this might seem a questionable choice. *Magnolia* represents the worst of the Los Angeles television-industry culture. It is shot through with promiscuity, profanity, and other sinful behaviors. Almost all the characters use the f-word with obsessive frequency. Two of the characters are drug addicts. A third is an unconfessed child molester. A fourth (Earl Partridge), the producer of a game show, has serially betrayed the wife of his youth and then, when she is dying of cancer, abandons her to the care of his fourteen-year-old son. Reflecting this family history of abuse, the producer's son becomes a "celebrity" in his own right and develops a video self-help program to teach men how to cynically dominate women. The world of *Magnolia* is literally and figuratively cancerous, with two characters dying of cancer and others suffering the effects of malignant paternal abuse.

If the Judeo-Christian tradition often likens God to a heavenly father and the faithful to his sons—as we say in the liturgical section that precedes *Ashamnu*, "We are your sons and You are our *father*"—then this is a world where fathering has become so corrupt and caustic an institution that it no longer serves as an apt metaphor for God or anything at all redemptive.

Precisely because of its sin-riven characters, however, *Magnolia* is such a powerful illustration of *t'shuvah* and *vidui*. Not just that: on the most basic level, this film reflects, albeit in secular, non-synagogue-based terms, the very experience of Yom Kippur. The impending death of Earl Partridge corresponds with the ways the daylong Yom Kippur privations simulate death. We dress in white; we desist from eating or drinking and give ourselves over to matters of the spirit—as if we were like Earl, about to die ourselves. Through the technique of doubling characters and repeated situations (e.g., there are two quiz kid contestants, two drug addicts, two cancer patients, several supposed coincidences and confessions) the film conveys the notion that even in our atomized, alienated world, where people sit alone watching their televisions, we have shared narratives and aspirations. As with Yom Kippur eve itself, where we declare our readiness to pray together with sinners, *Magnolia* juxtaposes our human experiences of virtue and sin as if they were conjoined. Specifically, in terms of the process of *vidui*, the film reinforces the notion that confessions work only if they are spoken aloud so that they can be heard. They are often best done in the presence of a group, in the first person plural.

This second lesson seems so counterintuitive today, when the group nature of the *Vidui* makes it seem, if anything, so inauthentic and formulaic. Who really bares her soul and confesses her sins in the presence of so many other people? Who really confesses in the first person plural? Doesn't it make more sense for me to confess in private to the sins I have actually committed rather than in the encyclopedic A-to-Z liturgical form of *Ashamnu* and *Al Chet*?

Magnolia illustrates, however, the power behind group confession. The verb used for Yom Kippur confession in the biblical account of the scapegoat sent into the wilderness is *l'hitvadot*, a *hitpa'el* verbal form[2] that often connotes reflexive or reciprocal action. The verb *l'hitpalel*, "to pray," takes the same form, suggesting that we should say our prayers and confessions to ourselves. Read as *reciprocal* verbs, however, *l'hitpalel* and *l'hitvadot* imply that God responds dialogically to our prayers and our *vidui* and that those who pray or confess together have a catalyzing effect on one another—they shore up one another's resolve to change, to do better.

In a climactic moment in the film, Earl (who, remember, is the terminally ill cancer patient who abandoned his wife when she was similarly sick, and left his child to deal with the physical and emotional repercussions) awakens long enough from his drug-induced haze to make a frank confession of his past sins. "I'm trying to say something, something," he says, a language doubling that can be attributed to the effects of his medication, but that also echoes the doubling that is common in the film and its general message about plural or interconnected experience. "Know," he says to Phil, his nurse, "that you should do better."

Earl's confession launches an instance of secular worship akin to Yom Kippur, as one by one, the nine characters in the film join in a serial singing of Aimee Mann's song "Wise Up," with each character taking up a part of the song that pertains most to his or her own vices or sins. They all sing the same song but find a way to identify their own experience within this collective chant. The sequence calls to mind the wondrous potential of *t'shuvah* to change one's nature and overturn the past. Two of the characters manage to sing while in a state of unconsciousness, suggesting that even a rote liturgical recitation with little or no consciousness of what the confession says may result in a seemingly miraculous coming to terms with one's actual sins—as one "wisens up."

In his *Hilkhot T'shuvah* ("Laws of Repentance"), Maimonides notes that "even a person who was wicked throughout his life but repented at the end does not have any of his wickedness remembered."[3] In dramatizing Earl's end-of-life confession, *Magnolia* echoes Maimonides: it is never too late to return to one's better self. And in keeping with the overall theme of reciprocity, Earl's own confession prompts others in its train—as well as a series of changes in the lives of those around Earl, some of whom he did not even know. All of this reinforces the idea of *vidui* as an authentic, communal act of breaking through the cycle of sin and effecting positive change.

Permit me another example of a modern *vidui*, this time from a more identifiably Jewish source. "*Dos kleyne mentschele*" ("The Little Man," 1864–65) by S. Y. Abramovitsch (aka Mendele Moycher Seforim) is considered the first work of modern Yiddish literature. It features the autobiography and last will and testament of Itzik Avram, a prominent and wealthy man in his community, and a hitherto unconfessed sinner—a lot like Earl Partridge, in fact. After recalling his personal history of childhood abuse and his eventual adoption of the vocation of "Little Man"—meaning a conniving middleman and practitioner of various forms of fraud—Itzik launches his own personalized *Al Chet*, requesting atonement for the sins of deceiving others, hardening his heart, hurrying to do evil—and more specifically for the sins of "slander and holding a lease ... for the sin of insolence and being a little man."[4] Only after this *Al Chet*, it turns out, is Itzik able to make concrete suggestions (and financial endowments) to (among other things) develop better Jewish schools with modern methods of education. Itzik's posthumous confession, publicly recited, thus becomes not merely a solipsistic exercise but also a gesture of communal engagement and improvement.

In his survey of philosophical approaches to *t'shuvah*, writer and literary critic Tzvi Luz notes that almost all modern thinkers see "the Jew's potential for *t'shuvah* as resting on his ability to reinterpret the religious significance of the tradition to make it applicable to a secular world."[5] *Magnolia* provides the inverse as well: in our pop-saturated

Appendix A

The Personal Prayers of the Rabbis (Talmud, Berakhot 16b–17a)

[Editor's note: Following the regular Amidah, *worshipers were encouraged to speak personally with God, offering whatever words they wished. The Talmud (Berakhot 16b–17a) provides several examples of such private prayers, as practiced by its Rabbinic masters. Although confession was not a mandatory part of these daily prayers, it is clear, nonetheless, that penitential piety dominated Rabbinic consciousness at the time of the Talmud's composition, circa 200–600 CE. Several parts of our current liturgy draw liberally on these prayers, but they are important in their own right, as a window into the penitential mentality of the Talmud.]*

The Personal Prayers

After completing his *Amidah*, Rabbi Elazar said, "May it be your will, Adonai our God, that You fill our destiny with love, amity, peace, and friendship; and expand our ranks with students. Prosper our end with a future and hope. And give us a portion in the Garden of Eden. Correct our way in your world with a good friend and a good inclination that we may awaken [in the morning] to find our heart yearning to fear your name. May our deepest desires / peace of mind [*korat nafsheinu*] come before You for good."

Upon completing his *Amidah*, Rabbi Yochanan said, "May it be your will, Adonai our God, that You look upon our shame and behold our evil. Then dress yourself in mercy, cover yourself with strength, wrap yourself in kindness, and gird yourself in grace. May your attribute of goodness and humility come before You."

Upon completing his *Amidah*, Rabbi Zeira said, "May it be your will, Adonai our God, that we do not sin and do not suffer shame and disgrace before our ancestors."

Upon completing his *Amidah*, Rabbi Chiya said, "May it be your will, Adonai our God, that your Torah be our craft, that our hearts not be pained and our vision not be dimmed."

Upon completing his *Amidah*, Rav said, "May it be your will, Adonai our God, that You give us long life, a life of peace, a life of goodness, a life of blessing, a life of earning a living, a life of health, a life with fear of sin, a life without shame and humiliation, a life of wealth and honor, a life in which we have love of Torah and fear of heaven, a life in which You fulfill our heart's yearnings for good."[1]

Upon completing his *Amidah*, Rabbi [Yehudah Hanasi] said, "May it be your will, Adonai our God, that You save us from shameless people and from shamelessness, from bad people and bad luck, bad companions and bad neighbors, from Satan the destructive one, from a hard judgment and a hard legal adversary, whether Jewish or not. ([This prayer was recited] even though guards [were posted] around Rabbi.)[2]

Upon completing his *Amidah*, Rav Safra said, "May it be your will, Adonai our God, that You make peace in the heavenly family above and in the earthly family below; and among students engaged in Torah study, whether for its own sake or not. But may it be your will that they engage in it for its own sake."

Upon completing his *Amidah*, Rabbi Alexandri said, "May it be your will, Adonai our God, that You place us in a corner with light, not a corner with darkness. Give us no heartache, and do not darken our eyes."

There are some who maintain that it was Rav Ham'nuna who said that prayer and when Rabbi Alexandri finished his *Amidah*, he said, "Lord of all worlds, it is known and revealed before You that we want what You want, so what prevents us from doing it? The yeast in the dough and our subjugation to ruling powers. May it be your will that You save us from them and that we return to perform the statutes of your will with a full heart."

Upon completing his *Amidah*, Rava said, "My God, until I was created I was unworthy, and now that I have been created it is as though I was not created. I am dust as I live, all the more so on my deathbed. Before You I am like a vessel full of shame and humiliation. May it be your will, Adonai my God and my ancestors' God, that I sin no more. And in your great mercy erase my previous sins before You, but not through punishment or terrible disease."[3]

This was the confession of Rav Ham'nuna Zuta on Yom Kippur.[4]

Upon completing his *Amidah*, Mar bar Chanina said, "My God, guard my tongue from evil and my lips from speaking deceit. To those who insult me may my soul be silent. May my soul be like dust to everyone. Open my heart to your Torah so that my soul might pursue your commandments. Save me from misfortune, the evil inclination, evil women, and all the evil that occurs in the world. As for those who think evil of me, quickly bring their advice to naught and frustrate their plans. May the words of my mouth and the thoughts of my heart be favorable before You, Adonai, my rock and my redeemer."[5]

When Rav Sheshet was observing a fast, he would follow his *Amidah* by saying, "Master of the worlds, it was known before You when the Temple was still standing that if someone committed a sin, he would offer a sacrifice. The sacrifice consisted of nothing but fat and blood, but nonetheless, it atoned for him. Now here I am, sitting and fasting, depleting my fat and blood. May it be your will that my fat and blood that I am depleting be as if it had been sacrificed by me before You on the altar, so that You look favorably on me."

Appendix B

Confessions of the Rabbis (Talmud, Yoma 87b)

[Editor's note: The tannaitic era (prior to 200 CE) provides no examples of standardized confessions for Yom Kippur. Its prime document, the Mishnah (c. 200 CE), demands confession but is silent as to what ought to be said. The Talmud (Yoma 87b), however, in the amoraic era following (after 200 CE), provides a few instances of confessions that were recited by some of the Rabbis. These are given in response to a secondary teaching from the tannaitic era—one not from the Mishnah, and called, therefore, a baraita*—that discusses the timing of confession but does not say what confession entails. Both the* baraita *and the Talmudic commentary are provided below.]*

The Confessions

The Rabbis taught in a *baraita*: The obligation to confess falls with the arrival of darkness. But the Sages say we should confess before eating and drinking [before dinner, that is], lest we get distracted by the meal. Even though we confess prior to eating and drinking, we should confess [again] after eating and drinking lest something inappropriate occur [lest we engage in something sinful] during the meal. And even though we confess in the *Ma'ariv* [evening] service, we should confess [again] in the *Shacharit* [morning] service; and even though we confess in the *Shacharit* service, we should confess [again] in the *Musaf* [additional] service; and even though we confess in the *Musaf* service, we should confess [again] in the *Minchah* [afternoon] service; and even though we confess in the *Minchah* service, we should confess again in the *N'ilah* [concluding] service.

Where do we do it?

The individual says it after reciting his *Amidah*. The prayer leader does it in the middle of his recitation of the *Amidah*.

What does one say?

Rav said, "You know the secrets of the universe," etc.[1]

Samuel said, "From the bottom of the heart," etc.[2]

Levi said, "In your Torah it is written …," etc.[3]

Rabbi Yochanan said, "Master of the worlds," etc.[4]

Rabbi Yehudah said, "For our iniquities are beyond count and our sins too numerous to tally."

Rav Ham'nuna said, "My God, until I was created I was unworthy, and now that I have been created, it is as *though* I was not created. I am dust as I live, all the more so on my deathbed. Before You I am like a vessel full of shame and humiliation. May it be your will, Adonai my God and my ancestors' God, that I sin no more. And in your great mercy erase my previous sins before You, but not through punishment or terrible disease."

This was the confession of Rava all year round and of Rav Ham'nuna Zuta on Yom Kippur.[5]

Mar Zutra said, "All of these prayers apply only to cases where one has not said, 'We have sinned' [*anachnu chatanu*], but if one has already said, 'But we have sinned' [*aval anachnu chatanu*], no more need be said,[6] for Bar Ham'dudei said: Once I was in the presence of Samuel who was sitting down. When the prayer leader got to 'But we have sinned,' Samuel stood up. He [Bar Ham'dudei] said: Learn from this that the essence of confession is that."

Notes

The Liturgy of Confession: What It Is and Why We Say It, by Rabbi Lawrence A. Hoffman, PhD

1. *Tur* 706:1.
2. Joel Sirkes to *Tur* 706:1, beginning *matzati.*
3. Maimonides, *Mishneh Torah*, Laws of Repentance 1:1.
4. Ibid.

From Penitence to Nobility: Modes of Jewish Piety, by Rabbi Lawrence A. Hoffman, PhD

1. Rev. Dr. K. Kohler, *Guide for Instruction in Judaism* (New York: Philip Cowan Publisher, 1899), 34.
2. An accessible summary of original sin as a doctrine and as a truism of human psychology can be found in Alan Jacobs, *Original Sin: A Cultural History* (New York: Harper Collins, 2008).
3. For metaphors of sin in the Bible and in Rabbinic Judaism, see Gary A. Anderson, *Sin: A History* (New Haven: Yale University Press, 2009).
4. Shakespeare, *Hamlet*, act 1, scene 3, line 78.
5. On which, see Charles Taylor, *The Ethics of Authenticity* (Cambridge: Harvard University Press, 1991).
6. Lionel Trilling, *Sincerity and Authenticity* (Cambridge: Harvard University Press, 1971).
7. Ibid. Trilling is responsible also for the understanding of Polonius as addressing the self below the various roles demanded by society, a matter that he calls sincerity. The reference to Machiavelli is also his. He locates authenticity as an outgrowth of an altogether different literary and philosophical trend, culminating in Rousseau's love of self and Hegel's "disintegrated" or "alienated consciousness"—what Hegel develops into his theory of the hero who scorns sincerity as a lower form of virtue and substitutes a higher ethic that moved the course of history forward. I do not altogether adhere to Trilling's view, but the authenticity I am describing here is indeed rooted in Hegel's heroic personality, as it is in Nietzsche's Superman (*Übermensch*), who would dismiss the calling of nobility as mere slave morality.

8. Shakespeare, *Hamlet*, act 1, scene 3, lines 78–80.
9. Jean Paul Sartre, *Nausea*. Trans. Lloyd Alexander (New York: New Directions, 1964), 96.
10. Dr. G. Salomon, *Predigten in dem neuen Israelitischen Tempel zu Hamburg gehalten*, 2nd collection (Hamburg, 1821), 45.

The Problem of Repentance: A Dilemma in Late Medieval Sephardic Preaching, by Rabbi Marc Saperstein, PhD

1. Don Isaac Abravanel, *Perush Hatorah*, vol. 3, reprint ed., *Deuteronomy* (Jerusalem: B'nei Arbel, 1964), 283c; cf. Isaac Arama, *Akedat Yitzchak*, vol. 3, *Deuteronomy* (Warsaw, 1883), 86c.
2. Shaul Regev, "D'rashot al Hat'shuvah L'Rabbi Yosef ibn Shem Tov," *Asufot* 5 (1991): 191; subsequent quotations are from 192 and 193.
3. This is taken up again in a later sermon: it is only "God's gracious compassion" that provides a way for human beings to return to their "pristine stature" following sin (ibid., 207). On grace, see also sources in Marc Saperstein, *Your Voice Like a Ram's Horn: Themes and Text in Traditional Jewish Preaching* (Cincinnati: HUC Press, 1996), 319n104.
4. Shem Tov ibn Shem Tov, *D'rashot R. Shem Tov ibn Shem Tov* (Salonika, 1525), 162b.
5. For example, "Some say this is said homiletically, in order to motivate people to repent, but the truth is that the level of the righteous is higher ..." (ibid., 163a). But this approach—that the Sages stated things they knew to be false in order to motivate Jews to act properly—is rejected.
6. Ibid., 163b. This confession on the part of someone obviously committed to philosophy of an utter inability to make sense of a Rabbinic statement that appears to be repugnant to reason, but nevertheless reaffirming its validity as an authentic tradition, echoes skeptical formulations of Abraham ibn Ezra.
7. Isaac Arama, *Akedat Yitzchak* (Warsaw, 1883), 84a.
8. Isaac Caro, *Toldot Yitzchak*, *Re'eh* (Riva di Trento, 1558), 103b.
9. See my translation of the entire sermon from which this passage is taken in Saperstein, *Your Voice Like a Ram's Horn*, 301–34; the passage quoted is on p. 317.
10. See the partial translation of this passage in Marc Saperstein, *Jewish Preaching 1200–1800* (New Haven: Yale University Press, 1989), 397, from Oxford Christ Church MS 197, fols. 175r–82v.
11. Abraham Saba, *Tseror ha-Mor*, reprint ed., *Deuteronomy* (Tel Aviv, 1975), 27b–c. Cf. Abraham Gross, *Iberian Jewry from Twilight to Dawn: The World of Rabbi Abraham Saba* (Leiden: Brill, 1995), 121n96, 159.
12. I am not convinced that such an interpretation is valid. The scholars I have cited were not radical philosophers. Isaac Aboab and Isaac Caro were distinguished Talmudists whose absolute commitment to Judaism is beyond any question; Shem Tov ibn Shem Tov, while a strong defender of Maimonidean philosophy, was not as far as we know attacked for heretical philosophical

doctrine in his sermons. The work of such preachers shows rather that rabbinic leaders of the generation incorporated philosophy and rational categories into their sermons and commentaries without viewing it as a threat.

13. See the German Franciscan Johannes von Werden, *Dormi Secure*, cited in *Models of Holiness in Medieval Sermons*, ed. Beverly Mayne Kienzle (Louvain-la-Neuve): Fédération internationale des instituts d'études médiévales, 1996), p. 308.
14. B. Netanyahu, "Homiletical and Exegetic Literature," in *The Marranos of Spain* (New York: AAJR, 1966). Abravanel introduces this category explicitly into his discussions of repentance, speaking, for example, of "the victims of duress who have left the category of religion. Regarding these it is said, 'You shall take it to heart' (Deuteronomy 30:1), for their repentance will be in the heart, not in the mouth, for they will not be able to proclaim their repentance and their faith publicly" (Abravanel, *Perush Hatorah*, 3:283a).
15. Marc Saperstein, "The Method of Doubts: Problematizing the Bible in Late Medieval Jewish Exegesis," in *With Reverence for the Word: Medieval Scriptural Exegesis in Judaism, Christianity, and Islam*, ed. Jane Dammen McAuliffe, Barry D. Walfish, and Joseph W. Goering (Oxford: Oxford University Press, 2003), 133–56.
16. Ibn Shem Tov, *D'rashot R. Shem Tov ibn Shem Tov*, 179a.

Six Understandings of Confession for Our Time, by Dr. Annette M. Boeckler

1. The academic term for the approach of this chapter is "hermeneutics": the philosophical analysis of ways of literary understandings. The German philosopher Hans Georg Gadamer (1900–2002) taught that understanding happens within a certain personal horizon, which is impossible to ever leave. To do a text justice means, therefore, not only to try to understand the meaning of a text and its horizon, but also to be aware of one's own horizon, that is, one's own presumptions, prejudices, and traditions, acquired by education, tradition, experience, and culture. This chapter introduces—academically spoken—six different hermeneutical horizons to understand the *Vidui*.
2. Quoted from the translation by Benjamin R. Forster, in William W. Hallo, *The Context of Scripture*, vol. 1, *Canonical Compositions from the Biblical World* (Leiden: Brill, 1997), 416–17f. The Akkadian original can be found in E. Ebeling, *Die akkadische Gebetsserie "Handerhebung"* (Berlin, 1953), 73–75. Further examples of Assyrian-Babylonian confessions of sins can be found in James B. Pritchard, *Ancient Near Eastern Texts Relating to the Old Testament* (Princeton, NJ: Princeton University Press, 1955), 390–92.
3. Nosson Scherman, *Vidui* (Brooklyn, NY: Mesorah, 1986), 5.
4. Cf., e.g., Zecheriah 7:2–3, 8:18; Jeremiah 41:5. For confessions, see Daniel 9:4–17; Ezra 9:6–15; Nehemiah 9:6–37; 1 Kings 8:47; 2 Chronicles 6:37; Psalm 106:6; Lamentations 3:42; Isaiah 59:12–14; Psalm 51:6; Nehemiah 1:6–7.

5. Quoted from a traditional *machzor* used in the United Kingdom: *Service of the Synagogue: Day of Atonement*, part 2, 9th ed. (London: Routledge, n.d.), 127. For an American example, see Philip Birnbaum, *High Holiday Prayer Book* (New York: Hebrew Publishing Company, 1951), 750.
6. Maimonides, *Mishneh Torah*, Laws of Repentance 1:1. Maimonides's sample text of a confession is based on the confession of the high priest in the *Avodah*, not on the *Vidui Zuta* (*Ashamnu*) or *Vidui Rabbah* (*Al Chet*).
7. Ibid., passages 2, 3, and 5.
8. *Mahzor Lev Shalem: Rosh Hashanah and Yom Kippur* (New York: Rabbinical Assembly, 2010), 235.
9. Ibid., 238.
10. Assembly of Rabbis of the Reform Synagogues of Great Britain, ed. *Forms of Prayer for Jewish Worship*, vol. 3, *Prayers for the High Holydays* (London: Reform Synagogues of Great Britain, 1985), 301f. passim. A German translation of this *machzor* is today used in many liberal congregations in Germany and in Zurich and Vienna.
11. For example, by Yehudah Halevi, p. 300; by Pamela Melnikoff, p. 421.
12. *Forms of Prayer*, vol. 3, 305–307.
13. *Gates of Repentance: The New Union Prayerbook for the Days of Awe*, rev. ed. (New York: Central Conference of American Rabbis, 1996), 325.
14. Ibid., p. 425.
15. Joseph G. Rosenstein, *Machzor Eit Ratzon: A Prayerbook for Rosh Hashanah and Yom Kippur* (Highland Park, NJ: Shiviti, 2010), 65–66f. A similar approach was taken until 2008 by the (discontinued) website SocialAction.com. It suggested the following family activity: "We can ... rewrite the alphabet of *Ashamnu* into an alphabet of hope and promise. Create a family alphabet of world repair, using the acrostic formula as a reminder of all of the ways that we can contribute to *tikkun olam*." This list may look like this: "Appreciate ..., Behave ..., Consider ..., Decide ..., Forgive ..., Give ..., Help ..., Imagine ..., Judge ..., Keep ..., Look ..., Make ..., Never ..., Often ..., Purchase ..., Quietly ..., Respond ..., Save ..., Try ..., Use ..., Value ..., Wish ..., Examine ..., Yield ..., Zealously ..."; one should add social activities. www.socialaction.com/1999andearly2000/family action yk 2000.phtml. (The page was stopped about 2008 according to the Internet archive but seems to be continued as repairtheworld.com.)
16. *Forms of Prayer*, vol. 3, 769–70.
17. *The Hirsch Siddur: The Order of Prayers for the Whole Year*, rev. ed., translation and commentary by Samson Raphael Hirsch (Jerusalem, New York: Feldheim Publishers, 1978), 656–57.
18. *Kol Haneshamah: Prayerbook for the Days of Awe* (Elkins Park, PA: Reconstructionist Press, 1999), 828. For further examples of this understanding, compare the comments on pp. 830, 832.
19. *Forms of Prayer*, vol. 3, 301–2.

20. Franz Rosenzweig, *The Star of Redemption*, trans. William W. Hallo (London: Routledge, 1970), 325. (In the German original it is clear that the confession is *Ashamnu* and *Al Chet* ("*an seine Brust schlaegt*"), which is interpreted in the light of Meir of Rothenburg's introduction to *Kol Nidre.*
21. For a modern example of this view, see Efrat Gal, ed., *Das Buch der juedischen Jahresfeste* (Frankfurt a. Main, 2001), 138: "Wer dieses Gebet [*Ashamnu*] mit der Erschuetterung, die es fordert, spricht, erkennt sich in einem Licht, das den Zugang zum hoeheren Selbst und zur eigentlichen Menschlichkeit eroeffnet."
22. *Machzor Ruach Chadashah: Services for the Days of Awe* (London: Liberal Judaism, 2003), 379.
23. *Mahzor Lev Shalem*, 238.
24. I translate *aval* as "but," following the translation provided in this volume. *Aval* can function as affirmation, however: see Genesis 42:21, "And they said one to the other [Joseph's brothers]: Indeed [*aval*], we have become sinners, as he cried, but we didn't listen." See also Genesis 17:19; 2 Samuel 14:5; 1 Kings 1:43; 2 Kings 4:14. Only in later biblical Hebrew (Daniel, Ezra, 2 Chronicles) does *aval* get the meaning that it has in Modern Hebrew—"but."
25. The following verses relate to situations in which a prophet accuses Israel of committing the sin in question or in which our ancestors actually confessed to having committed the sin: *ashamnu* (Ezekiel 22:4; Genesis 42:21); *bagadnu* (Hosea 1–3; Jeremiah 3:8, 3:11, 3:20; 1 Samuel 14:33; Isaiah 48:8; Jeremiah 5:11, 9:1; Malachi 2:14); *gazalnu* (Micah 2:2); *dibarnu dofi* (Psalm 50:20); *he'evinu* (1 Kings 8:47; 2 Chronicles 6:37; Psalm 106:6); *hirshanu* (Daniel 9:5; Psalm 106:6; Nehemiah 9:33); *zadnu* (Daniel 1:43; Nehemiah 9:16, 9:29); *chamasnu* (Ezekiel 22:26; Zephaniah 3:4); *tafalnu sheker* (Job 13:4); *ya'atznu ra* (Ezekiel 11:2); *kizavnu* (Psalm 78:36; Isaiah 57:11); *latznu* (Hosea 7:5); *maradnu*—Ashkenazi (Daniel 9:5, 9:9; Nehemiah 9:26; Ezekiel 2:3, 20:38); *marinu*—Sephardic (Psalm 106:7, 106:43; Lamentations 3:42; Isaiah 63:10; often about Israel's behavior in the desert, e.g., Numbers 20:10, 20:24); *ni'atznu*—Ashkenazi (Numbers 14:11; Deuteronomy 31:20; Jeremiah 23:17); *ni'afnu*—Sephardic (Isaiah 57:3; Jeremiah 3:8, 5:7, 23:10; Ezekiel 23:37; Hosea 3:1, 4:13–14; Malachi 3:5; Psalm 50:18); *sararnu* (Hosea 4:16; Zechariah 7:11; Nehemiah 9:29; Isaiah 65:2; Zechariah 7:10, 7:13; in several places Israel is compared with a stubborn son, e.g., Isaiah 30:1); *avinu* (Daniel 9:5); *pashanu* (Isaiah 59:12–13; Lamentations 3:42; Isaiah 1:2; Jeremiah 2:29, 3:13; Ezra 2:3; Hoses 7:13, 8:1); *tzararnu* (Amos 5:12); *kishinu oref* (often about Israel in the story of the golden calf, Exodus 32–34, e.g., Exodus 32:9, 33:3, 33:5; further Daniel 9:6, 9:13, 31:27; Jeremiah 7:26; Nehemiah 9:16); *rashanu* (1 Kings 8:47; Daniel 9:15; 2 Chronicles 6:37); *shichatnu* (Exodus 32:7; Deuteronomy 9:12, both in regard to the golden calf); *ti'avnu* (Amos 5:10; Micah 3:9; Ezra 16:25); *ta'inu* (Isaiah 53:6; Psalm 95:10); *titanu* (2 Chronicles 36:16). For a detailed analysis of each verb, see Annette M. Boeckler, "Haben wir gelogen oder waren wir schwerhoerig? Zur Textgeschichte und Bedeutung des Ashamnu-Gebets," *Frankfurter Judaistische Beitraege* 31 (2004): S. 123–53.

26. *Mahzor Lev Shalem*, 239.
27. S. Baer, ed., *Seder Avodat Yisrael* (New York: Schocken, 1957), 415.

Al Chet in Israeli Culture: Israeli Confessions over Everything, by Rabbi Dalia Marx, PhD

1. Chayim Nachman Bialik, *Letters*, vol. 1 (Tel Aviv, 1890), 21 (in Hebrew). Every effort has been made to trace and acknowledge the copyright holders for the material included in this chapter. I apologize for any errors or omissions that may remain and ask that any omissions be brought to my attention so that they may be corrected in future editions. I thank Dr. Joel M. Hoffman for translating the Hebrew texts, a task that in some cases was especially demanding.
2. *Kavanat Halev: Machzor Ha-T'fillot Leyamin Nora'im* (*The Intention of the Heart: A* Machzor *for High Holy Days*) (Jerusalem: Israel Movement for Progressive Judaism, 1989), 285.
3. Ibid., 286.
4. *K'rovah* is a type of *piyyut* (a liturgical hymn). The word may stem from *karov* ("near"), but some commentators derive it from *k'rav* ("battle"). Rabbi Menachem of Galia says that the way a cantor would be called to conduct the service was, "Come, draw near [*k'rav*], bring our offering, do our deeds, fight our wars [*k'rav*]" (Jerusalem Talmud, Berakhot 4:4, 8b; *Genesis Rabbah* 49:23 [Theodor-Albeck, pp. 506–7]).
5. See Dalia Marx, "*Un'taneh Tokef* through Israeli Eyes," in *Who by Fire, Who by Water—Un'taneh Tokef*, ed. Lawrence Hoffman (Woodstock, VT: Jewish Lights, 2010), 117–21.
6. *Mishpahag: Yom Hakippurim (Celebrating Holidays in the Family Circle)* (Tel-Aviv: *Shitim*), 13.
7. Rabbis for Human Rights website, http://rhr.org.il/eng/index.php/about.
8. The full text can be found in English and in Hebrew on the Rabbis for Human Rights website, http://rhr.org.il/heb/?p=3935.
9. Rosenthal published his text initially in his blog, *Hazirah Haleshonit*, September 22, 2004.
10. This confession was published online, and it was later printed in *Olam Katan*, a magazine for Orthodox youth, Fall 2008.
11. The text was originally published on the YNET website, September 19, 2007.
12. The text was published at www.ynet.co.il/articles/0,7340,L-4131935,00.html. In spite of my efforts, I could not find out who wrote this text.
13. Moshe Meir, *Sefer Habayit V'ham'nuchah: Shirim Be'ikvot Yirmiyahu (The Book of Home and of Rest: Poems as Response to Jeremiah)* (Jerusalem: 1995), 55.
14. See Dalia Marx, "When *L'shon HaKodesh* Is Also the Vernacular: The Development of Israeli Reform Liturgy," *CCAR Journal* (Fall 2009): 31–62; Dalia Marx, "Ideology, Theology, and Style in Israeli Reform Liturgy," *CCAR Journal* (Winter 2010): 48–83.

Finding Ourselves in God, by Rabbi Elyse D. Frishman

1. From Tom Wolfe, *Bonfire of the Vanities* (New York: Farrar, Straus and Giroux, 1987).

Multiplying the Sins, by Rabbi Andrew Goldstein, PhD

1. Ismar Elbogen, *Jewish Liturgy: A Comprehensive History* (Philadelphia: Jewish Publication Society, 1993), 125, 419n47.
2. Ibid., 419n49.
3. *The Union Prayer Book for Jewish Worship*, part 2, rev. ed. (Cincinnati: Central Conference of American Rabbis, 1922), 108–9.
4. *Liberal Jewish Prayer Book*, vol. 2 (London: Liberal Jewish Synagogue, 1923), 106–7.
5. *Gates of Repentance: Services for the High Holydays* (London: Union of Liberal and Progressive Synagogues, 1973), 159–61.
6. *Gates of Repentance* (New York: Central Conference of American Rabbis, 1978), 271–72. There are twelve sins in the evening and fifteen in the morning service (pp. 330–31).
7. *High Holiday Prayer Book*, vol. 2 (Jewish Reconstructionist Foundation, 1948), 82–83. This list is followed by a list of forty-four sins from the traditional list.
8. Ronald S. Aigen, *Renew Our Days: A Prayer-Cycle for Days of Awe* (Quebec: Congregation Dorshei Emet, 2001), 447–48.
9. *Mahzor Lev Shalem: For Rosh Hashanah and Yom Kippur* (New York: Rabbinical Assembly, 2010), 267.
10. *The Complete ArtScroll Machzor*, trans. Rabbi Nosson Scherman (Brooklyn, NY: Mesorah Publications, 1986), 849–64.
11. *Union Prayer Book*, 212–21.
12. *Gates of Repentance*, 217–19.

For the Sin of "Unattempted Loveliness," by Rabbi Edwin Goldberg

1. M. Scott Peck, *The People of the Lie: The Hope for Healing Human Evil* (New York: Simon and Schuster, 1983).
2. From "Guilty" by Marguerite Wilkinson, cited in Sidney Greenberg, *High Holiday Bible Themes*, vol. 2 (New York: Hartmore, 1974), 52.
3. Christian Smith, with Kari Christoffersen, Hillary Davidson, and Patricia Snell Herzog, *Lost in Transition: The Dark Side of Emerging Adulthood* (New York: Oxford University press, 2011).
4. David Brooks, "If It Feels Right," The Opinion Pages, *New York Times*, September 13, 2011, New York edition, A31. See also Smith, *Lost in Transition.*
5. From Liz Allen Fey, CEO of Management Solutions Group, LLC.

Manifesting as Jews, by Rabbi Jonathan Magonet, PhD

1. Sir Victor Gollancz (1893–1967) was a London-born and -based publisher, socialist, and humanitarian. He drew attention to the plight of European Jews at the hands of the Nazis already in 1942 in an influential pamphlet *Let My People Go*. After the war, he courted unpopularity by campaigning to send food and clothing to Germany and Italy. He edited the spiritual anthology *A Year of Grace: Passages Chosen and Arranged to Express a Mood about God and Man.*
2. The passages in this article are from Gollancz's autobiography *My Dear Timothy*, quoted in *Forms of Prayer for Jewish Worship*, vol. 3, *Prayers for the High Holydays*, ed. Assembly of Rabbis of the Reform Synagogues of Great Britain (London: Reform Synagogues of Great Britain, 1985), 835–836.
3. *Forms of Prayer for Jewish Worship*, vol. 3, *Prayers for the High Holydays*, ed. Assembly of Rabbis of the Reform Synagogues of Great Britain (London: Reform Synagogues of Great Britain, 1985), 304–6.

From Staid Sins of Yesteryear to Wrongdoings of Today, by Rabbi Charles H. Middleburgh, PhD

1. Rabbi John D. Rayner, CBE, DD, editor of *Service of the Heart*, *Gates of Repentance*, and *Siddur Lev Chadash*, the prayer books of the Union of Liberal and Progressive Synagogues (Liberal Judaism).
2. Rabbi Chaim Stern, coeditor with John D. Rayner of the above prayer books.

We Are All Unrepentant Humanists, by Rabbi Tony Bayfield, CBE, DD

1. Byron Sherwin (*Studies in Jewish Theology* [London: Vallentine Mitchell, 2007], p. 17) assigns authority over theology only to the small minority who constitute the believing community and quotes, in support, Arthur A. Cohen's appeal to the "supernatural vocation of the Jew."
2. Cf. Streep's 2012 Oscar-winning performance as Margaret Thatcher in *The Iron Lady*.
3. Cf. the familiar folktale about the great sin (boulder) and the little sins (pebbles). It appears in many guises, including Hasidic literature and a story by Leo Tolstoy.
4. "Aggregate" as in the construction industry term meaning, "an amalgam of pebbles, stones, minerals, etc."
5. See *Forms of Prayer for Jewish Worship*, vol. 3, *Prayers for the High Holydays*, 8th ed., ed. Assembly of Rabbis of the Reform Synagogues of Great Britain (London: Reform Synagogue of Great Britain, 1985), 304, and subsequently.
6. Talmud, Niddah 16b. The last line and proof text are repeated in Berakhot 33b.
7. I am not suggesting that all moral choices are absolutely free—instinct and conditioning play a significant part in decision making. But they are not the whole story by any means, and personal, ethical responsibility still lies at the heart of Jewish teaching.

8. *Avot D'rabbi Natan* 39.
9. *Pirkei Avot* 3:19.
10. John Gray, *Straw Dogs: Thoughts on Humans and Other Animals* (London: Granta Books, 2002), 66.
11. Raymond Tallis, *Aping Mankind: Neuromania, Darwinitis and the Misrepresentation of Humanity* (Durham, UK: Acumen, 2011), 16.
12. Quoted in ibid., 41.
13. Yeats, "The Second Coming," line 8.
14. Tallis, *Aping Mankind*, 41.
15. Gray, *Straw Dogs*, 5, 3, 12, 120, 116, 110, 76.
16. Yiddish: "despite everything," "in defiance of what you would expect."

For the Sin of … Poor Leadership, by Dr. Erica Brown

1. Tom Peters and Nancy Austin, *A Passion for Excellence* (New York: Warner Books, 1986), 383.
2. Martin Heifetz and Ronald Linsky, *Leadership on the Line: Staying Alive through the Dangers of Leading* (Boston: Harvard Business Review Press, 2002), 167.
3. Michael Marquardt, *Leading with Questions* (San Francisco: Jossey-Bass, 2005), 114.
4. Chalmers Brothers, *Language and the Pursuit of Happiness* (Naples, FL: New Possibilities Press, 2005), 89–90.
5. Ibid., 90.

We Can't Really Be That Evil!, by Rabbi Lawrence A. Englander, DHL

1. Ian Barbour, *Issues in Science and Religion* (New York: Harper and Row, 1971), 285.
2. Henry Slonimsky, *Essays* (Cincinnati: Hebrew Union College Press, 1967), 123–34.
3. Ibid., 125–26.
4. For a more detailed discussion of this idea, see Rabbi Lawrence A. Englander, DHL, "How Powerful Is God? Lurianic Kabbalah and Process Thought," *CCAR Journal* (Fall 2007): 27ff.
5. On which, see Rabbi Lawrence A. Hoffman, PhD, ed., *Who by Fire, Who by Water—Un'taneh Tokef* (Woodstock, VT: Jewish Lights, 2010).

We Have Sinned: *T'shuvah* in a Globalized World, by Lisa Exler and Ruth Messinger

1. Maimonides, *Mishneh Torah*, Laws of Repentance 1:1.
2. Gustavo Gutierrez, *The Power of the Poor in History*, trans. Robert R. Barr (New York: Orbis Books, 1988), 44–45.

Aval Chatanu ("But / In Truth, We Have Sinned"): A Literary Investigation, by Rabbi Elie Kaunfer

1. In most manuscripts of the Talmud the text reads only *aval chatanu*. See Daniel Goldschmidt, *Machzor for Yom Kippur* (Jerusalem: Koren, 1970), 11.
2. *Seder Rav Amram Gaon*, ed. Daniel Goldschmidt (Jerusalem: Mossad HaRav Kook, 2004), 56, 160. For more variations, see Goldschmidt, *Machzor for Yom Kippur*, 11n18.
3. *Aval* also means "in truth" in some passages in Rabbinic literature. See Babylonian Talmud, Eruvin 30b, Niddah 3b; Rashi to Eruvin 38a, s.v. *aval*; Rashi to M'ilah 6b, s.v. *v'chayavin alav*.
4. Interestingly, the Midrash (*Genesis Rabbah* 91) reports that the people of the south translated *aval* as "but," indicating that it was not a universally accepted translation, but limited to a certain group.
5. See Rabbi Lawrence A. Hoffman, PhD, ed., *My People's Prayer Book*, vol. 5, *Birkhot Hashachar (Morning Blessings)* (Woodstock, VT: Jewish Lights, 2001), 157.
6. Ismar Elbogen, *Jewish Liturgy*, trans. Raymond Scheindlin (Philadelphia: Jewish Publication Society, 1993), 79; Seligman Baer, *Seder Avodat Yisrael* (Redelheim, 1865), 45.
7. *Mekhilta D'rabbi Yishmael, Masekhta Deshira* 10 (ed. Horowitz-Rabin, 150; ed. Lauterbach, 2:80); *Mekhilta D'rabbi Shimon bar Yochai, B'shalach* 15 (ed. Hoffmann, 70; ed. Epstein-Melamed, 100); *Yalkut Shimoni, B'shalach* 252 (ed. Hyman, 3:342).

Confession and Its Discontents, by Rabbi Reuven Kimelman, PhD

1. They should be considered along with a similarly disturbing prayer from Rosh Hashanah (and again on Yom Kippur): *Un'taneh Tokef.* On their relationship, see Reuven Kimelman, "*Un'taneh Tokef* as a Midrashic Poem," in *The Experience of Jewish Liturgy: Studies Dedicated to Menachem Schmelzer*, ed. Debra Blank (Leiden: Brill, 2011), 115–46. On *Un'taneh Tokef* alone, see the previous volume in this series, Rabbi Lawrence A. Hoffman, PhD, ed., *Who by Fire, Who by Water—Un'taneh Tokef* (Woodstock, VT: Jewish Lights, 2010).
2. See Tosefta Kippurim 4:14.
3. For the whole process and its historical development, see Reuven Kimelman, "Leadership and Community in Judaism," *Tikkun* 2, no. 5 (Nov. 1987): 26–30, 88–91; and Reuven Kimelman, "Rabbinic Prayer in Late Antiquity," in *The Cambridge History of Judaism*, vol. 4, *The Late Roman-Rabbinic Period*, ed. Steven Katz (Cambridge: Cambridge University Press, 2006), 573–611.
4. Following the version in Tosefta Kippurim 4:15, ed. Lieberman, 255, l. 75.
5. *The Midrash on Psalms* 32:2, adapted from the translation of William Braude, *The Midrash on Psalms* (New Haven, CT: Yale University Press, 1959), 1:403.
6. See David Abudarham, *Abudarham Hashaleim* (Jerusalem: Usha, 1963), 282.
7. See Rashi ad loc.

On Hitting Yourself, by Rabbi Lawrence Kushner

1. *Mahzor Lev Shalem* (New York: Rabbinical Assembly, 2010), 219.
2. *Tzava'at Harivash* (*The Testament of Rabbi Israel Baal Shem Tov*) (Brooklyn, NY: Kehot Publication Society, 1998), par. #44.
3. Alexander Altmann, "God and the Self in Jewish Mysticism," *Judaism*, vol. III, no. 2 (1954).
4. *Tsidkat haTsaddik*, Jerusalem, 1987.
5. Daniel Matt in *Studia Mystica*, vol. X, no. 2 (Summer 1987): 7, citing Yaakov Yosef of Polnoye, *Ben Porat Yosef*, 50b–d; and Dov Baer of Mezritch, *Likkutey Amarim*, par. #232 (Jerusalem, 1971); *Maggid Devarav Leyakov*, ed. Rivka Shatz-Uffenheimer (Jerusalem: Magnes Press, 1976), par. #167.
6. Daniel Matt in *Studia Mystica*, vol. x, no. 2 (Summer 1987): 7, citing Yaakov Yosef of Polnoye, *Ben Porat Yosef*, 122b–d.

Vidui and Its Halakhic Contexts, by Rabbi Daniel Landes

1. Nachmanides on Leviticus 1:9.
2. Maimonides, *Mishneh Torah*, Laws of Sacrifice 3:15.
3. Ibid., Laws of the Yom Kippur Service 2:6.
4. Ibid., 16:17.
5. Ibid., Laws of Repentance 1:3.
6. Ibid., 1:1.
7. Ibid.
8. Ibid., 2:3.
9. Ibid., Laws of Yom Kippur Service.

Putting the Performance of the *Vidui* in Its Context, by Rabbi Ruth Langer, PhD

1. Technically called *s'lichot* (poems of penitence) and *tokh'chot* (poems of rebuke). Note that the American Reform movement's *Gates of Repentance* not only abbreviates but also transposes the order of all these sections.
2. One thinks here most powerfully of the collection of biblical verses recited by the cantor and repeated by the community beginning *Sh'ma koleinu* ("Hear our voice"). Of course, the immediate framing of the *Vidui* itself is inherently petitionary. All of these themes appear also in the various *piyyutim*.
3. I have included significant expansions in square brackets.
4. And probably also line 5, as its proof text comes from the same discussion of the effects of Israelite sin.
5. This last has been omitted in *Mahzor Lev Shalem* in favor of a first passage calling on Hannah as a model of prayer.
6. *Mahzor Lev Shalem*, 239, 386.

Secrets and Silence: The Hidden Power of the Un-confessional *Vidui*, by Rabbi Jay Henry Moses

1. On the dimension of mystery/secrets in the *Zohar*, see Melila Hellner-Eshed, *A River Flows from Eden: The Language of Mystical Experience in the Zohar*, trans. Nathan Wolski (Stanford: Stanford University Press, 2009), 157–88.

The Remembrance of Things Past (and Future), Private (and Public), by Rabbi Aaron D. Panken, PhD

1. Saul Lieberman, *Hellenism in Jewish Palestine* (New York: Jewish Theological Seminary of America, 1994), 140–11.
2. Joseph Tabory, "The Early History of the Liturgy of Yom Kippur," in *The Experience of Jewish Liturgy*, ed. Debra Reed Blank (Leiden: Brill, 2011), 288, and see the notes there.
3. *Shulchan Arukh, Yoreh De'ah* 607:2.

Can "Sin" Be Redeemed? New Metaphors for an Old Problem, by Rabbi Jeffrey K. Salkin, DMin

1. Gary Anderson, *Sin: A History* (New Haven: Yale University Press, 2010), 13.
2. Pinchas H. Peli, trans., *Soloveitchik on Repentance: The Thought and Oral Discourses of Rabbi Joseph B. Soloveitchik* (New York: Paulist Press, 1984), 78.
3. Louis Jacobs, *The Book of Jewish Practice* (West Orange, NJ: Behrman House, 1987), 116.
4. Chaim Stern, ed., *Gates of Repentance: The New Union Prayerbook for the Days of Awe* (New York: Central Conference of American Rabbis, 1978), 106.

"Later He Realizes His Guilt," by Rabbi Jonathan P. Slater, DMin

1. *The JPS Torah Commentary: Leviticus*, commentary by Baruch A. Levine (Philadelphia: Jewish Publication Society, 1989), Varda Books digital edition (2004), 22.

Some Are Guilty, All Are Responsible, by Dr. Ellen M. Umansky

1. Michael S. Kogan, *Opening the Covenant: A Jewish Theology of Christianity* (New York: Oxford University Press, 2008), 26.
2. Abraham Joshua Heschel, "Introduction to Martin Luther King [Jr.] at Riverside [Church NYC] (1967)," in *Abraham Joshua Heschel: Essential Writings*, ed. Susannah Heschel (Maryknoll, NY: Orbis Books, 2011), 83.

Sin, Confession, and … Forgiveness?, by Rabbi Margaret Moers Wenig, DD

1. When I write about "God," I acknowledge that we mortals cannot truly know God; we can only *imagine* God. And the ways in which we imagine God probably say more about us than about God. Language I use for God is figurative.

2. Or, if you wish, "to our better selves."
3. *Machzor Hashaleim L'Rosh Hashanah v'Yom Kippur, High Holiday Prayer Book*, translated and annotated by Philip Birnbaum (New York: Hebrew Publishing Company, 1951), 551, 679, 853, 907.
4. Ibid., 987, 992, 993, 995, 997, 999, 1001.
5. Ibid., 997. Thank you to Cantors Goldstein, Lefkowitz, Mendelson, and Schall for explaining this to me.
6. *Taharah* ("cleansing") alludes here to two forms of cleansing: the cleansing provided by immersion in a *mikveh*, and the washing of a dead body before burial and new life for the soul.
7. This is the verse announcing the day of Yom Kippur.
8. In the stanza of *Un'taneh Tokef* that begins "*Ki kh'shimkha …*" recited by some during the morning service, by others during *Musaf*.
9. With thanks to Steven Rosenberg for his insightful feedback on an earlier draft.

Trying to Say Something, Something: *Magnolia* and Confession, by Dr. Wendy Zierler

1. Franz Rosenzweig presented a similar idea in his essay "Upon the Opening of the Jüdisches Lehrhaus," in which he suggested that a "new learning was about to be born.… It is a learning in reverse order. A learning that no longer starts from the Torah and leads into life, but the other way around: from life, from a world that knows nothing of the Law, or pretends to know nothing, back to the Torah." See Franz Rosenzweig, *On Jewish Learning*, ed. N. N. Galtzer (New York: Schocken Press, 1955), 98.
2. See, for example, Leviticus 16:21, where the high priest is instructed to "lay both his hands upon the head of the live goat, and confess over him [*v'hitvadah alav*] all the iniquities of the children of Israel, and all their transgressions."
3. Maimonides, *Mishneh Torah*, Laws of Repentance 1:3.
4. S. Y. Abramovitsch, "The Little Man," in *Classic Yiddish Stories of S. Y Abramovitsch, Sholem Aleichem and Y. L. Peretz*, ed. Ken Frieden (Syracuse, NY: Syracuse University Press, 2004), 26.
5. Tzvi Luz, "Repentance," in *Contemporary Jewish Religious Thought*, ed. Arthur Cohen and Paul Mendes-Flohr (New York: Free Press, 1988), 787.

Appendix A: The Personal Prayers of the Rabbis (Talmud, Berakhot 16b–17a)

1. Now recited regularly for Shabbat M'vorakhin ("The Sabbath of Blessing"), the Sabbath preceding Rosh Chodesh (the new moon).
2. Presumably because he was the patriarch and the official representative, therefore, to the Roman authorities. Guards were present for his protection, not because he was incarcerated.
3. Now the conclusion to *Al Chet*.

4. Printed editions of the Talmud call him Ham'nuna Zuti; manuscripts call him simply Ham'nuna. It is assumed that he is the same Ham'nuna Zuta as we find mentioned in Yoma 87b, advocating the same prayer. See p. 255.
6. Now recited daily as the silent prayer that follows the *Amidah.*

Appendix B: Confessions of the Rabbis (Talmud, Yoma 87b)

1. This is at least the beginning of the prayer we now say as the introduction to *Al Chet.* Whether our wording in its entirety is exactly what Rav had in mind is possible, but we cannot know for sure.
2. We have no way of knowing how this prayer continues. Its text is lost to us.
3. Probably a citation of Leviticus 16:30, "For on this day, atonement will be made for you to cleanse you of all your sins; you shall be clean before Adonai." We do not know what, if anything, followed.
4. Maimonides suggests the prayer continued as follows: "Not on account of our own righteousness do we cast our supplications before You, but on account of your abundant compassion."
5. See appendix A, p. 253.
6. Clearly, even by the time of the Talmud, no lengthy confessions were yet in place everywhere. The essence of confession—the admission of sin—was sufficient. But the Rabbis were already experimenting with lengthier prayers, and eventually, the long confessions we now have were put together with some of these Rabbinic prototypes to give us our current order of confession. Manuscripts of the Talmud and the first prayer book to quote the confession (*Seder Rav Amram*, c. 860) omit the word *anachnu*. For discussion, see Lawrence A. Hoffman, pp. 13–31, and Elie Kaunfer, pp. 181–185.

Glossary

The glossary presents names and Hebrew words used regularly throughout this volume and provides the way they are pronounced. Sometimes two pronunciations are common, in which case the first is the way the word is sounded in Hebrew, and the second is the way it is sometimes heard in common speech, under the influence of English or, sometimes, of Yiddish, the folk language of Jews in northern and Eastern Europe (a combination, mostly, of Hebrew and German). Our goal is to provide the way that many Jews actually use these words, not just the technically correct version.

- The pronunciations are divided into syllables by dashes.
- The accented syllable is written in capital letters.
- "Kh" represents a guttural sound, similar to the German (as in "sprach").
- The most common vowel is "a" as in "father," which appears here as "ah."
- The short "e" (as in "get") is written as either "e" (when it is in the middle of a syllable) or "eh" (when it ends a syllable).
- Similarly, the short "i" (as in "tin") is written as either "i" (when it is in the middle of a syllable) or "ih" (when it ends a syllable).
- A long "o" (as in "Moses") is written as "oe" (as in the word "toe") or "oh" (as in the word "Oh!").

Adonai (pronounced ah-doh-NA'I): The pronunciation for the tetragrammaton. See **Tetragrammaton**.

Al Chet (pronounced ahl-CHET): Literally, "For the sin," the larger of the two confessions that mark the Yom Kippur liturgy. See ***Vidui Rabbah***.

Alenu (pronounced ah-LAY-noo): The first word and, therefore, the title of a well-known prayer, compiled in the second or third century as part of the New Year (Rosh Hashanah) service, but from about 1300 CE on, used also as a concluding prayer for every daily service. *Alenu* means "it is incumbent upon us ..." and introduces the prayer's theme: our duty to praise God.

Amidah (pronounced either ah-mee-DAH or, commonly, ah-MEE-dah): One of three titles for the second of two central units in the worship service, the first being the *Sh'ma* and Its Blessings. It is composed of a series of blessings, many of which are petitionary, except on Sabbaths and holidays, when the petitions are removed out of deference to the holiness of the day. Also called *T'fillah* (pronounced t'-fee-LAH or, commonly, t'-FEE-lah) and *Sh'moneh Esreh* (pronounced sh'-moh-NEH es-RAY or, commonly, sh'-MOH-neh ES-ray). *Amidah* means "standing," and refers to the fact that the prayer is said standing up.

Amram (pronounced ahm-RAHN, but commonly, AHM-rahm): Rabbi in Baghdad, who authored the first-known comprehensive Jewish prayer book, c. 860 CE.

Ashamnu (pronounced ah-SHAMN-noo): Literally, "We have sinned," the smaller of the two confessions that mark the Yom Kippur liturgy. See ***Vidui Zuta.***

Ashkenazi (pronounced ahsh-k'-nah-ZEE or, commonly, ahsh-k'-NAH-zee): From the Hebrew word *Ashkenaz,* denoting the geographic area of northern and Eastern Europe. Ashkenazi is the adjective, describing not just the inhabitants but also the liturgical rituals and customs practiced there, as opposed to Sephardi (pronounced s'-fahr-DEE or, commonly, s'-FAHR-dee), meaning those derived from *Sefarad,* modern-day Spain and Portugal (see **Sephardi**).

Atah noten yad (pronounced ah-TAH noh-TAYN YAHD): Literally, "You extend a hand," the opening words of the prayer that takes the place of the Long Confession (*Al Chet*) at *N'ilah,* indicating the change in mood from sinful penitence, with which Yom Kippur begins, to divine promise of pardon, with which it ends.

Ba'al Shem Tov (pronounced bah-AHL shem TOHV, or, commonly, BAH-ahl shem TOHV): Literally, "Master of the Good Name," a reference to Rabbi Israel ben Eliezer (Ukraine, 1698–1760), also known as the BeSHT (pronounced besht), an acronym of **Ba**'al **SH**em **T**ov; the founder of modern-day Hasidism.

BaCH (pronounced BAHKH): An acronym of the Hebrew initials for *Bayit Chadash,* the name of a legal commentary to the thirteenth-century law code known as the *Tur*; composed by Rabbi Joel Sirkes of Poland (1561–1640). *BaCH* refers to Sirkes and to his commentary.

Bar'khu (pronounced bah-r'KHU, or, commonly, BAHR'khu): The first word, and, therefore, the title of the formal call to prayer for the morning and evening services. *Bar'khu* means "praise" and introduces the invitation to the assembled congregation to praise God.

Bein adam lachavero / bein adam lamakom (pronounced bayn ah-DAHM l'-chah-vay-ROH / bein ah-DAHM lah-mah-KOHM): Literally, "between one person and another" / "between human beings and God," two categories of relationship and, therefore, two categories of responsibilities and of potential sins for which one is to atone.

Bimah (pronounced bee-MAH or, commonly, BEE-mah): Literally, "stage," "platform," or "pulpit"; in context here, the area in a worship space from which the worship service is led and the Torah publicly read.

Chametz (pronounced khah-MAYTS): Literally, "leaven." Hence, products forbidden on Passover because they are made with wheat, barley, spelt, oats, or rye that may have fermented or leavened through having come into contact with water for more than eighteen minutes.

Charatah (pronounced khah-rah-TAH or, commonly, khah-RAH-tah): Literally, "regret," that is, the regret one feels when recognizing oaths and vows that one has taken and wishes to annul.

Chazzan (pronounced chah-ZAHN, or, commonly CHAH-zahn): Cantor.

Converso (pronounced kon-VEHR-soh): A Jew forced to convert to Christianity during the period of the Spanish Inquisition.

Dayyenu (pronounced dah-YAY-noo): Literally, "It would have been enough," a medieval addition to the liturgy of the Passover Haggadah, listing the various acts of deliverance God bestowed on Israel, beginning with the Exodus from Egypt and culminating in the building of the Temple in Jerusalem. The name derives from the refrain that follows recollection of each act: *Dayyenu!*—"[That deed alone] would have been enough."

Elul (pronounced eh-LOOL, and, commonly EH-lool): The month prior to Rosh Hashanah, and, therefore, a month of penitential prayer and introspection.

Gaon (pronounced gah-OHN; pl. *geonim*, pronounced g'-oh-NEEM): Title for the leading rabbis in Babylon (present-day Iraq) from about 750 to 1038 CE. From a biblical word meaning "glory," equivalent (in the title) to saying, "Your Excellence."

Halakhah (pronounced hah-lah-KHAH or, commonly, hah-LAH-khah): The Hebrew word for Jewish law. Used adjectivally in the anglicized form, "halakhic" (pronounced hah-LAH-khic), meaning "legal." From the Hebrew root *h.l.kh*, meaning "to walk," or "to go," denoting the way one should walk or go through life.

Kaddish (pronounced kah-DEESH or, commonly, KAH-dish): From the Hebrew root *k.d.sh*, meaning "holy," and, therefore, the name given to a first-century prayer affirming God's holiness. It eventually found its way into the service in several forms, including one known as the Mourner's *Kaddish* (*Kaddish Yatom*, pronounced kah-DEESH yah-TOHM). It functions also as a form of oral punctuation, a "Full *Kaddish*" (*Kaddish Shalem*, pronounced kah-DEESH shah-LAYM) representing a complete break between sections (a "period") and the "Half *Kaddish*" (*Chatzi Kaddish*, pronounced khah-TSEE kah-DEESH or, commonly, KHAH-tsee KAH-dish), a minor break (a "semicolon").

Ki anu amekha (pronounced kee ah-NOO an-MEH-khah, but, commonly, kee AH-noo ah-MEH-khah): Literally, "For we are your people," and hence, the poetic introduction to the confessions, affirming the covenantal relationship between God and Israel.

Machzor (pronounced mahkh-ZOHR or, commonly, MAHKH-zohr; pl. *machzorim*, pronounced mahkh-zoh-REEM): Literally, "cycle," as in the annual cycle of time; hence, the name given to the prayer book for holy days that occur once annually and that mark the passing of the year. Separate *machzorim* exist for Rosh Hashanah and Yom Kippur.

Matzah (pronounced mah-TZAH but, commonly, MAH-tzuh): Unleavened bread consumed during Passover as a recollection of the fact that the Israelites hastened out of Egypt without time to let their bread for the journey rise.

M'chilah (pronounced m'-khee-LAH, or, commonly, m'-KHEE-lah): Literally, "forgiveness."

Mikveh (pronounced mihk-VEH, or, commonly MIHK-v'h): Ritual bath.

Minchah (pronounced meen-KHAH or, commonly, MIN-khah): Literally, "afternoon." Originally, the name of a type of sacrifice, but the name now of the afternoon service usually scheduled just before nightfall.

Mitzvah (pronounced meetz-VAH or, commonly, MITZ-vah; pl. *mitzvot*, pronounced meetz-VOHT): A Hebrew word used commonly to mean "good deed," but in the more technical sense, a commandment from God; from its Hebrew root *tz.v.h*, meaning "command."

Musaf (pronounced moo-SAHF or, commonly, MOO-sahf): The Hebrew word meaning "extra" or "added," and, therefore, the title of the additional sacrifice that was offered in the Temple on Shabbat and holy days; now the name given to the additional service of worship appended to the morning service on those days.

Musar (pronounced moo-SAHR, but, commonly, MOO-sahr): Literally, "ethics" or "morality." By extension, a body of literature on ethical behavior, and even a nineteenth-century movement for educational reform that emphasized ethical/spiritual discernment, not just Talmudic learning.

N'ilah (pronounced n'-ee-LAH or, commonly, n'-EE-lah): Literally, "locking," hence, (1) the time at night when the gates to the sacrificial Temple of late antiquity were closed; and (2) an additional worship service that developed then just for fast days, one of which, the final service for Yom Kippur, is still the norm today.

Perut hachet (pronounced pay-ROOT hah-KHEHT): Literally, "specifying the sin," the halakhically required act of stipulating the sin for which one is seeking atonement, rather than requesting blanket forgiveness for sin in general.

Piyyut (pronounced pee-YOOT; pl. *piyyutim*, pronounced pee-yoo-TEEM): A poem. In a liturgical context specifically, poetry added to the main prayers of the liturgy, and embedded in those prayers according to a complex set of rules that combine the nature of the poem in question with the content and structure of the prayer for which it is composed.

Rosh Chodesh (pronounced rohsh KHOH-desh): Literally, "head of the moon or month," hence, the twenty-four-hour holy-day period introduced by the new moon, the first of the month.

Rosh Hashanah (pronounced rohsh hah-shah-NAH or, commonly ROHSH hah-SHAH-nah): Literally, "head of the year," hence, the new year.

Sefer Torah (pronounced SAY-fer toh-RAH or, commonly, SAY-fer TOH-rah; pl. *sifrei Torah* (pronounced seef-RAY toh-RAH or, commonly, SIF-ray-TOH-rah): A Torah scroll.

Sephardi (pronounced s'-fahr-DEE or, commonly, s'-FAHR-dee): From the Hebrew word *Sefarad*, pronounced s'-fah-RAHD), denoting the geographic area of modern-day Spain and Portugal. Sephardi is the adjective describing not just the inhabitants but also the liturgical rituals and customs practiced there, as opposed to Ashkenazi, meaning those derived from *Ashkenaz*, northern and Western Europe (see **Ashkenazi**).

Shabbat Shuvah (pronounced shah-BAHT shuh-VAH, but, commonly, SHAH-baht SHOO-vah): Literally, "the Sabbath of Return," and hence, the Shabbat between Rosh Hashanah and Yom Kippur, given over to the theme of repentance (return to God).

Sh'khinah (pronounced sh'-khee'NAH or, commonly, sh'-KHEE-nah): From the Hebrew root *sh.kh.n*, "to dwell." In Talmudic literature, therefore, the "indwelling" aspect of God, most immediately empathetic to human experience. As the feminine side of God, it appears in Kabbalah as the tenth, and final, emanation.

Shogeg (pronounced shoh-GAYG): "Mistakenly," denoting a sin that has been mistakenly committed. This is the opposite of *mezid* (pronounced may-ZEED).

Shulchan Arukh (pronounced shool-KHAN ah-ROOKH or, commonly, SHOOL-khahn AH-rookh): Literally, "the set table"; a compendium of law written by Joseph Caro (1488–1575), a prominent Sephardi rabbi and mystical teacher in medieval Safed, and published in 1565. The name refers to the ease with which the laws are presented—like a table set with food that is ready for consumption. Rabbi Moses Isserles of Cracow, Poland (1520–1572)—called, also, the *mapa* (pronounced mah-PAH, and meaning "tablecloth")—provided "corrective" glosses that fill in points where Ashkenazi custom differed from Caro's Sephardi practice.

Sifrei Torah: See ***Sefer Torah***.

S'lichah (pronounced s'-lee-KHAH or, commonly s'-LEE-khah; pl. *s'lichot*, pronounced s'-lee-KHOT): Literally, "pardon"; hence, the name given to (1) the blessing for pardon within the daily *Amidah* (see ***Amidah***) and (2) a liturgical poem (*piyyut*, pronounced pee-YOOT) inserted into the liturgy on the theme of pardon (see ***piyyut***).

Tachanun (pronounced TAH-khah-noon): A Hebrew word meaning "supplications," and, therefore, the title of a large unit of prayer that follows the *Amidah*, and which is largely supplicatory in nature.

Tallit (pronounced tah-LEET or, commonly, TAH-lis): The prayer shawl worn for morning worship, featuring tassels called *tzitzit* (pronounced tsee-TSEET or, commonly, TSIH-tsis) on the corners. See ***tzitzit***. In context here, worn also for just one evening service in the year, the one introduced by *Kol Nidre*.

T'fillah (pronounced t'-fee-LAH or, commonly, t'-FEE-lah): A Hebrew word meaning "prayer," but used technically to denote a specific prayer, namely, the second of the two main units in the worship service; known also as the *Amidah* or the *Sh'moneh Esreh* (see ***Amidah***). Also the title of the sixteenth blessing of the *Amidah*, a petition for God to accept our prayer.

Thirteen attributes: Attributes of God mentioned in Exodus 34:6–7, taken to be God's thirteen attributes of mercy, and recited liturgically, especially on the High Holy Days, as a reminder that God approaches sin and sinners with divine compassion, and that God (according to the Talmud) has even made a covenant with us with the thirteen attributes at the center.

Tikkun olam (pronounced tee-KOON oh-LAHM, but, commonly, TEE-koon oh-LAHM): Literally, "correction of the world," a term from late antiquity that takes on special resonance with medieval Kabbalah as the act of ending (or, correcting) the world's evil; used nowadays as a generalized term for social action or social justice.

Tokh'chah (pronounced toh-kh'KHAH): Literally, "admonition," the act of admonishing someone against sin.

T'shuvah (pronounced t'-shoo-VAH or, commonly, t'-SHOO-vah): Literally "repentance"; also the title of the fifth blessing in the daily *Amidah*, a petition by worshipers that they successfully turn to God in heartfelt repentance.

Tur (pronounced TOOR): The shorthand title applied to the fourteenth-century code of Jewish law compiled by Jacob Ben Asher of Spain, and the source for much of our knowledge about medieval liturgical practice. *Tur* means "row" or "column." The full name of the code is *Arba'ah Turim* (pronounced ahr-bah-AH too-REEM), "The Four Rows," with each row (or *tur*) being a separate section of law on a given broad topic.

Tz'dakah (pronounced ts'-dah-KAH or, commonly, ts'-DAH-kah): Charity.

Un'taneh Tokef (pronounced oo-n'-TAH-neh TOH-kehf): A *piyyut* (liturgical poem) for the High Holy Days emphasizing the awesome nature of these days when we stand before God for judgment; but originally, the climactic part of a longer poem for the *Amidah* called *k'dushta* (pronounced k'-doosh-TAH or, commonly, k'-DOOSH-tah). Although widely connected with a legend of Jewish martyrdom in medieval Germany, the poem more likely derives from a Byzantine poet, circa sixth century. It is known for its conclusion: "Penitence, prayer, and charity help the misfortune of the decree pass." See full treatment in Rabbi Lawrence A. Hoffman, PhD, ed., *Who by Fire, Who by Water—Un'taneh Tokef* (Woodstock, VT: Jewish Lights Publishing, 2010).

Vidui (pronounced vee-DOO'i): Literally, "confession."

Vidui Rabbah (pronounced vee-DOO'i rah-BAH, but, commonly, VEE-doo'i RAH-bah): Literally, "long" or "great confession," and, hence, the name of the larger of the two confessions that mark the Yom Kippur liturgy. Also known as *Al Chet* ("For the sin..."), the opening two Hebrew words of the prayer.

Vidui Zuta (pronounced vee-DOO'i zoo-TAH, but, commonly, VEE-doo'i ZOO-tah): Literally, "short confession," and, hence, the name of the smaller of the two confessions that mark the Yom Kippur liturgy. Also known as *Ashamnu* ("We have sinned"), the opening Hebrew word of the prayer.

Yetzer (pronounced YAY-tser): A psychological inclination. According to the Rabbis, all human beings have two of them, a *yetzer hatov* (pronounced YAY-tser hah-TOHV) and a *yetzer hara* (pronounced YAY-tser hah-RAH), a "good" and an "evil" inclination that struggle within us for moral dominance, as we act in the world.

Yom Hakippurim (pronounced YOHM hah-kee-poo-REEM): The formal Rabbinic term for "Day of Atonement," nowadays, shortened in common speech to Yom Kippur.

Yom Kippur (pronounced yohm kee-POOR or, commonly, yohm KIH-p'r): Day of Atonement.

Z'khut avot (pronounced z'-KHOOT ah-VOHT): Literally, "merit of the fathers," the classic theological doctrine of the Rabbis that attributes merit to our ancestors (primarily Abraham, Isaac, and Jacob), that we (who are more sinful than they and who, therefore, have little merit of our own) may draw upon to provide pardon for our sins.

Bar/Bat Mitzvah

The Mitzvah Project Book
Making Mitzvah Part of Your Bar/Bat Mitzvah ... and Your Life
By Liz Suneby and Diane Heiman; Foreword by Rabbi Jeffrey K. Salkin; Preface by Rabbi Sharon Brous
The go-to source for Jewish young adults and their families looking to make the world a better place through good deeds—big or small.
6 x 9, 224 pp, Quality PB Original, 978-1-58023-458-0 **$16.99** For ages 11–13

The Bar/Bat Mitzvah Memory Book, 2nd Edition: An Album for Treasuring the Spiritual Celebration
By Rabbi Jeffrey K. Salkin and Nina Salkin
8 x 10, 48 pp, 2-color text, Deluxe HC, ribbon marker, 978-1-58023-263-0 **$19.99**

For Kids—Putting God on Your Guest List, 2nd Edition: How to Claim the Spiritual Meaning of Your Bar or Bat Mitzvah *By Rabbi Jeffrey K. Salkin*
6 x 9, 144 pp, Quality PB, 978-1-58023-308-8 **$15.99** For ages 11–13

The Jewish Prophet: Visionary Words from Moses and Miriam to Henrietta Szold and A. J. Heschel *By Rabbi Dr. Michael J. Shire*
6½ x 8½, 128 pp, 123 full-color illus., HC, 978-1-58023-168-8 **$14.95**

Putting God on the Guest List, 3rd Edition: How to Reclaim the Spiritual Meaning of Your Child's Bar or Bat Mitzvah *By Rabbi Jeffrey K. Salkin*
6 x 9, 224 pp, Quality PB, 978-1-58023-222-7 **$16.99**; HC, 978-1-58023-260-9 **$24.99**

Putting God on the Guest List Teacher's Guide
8½ x 11, 48 pp, PB, 978-1-58023-226-5 **$8.99**

Teens / Young Adults

Text Messages: A Torah Commentary for Teens
Edited by Rabbi Jeffrey K. Salkin
Shows today's teens how each Torah portion contains worlds of meaning for them, for what they are going through in their lives, and how they can shape their Jewish identity as they enter adulthood.
6 x 9, 304 pp (est), HC, 978-1-58023-507-5 **$24.99**

Hannah Senesh: Her Life and Diary, the First Complete Edition
By Hannah Senesh; Foreword by Marge Piercy; Preface by Eitan Senesh; Afterword by Roberta Grossman
6 x 9, 368 pp, b/w photos, Quality PB, 978-1-58023-342-2 **$19.99**

I Am Jewish: Personal Reflections Inspired by the Last Words of Daniel Pearl
Edited by Judea and Ruth Pearl 6 x 9, 304 pp, Deluxe PB w/ flaps, 978-1-58023-259-3 $18.99
Download a free copy of the ***I Am Jewish Teacher's Guide*** at www.jewishlights.com.

The JGirl's Guide: The Young Jewish Woman's Handbook for Coming of Age
By Penina Adelman, Ali Feldman and Shulamit Reinharz
6 x 9, 240 pp, Quality PB, 978-1-58023-215-9 **$14.99** For ages 11 & up

The JGirl's Teacher's and Parent's Guide
8½ x 11, 56 pp, PB, 978-1-58023-225-8 **$8.99**

Tough Questions Jews Ask, 2nd Edition: A Young Adult's Guide to Building a Jewish Life *By Rabbi Edward Feinstein*
6 x 9, 160 pp, Quality PB, 978-1-58023-454-2 **$16.99** For ages 11 & up

Tough Questions Jews Ask Teacher's Guide
8½ x 11, 72 pp, PB, 978-1-58023-187-9 **$8.95**

Pre-Teens

Be Like God: God's To-Do List for Kids
By Dr. Ron Wolfson
Encourages kids ages eight through twelve to use their God-given superpowers to find the many ways they can make a difference in the lives of others and find meaning and purpose for their own.
7 x 9, 144 pp, Quality PB, 978-1-58023-510-5 **$15.99** For ages 8–12

The Book of Miracles: A Young Person's Guide to Jewish Spiritual Awareness
By Lawrence Kushner, with all-new illustrations by the author.
6 x 9, 96 pp, 2-color illus., HC, 978-1-879045-78-1 **$16.95** For ages 9–13

Congregation Resources

A Practical Guide to Rabbinic Counseling
Edited by Rabbi Yisrael N. Levitz, PhD, and Rabbi Abraham J. Twerski, MD
Provides rabbis with the requisite knowledge and practical guidelines for some of the most common counseling situations.
6 x 9, 432 pp, HC, 978-1-58023-562-4 **$40.00**

Professional Spiritual & Pastoral Care: A Practical Clergy and Chaplain's Handbook
Edited by Rabbi Stephen B. Roberts, MBA, MHL, BCJC
An essential resource integrating the classic foundations of pastoral care with the latest approaches to spiritual care, specifically intended for professionals who work or spend time with congregants in acute care hospitals, behavioral health facilities, rehabilitation centers and long-term care facilities.
6 x 9, 480 pp, HC, 978-1-59473-312-3 **$50.00**

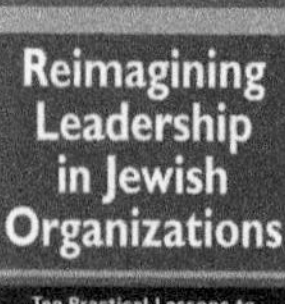

Reimagining Leadership in Jewish Organizations: Ten Practical Lessons to Help You Implement Change and Achieve Your Goals
By Dr. Misha Galperin
Serves as a practical guidepost for lay and professional leaders to evaluate the current paradigm with insights from the world of business, psychology and research in Jewish demographics and sociology. Supported by vignettes from the field that illustrate the successes of the lessons as well as the consequences of not implementing them.
6 x 9, 192 pp, Quality PB, 978-1-58023-492-4 **$16.99**

Empowered Judaism: What Independent Minyanim Can Teach Us about Building Vibrant Jewish Communities
By Rabbi Elie Kaunfer; Foreword by Prof. Jonathan D. Sarna
6 x 9, 224 pp, Quality PB, 978-1-58023-412-2 **$18.99**

Building a Successful Volunteer Culture: Finding Meaning in Service in the Jewish Community *By Rabbi Charles Simon; Foreword by Shelley Lindauer; Preface by Dr. Ron Wolfson*
6 x 9, 192 pp, Quality PB, 978-1-58023-408-5 **$16.99**

The Case for Jewish Peoplehood: Can We Be One?
By Dr. Erica Brown and Dr. Misha Galperin; Foreword by Rabbi Joseph Telushkin
6 x 9, 224 pp, HC, 978-1-58023-401-6 **$21.99**

Finding a Spiritual Home: How a New Generation of Jews Can Transform the American Synagogue *By Rabbi Sidney Schwarz*
6 x 9, 352 pp, Quality PB, 978-1-58023-185-5 **$19.95**

Inspired Jewish Leadership: Practical Approaches to Building Strong Communities
By Dr. Erica Brown 6 x 9, 256 pp, HC, 978-1-58023-361-3 **$27.99**

Jewish Pastoral Care, 2nd Edition: A Practical Handbook from Traditional & Contemporary Sources *Edited by Rabbi Dayle A. Friedman, MSW, MAJCS, BCC*
6 x 9, 528 pp, Quality PB, 978-1-58023-427-6 **$30.00**

Jewish Spiritual Direction: An Innovative Guide from Traditional and Contemporary Sources
Edited by Rabbi Howard A. Addison, PhD, and Barbara Eve Breitman, MSW
6 x 9, 368 pp, HC, 978-1-58023-230-2 **$30.00**

Rethinking Synagogues: A New Vocabulary for Congregational Life
By Rabbi Lawrence A. Hoffman, PhD 6 x 9, 240 pp, Quality PB, 978-1-58023-248-7 **$19.99**

Spiritual Community: The Power to Restore Hope, Commitment and Joy
By Rabbi David A. Teutsch, PhD
5½ x 8½, 144 pp, HC, 978-1-58023-270-8 **$19.99**

Spiritual Boredom: Rediscovering the Wonder of Judaism By Dr. Erica Brown
6 x 9, 208 pp, HC, 978-1-58023-405-4 **$21.99**

The Spirituality of Welcoming: How to Transform Your Congregation into a Sacred Community *By Dr. Ron Wolfson* 6 x 9, 224 pp, Quality PB, 978-1-58023-244-9 **$19.99**

Children's Books

Around the World in One Shabbat
Jewish People Celebrate the Sabbath Together
By Durga Yael Bernhard
Takes your child on a colorful adventure to share the many ways Jewish people celebrate Shabbat around the world.
11 x 8½, 32 pp, Full-color illus., HC, 978-1-58023-433-7 **$18.99** *For ages 3–6*

It's a … It's a … It's a Mitzvah
By Liz Suneby and Diane Heiman; Full-color Illus. by Laurel Molk
Join Mitzvah Meerkat and friends as they introduce children to the everyday kindnesses that mark the beginning of a Jewish journey and a lifetime commitment to *tikkun olam* (repairing the world). 9 x 12, 32 pp, Full-color illus., HC, 978-1-58023-509-9 **$18.99** *For ages 3–6*

What You Will See Inside a Synagogue
By Rabbi Lawrence A. Hoffman, PhD, and Dr. Ron Wolfson; Full-color photos by Bill Aron
A colorful, fun-to-read introduction that explains the ways and whys of Jewish worship and religious life. 8½ x 10½, 32 pp, Full-color photos, Quality PB, 978-1-59473-256-0 **$8.99** *For ages 6 & up*
(A book from SkyLight Paths, Jewish Lights' sister imprint)

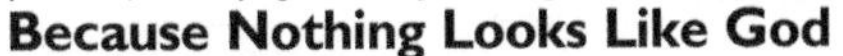

Because Nothing Looks Like God
By Lawrence Kushner and Karen Kushner
Real-life examples of happiness and sadness—from goodnight stories, to the hope and fear felt the first time at bat, to the closing moments of someone's life—invite parents and children to explore, together, the questions we all have about God, no matter what our age. 11 x 8½, 32 pp, Full-color illus., HC, 978-1-58023-092-6 **$18.99** *For ages 4 & up*

The Book of Miracles: A Young Person's Guide to Jewish Spiritual Awareness
Written and illus. by Lawrence Kushner
Easy-to-read, imaginatively illustrated book encourages kids' awareness of their own spirituality. Revealing the essence of Judaism in a language they can understand and enjoy. 6 x 9, 96 pp, 2-color illus., HC, 978-1-879045-78-1 **$16.95** *For ages 9–13*

In God's Hands *By Lawrence Kushner and Gary Schmidt*
Brings new life to a traditional Jewish folktale, reminding parents and kids of all faiths and all backgrounds that each of us has the power to make the world a better place—working ordinary miracles with our everyday deeds.
9 x 12, 32 pp, Full-color illus., HC, 978-1-58023-224-1 **$16.99** For ages 5 & up

In Our Image: God's First Creatures
By Nancy Sohn Swartz
A playful new twist to the Genesis story, God asks all of nature to offer gifts to humankind—with a promise that the humans would care for creation in return. 9 x 12, 32 pp, Full-color illus., HC, 978-1-879045-99-6 **$16.95** *For ages 4 & up*

The Jewish Family Fun Book, 2nd Ed.
Holiday Projects, Everyday Activities, and Travel Ideas with Jewish Themes
By Danielle Dardashti and Roni Sarig
The complete sourcebook for families wanting to put a new spin on activities for Jewish holidays, holy days and the everyday. It offers dozens of easy-to-do activities that bring Jewish tradition to life for kids of all ages.
6 x 9, 304 pp, w/ 70+ b/w illus., Quality PB, 978-1-58023-333-0 **$18.99**

The Kids' Fun Book of Jewish Time *By Emily Sper*
A unique way to introduce children to the Jewish calendar—night and day, the seven-day week, Shabbat, the Hebrew months, seasons and dates.
9 x 7½, 24 pp, Full-color illus., HC, 978-1-58023-311-8 **$16.99** *For ages 3–6*

What Makes Someone a Jew? *By Lauren Seidman*
Reflects the changing face of American Judaism. Helps preschoolers and young readers (ages 3–6) understand that you don't have to look a certain way to be Jewish. 10 x 8½, 32 pp, Full-color photos, Quality PB, 978-1-58023-321-7 **$8.99** *For ages 3–6*

When a Grandparent Dies: A Kid's Own Remembering Workbook for Dealing with Shiva and the Year Beyond *By Nechama Liss-Levinson*
8 x 10, 48 pp, 2-color text, HC, 978-1-879045-44-6 **$15.95** *For ages 7–13*

Children's Books by Sandy Eisenberg Sasso

The *Shema* in the Mezuzah: Listening to Each Other
By Sandy Eisenberg Sasso; Full-color Illus. by Joani Keller Rothenberg
This playful yet profound story of conflict and compromise introduces children ages 3 to 6 to the words of the *Shema* and the custom of putting up the mezuzah.
9 x 12, 32 pp, Full-color illus., HC, 978-1-58023-506-8 **$18.99**

Adam & Eve's First Sunset: God's New Day
Explores fear and hope, faith and gratitude in ways that will delight kids and adults—inspiring us to bless each of God's days and nights.
9 x 12, 32 pp, Full-color illus., HC, 978-1-58023-177-0 **$17.95** *For ages 4 & up*
Also Available as a Board Book: **Adam and Eve's New Day**
5 x 5, 24 pp, Full-color illus., Board Book, 978-1-59473-205-8 **$7.99** *For ages 0–4*
(A book from SkyLight Paths, Jewish Lights' sister imprint)

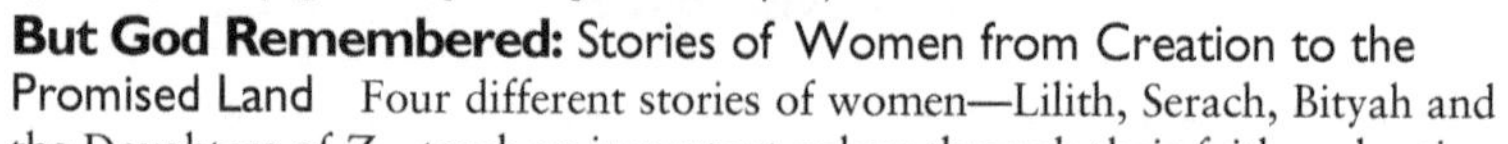

But God Remembered: Stories of Women from Creation to the Promised Land Four different stories of women—Lilith, Serach, Bityah and the Daughters of Z—teach us important values through their faith and actions.
9 x 12, 32 pp, Full-color illus., Quality PB, 978-1-58023-372-9 **$8.99** *For ages 8 & up*

For Heaven's Sake
Heaven is often found where you least expect it.
9 x 12, 32 pp, Full-color illus., HC, 978-1-58023-054-4 **$16.95** *For ages 4 & up*

God in Between
If you wanted to find God, where would you look? This magical, mythical tale teaches that God can be found where we are: within all of us and the relationships between us. 9 x 12, 32 pp, Full-color illus., HC, 978-1-879045-86-6 **$16.95** *For ages 4 & up*

God Said Amen
An inspiring story about hearing the answers to our prayers.
9 x 12, 32 pp, Full-color illus., HC, 978-1-58023-080-3 **$16.95** *For ages 4 & up*

God's Paintbrush: Special 10th Anniversary Edition
Wonderfully interactive, invites children of all faiths and backgrounds to encounter God through moments in their own lives. Provides questions adult and child can explore together. 11 x 8½, 32 pp, Full-color illus., HC, 978-1-58023-195-4 **$17.95** *For ages 4 & up*
Also Available as a Board Book: **I Am God's Paintbrush**
5 x 5, 24 pp, Full-color illus., Board Book, 978-1-59473-265-2 **$7.99** *For ages 0–4*
(A book from SkyLight Paths, Jewish Lights' sister imprint)
Also Available: **God's Paintbrush Teacher's Guide**
8½ x 11, 32 pp, PB, 978-1-879045-57-6 **$8.95**
God's Paintbrush Celebration Kit
A Spiritual Activity Kit for Teachers and Students of All Faiths, All Backgrounds
9½ x 12, 40 Full-color Activity Sheets & Teacher Folder w/ complete instructions
HC, 978-1-58023-050-6 **$21.95**
8-Student Activity Sheet Pack (40 sheets/5 sessions), 978-1-58023-058-2 **$19.95**

In God's Name
Like an ancient myth in its poetic text and vibrant illustrations, this award-winning modern fable about the search for God's name celebrates the diversity and, at the same time, the unity of all people.
9 x 12, 32 pp, Full-color illus., HC, 978-1-879045-26-2 **$16.99** *For ages 4 & up*
Also Available as a Board Book: **What Is God's Name?**
5 x 5, 24 pp, Full-color illus., Board Book, 978-1-893361-10-2 **$7.99** *For ages 0–4*
(A book from SkyLight Paths, Jewish Lights' sister imprint)
Also Available in Spanish: **El nombre de Dios**
9 x 12, 32 pp, Full-color illus., HC, 978-1-893361-63-8 **$16.95** *For ages 4 & up*

Noah's Wife: The Story of Naamah
9 x 12, 32 pp, Full-color illus., HC, 978-1-58023-134-3 **$16.95** *For ages 4 & up*
Also Available as a Board Book: **Naamah, Noah's Wife**
5 x 5, 24 pp, Full-color illus., Board Book, 978-1-893361-56-0 **$7.95** *For ages 0–4*
(A book from SkyLight Paths, Jewish Lights' sister imprint)

Ecology/Environment

A Wild Faith: Jewish Ways into Wilderness, Wilderness Ways into Judaism
By Rabbi Mike Comins; Foreword by Nigel Savage 6 x 9, 240 pp, Quality PB, 978-1-58023-316-3 **$16.99**

Ecology & the Jewish Spirit: Where Nature & the Sacred Meet
Edited by Ellen Bernstein 6 x 9, 288 pp, Quality PB, 978-1-58023-082-7 **$18.99**

Torah of the Earth: Exploring 4,000 Years of Ecology in Jewish Thought
Vol. 1: Biblical Israel & Rabbinic Judaism; Vol. 2: Zionism & Eco-Judaism
Edited by Rabbi Arthur Waskow Vol. 1: 6 x 9, 272 pp, Quality PB, 978-1-58023-086-5 **$19.95**
Vol. 2: 6 x 9, 336 pp, Quality PB, 978-1-58023-087-2 **$19.95**

The Way Into Judaism and the Environment *By Jeremy Benstein, PhD*
6 x 9, 288 pp, Quality PB, 978-1-58023-368-2 **$18.99**; HC, 978-1-58023-268-5 **$24.99**

Graphic Novels/Graphic History

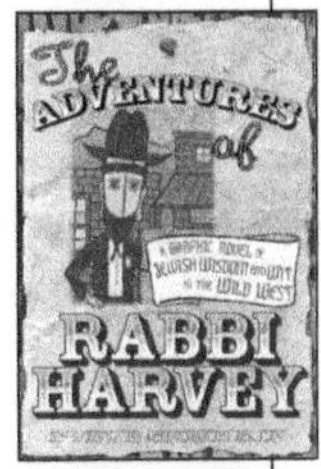

The Adventures of Rabbi Harvey: A Graphic Novel of Jewish Wisdom and Wit in the Wild West *By Steve Sheinkin* 6 x 9, 144 pp, Full-color illus., Quality PB, 978-1-58023-310-1 **$16.99**

Rabbi Harvey Rides Again: A Graphic Novel of Jewish Folktales Let Loose in the Wild West *By Steve Sheinkin* 6 x 9, 144 pp, Full-color illus., Quality PB, 978-1-58023-347-7 **$16.99**

Rabbi Harvey vs. the Wisdom Kid: A Graphic Novel of Dueling Jewish Folktales in the Wild West *By Steve Sheinkin*
Rabbi Harvey's first book-length adventure—and toughest challenge.
6 x 9, 144 pp, Full-color illus., Quality PB, 978-1-58023-422-1 **$16.99**

The Story of the Jews: A 4,000-Year Adventure—A Graphic History Book
By Stan Mack 6 x 9, 288 pp, Illus., Quality PB, 978-1-58023-155-8 **$16.99**

Grief/Healing

Facing Illness, Finding God: How Judaism Can Help You and Caregivers Cope When Body or Spirit Fails *By Rabbi Joseph B. Meszler*
Will help you find spiritual strength for healing amid the fear, pain and chaos of illness. 6 x 9, 208 pp, Quality PB, 978-1-58023-423-8 **$16.99**

Midrash & Medicine: Healing Body and Soul in the Jewish Interpretive Tradition *Edited by Rabbi William Cutter, PhD; Foreword by Michele F. Prince, LCSW, MAJCS*
Explores how midrash can help you see beyond the physical aspects of healing to tune in to your spiritual source.
6 x 9, 352 pp, Quality PB, 978-1-58023-484-9 **$21.99**

Healing from Despair: Choosing Wholeness in a Broken World
By Rabbi Elie Kaplan Spitz with Erica Shapiro Taylor; Foreword by Abraham J. Twerski, MD
5½ x 8½, 208 pp, Quality PB, 978-1-58023-436-8 **$16.99**

Healing and the Jewish Imagination: Spiritual and Practical Perspectives on Judaism and Health *Edited by Rabbi William Cutter, PhD*
6 x 9, 240 pp, Quality PB, 978-1-58023-373-6 **$19.99**

Grief in Our Seasons: A Mourner's Kaddish Companion *By Rabbi Kerry M. Olitzky*
4½ x 6½, 448 pp, Quality PB, 978-1-879045-55-2 **$15.95**

Healing of Soul, Healing of Body: Spiritual Leaders Unfold the Strength & Solace in Psalms *Edited by Rabbi Simkha Y. Weintraub, LCSW*
6 x 9, 128 pp, 2-color illus. text, Quality PB, 978-1-879045-31-6 **$16.99**

Mourning & Mitzvah, 2nd Edition: A Guided Journal for Walking the Mourner's Path through Grief to Healing *By Rabbi Anne Brener, LCSW*
7½ x 9, 304 pp, Quality PB, 978-1-58023-113-8 **$19.99**

Tears of Sorrow, Seeds of Hope, 2nd Edition: A Jewish Spiritual Companion for Infertility and Pregnancy Loss *By Rabbi Nina Beth Cardin*
6 x 9, 208 pp, Quality PB, 978-1-58023-233-3 **$18.99**

A Time to Mourn, a Time to Comfort, 2nd Edition: A Guide to Jewish Bereavement *By Dr. Ron Wolfson; Foreword by Rabbi David J. Wolpe*
7 x 9, 384 pp, Quality PB, 978-1-58023-253-1 **$21.99**

When a Grandparent Dies: A Kid's Own Remembering Workbook for Dealing with Shiva and the Year Beyond *By Nechama Liss-Levinson, PhD*
8 x 10, 48 pp, 2-color text, HC, 978-1-879045-44-6 **$15.95** *For ages 7–13*

Inspiration

God of Me: Imagining God throughout Your Lifetime
By Rabbi David Lyon Helps you cut through preconceived ideas of God and dogmas that stifle your creativity when thinking about your personal relationship with God. 6 x 9, 176 pp, Quality PB, 978-1-58023-452-8 **$16.99**

The God Upgrade: Finding Your 21st-Century Spirituality in Judaism's 5,000-Year-Old Tradition *By Rabbi Jamie Korngold; Foreword by Rabbi Harold M. Schulweis*
A provocative look at how our changing God concepts have shaped every aspect of Judaism. 6 x 9, 176 pp, Quality PB, 978-1-58023-443-6 **$15.99**

The Seven Questions You're Asked in Heaven: Reviewing and Renewing Your Life on Earth *By Dr. Ron Wolfson* An intriguing and entertaining resource for living a life that matters. 6 x 9, 176 pp, Quality PB, 978-1-58023-407-8 **$16.99**

Happiness and the Human Spirit: The Spirituality of Becoming the Best You Can Be *By Rabbi Abraham J. Twerski, MD*
Shows you that true happiness is attainable once you stop looking outside yourself for the source. 6 x 9, 176 pp, Quality PB, 978-1-58023-404-7 **$16.99**; HC, 978-1-58023-343-9 **$19.99**

A Formula for Proper Living: Practical Lessons from Life and Torah
By Rabbi Abraham J. Twerski, MD 6 x 9, 144 pp, HC, 978-1-58023-402-3 **$19.99**

The Bridge to Forgiveness: Stories and Prayers for Finding God and Restoring Wholeness *By Rabbi Karyn D. Kedar* 6 x 9, 176 pp, Quality PB, 978-1-58023-451-1 **$16.99**

The Empty Chair: Finding Hope and Joy—Timeless Wisdom from a Hasidic Master, Rebbe Nachman of Breslov *Adapted by Moshe Mykoff and the Breslov Research Institute*
4 x 6, 128 pp, Deluxe PB w/ flaps, 978-1-879045-67-5 **$9.99**

The Gentle Weapon: Prayers for Everyday and Not-So-Everyday Moments—Timeless Wisdom from the Teachings of the Hasidic Master, Rebbe Nachman of Breslov
Adapted by Moshe Mykoff and S. C. Mizrahi, together with the Breslov Research Institute
4 x 6, 144 pp, Deluxe PB w/ flaps, 978-1-58023-022-3 **$9.99**

God Whispers: Stories of the Soul, Lessons of the Heart *By Rabbi Karyn D. Kedar*
6 x 9, 176 pp, Quality PB, 978-1-58023-088-9 **$15.95**

God's To-Do List: 103 Ways to Be an Angel and Do God's Work on Earth
By Dr. Ron Wolfson 6 x 9, 144 pp, Quality PB, 978-1-58023-301-9 **$16.99**

Jewish Stories from Heaven and Earth: Inspiring Tales to Nourish the Heart and Soul *Edited by Rabbi Dov Peretz Elkins* 6 x 9, 304 pp, Quality PB, 978-1-58023-363-7 **$16.99**

Life's Daily Blessings: Inspiring Reflections on Gratitude and Joy for Every Day, Based on Jewish Wisdom *By Rabbi Kerry M. Olitzky* 4½ x 6½, 368 pp, Quality PB, 978-1-58023-396-5 **$16.99**

Restful Reflections: Nighttime Inspiration to Calm the Soul, Based on Jewish Wisdom
By Rabbi Kerry M. Olitzky and Rabbi Lori Forman-Jacobi 5 x 8, 352 pp, Quality PB, 978-1-58023-091-9 **$16.99**

Sacred Intentions: Morning Inspiration to Strengthen the Spirit, Based on Jewish Wisdom
By Rabbi Kerry M. Olitzky and Rabbi Lori Forman-Jacobi 4½ x 6½, 448 pp, Quality PB, 978-1-58023-061-2 **$16.99**

Kabbalah/Mysticism

Jewish Mysticism and the Spiritual Life: Classical Texts, Contemporary Reflections *Edited by Dr. Lawrence Fine, Dr. Eitan Fishbane and Rabbi Or N. Rose*
Inspirational and thought-provoking materials for contemplation, discussion and action. 6 x 9, 256 pp, HC, 978-1-58023-434-4 **$24.99**

Ehyeh: A Kabbalah for Tomorrow
By Rabbi Arthur Green, PhD 6 x 9, 224 pp, Quality PB, 978-1-58023-213-5 **$18.99**

The Gift of Kabbalah: Discovering the Secrets of Heaven, Renewing Your Life on Earth
By Tamar Frankiel, PhD 6 x 9, 256 pp, Quality PB, 978-1-58023-141-1 **$16.95**

Seek My Face: A Jewish Mystical Theology *By Rabbi Arthur Green, PhD*
6 x 9, 304 pp, Quality PB, 978-1-58023-130-5 **$19.95**

Zohar: Annotated & Explained *Translation & Annotation by Dr. Daniel C. Matt; Foreword by Andrew Harvey* 5½ x 8½, 176 pp, Quality PB, 978-1-893361-51-5 **$15.99**
(A book from SkyLight Paths, Jewish Lights' sister imprint)

See also *The Way Into Jewish Mystical Tradition* in The Way Into… Series.

Holidays/Holy Days

Prayers of Awe Series

An exciting new series that examines the High Holy Day liturgy to enrich the praying experience of everyone—whether experienced worshipers or guests who encounter Jewish prayer for the very first time.

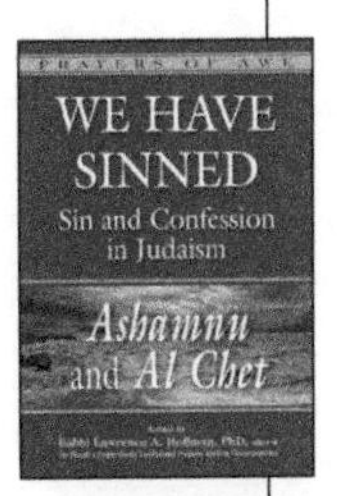

We Have Sinned—Sin and Confession in Judaism: *Ashamnu* and *Al Chet*
Edited by Rabbi Lawrence A. Hoffman, PhD
A varied and fascinating look at sin, confession and pardon in Judaism, as suggested by the centrality of *Ashamnu* and *Al Chet*, two prayers that people know so well, though understand so little. 6 x 9, 304 pp, HC, 978-1-58023-612-6 **$24.99**

Who by Fire, Who by Water—*Un'taneh Tokef*
Edited by Rabbi Lawrence A. Hoffman, PhD 6 x 9, 272 pp, HC, 978-1-58023-424-5 **$24.99**

All These Vows—*Kol Nidre*
Edited by Rabbi Lawrence A. Hoffman, PhD 6 x 9, 288 pp, HC, 978-1-58023-430-6 **$24.99**

Rosh Hashanah Readings: Inspiration, Information and Contemplation
Yom Kippur Readings: Inspiration, Information and Contemplation
Edited by Rabbi Dov Peretz Elkins; Section Introductions from Arthur Green's These Are the Words
Rosh Hashanah: 6 x 9, 400 pp, Quality PB, 978-1-58023-437-5 **$19.99**
Yom Kippur: 6 x 9, 368 pp, Quality PB, 978-1-58023-438-2 **$19.99**; HC, 978-1-58023-271-5 **$24.99**

Reclaiming Judaism as a Spiritual Practice: Holy Days and Shabbat
By Rabbi Goldie Milgram 7 x 9, 272 pp, Quality PB, 978-1-58023-205-0 **$19.99**

The Sabbath Soul: Mystical Reflections on the Transformative Power of Holy Time
Selection, Translation and Commentary by Eitan Fishbane, PhD
6 x 9, 208 pp, Quality PB, 978-1-58023-459-7 **$18.99**

Shabbat, 2nd Edition: The Family Guide to Preparing for and Celebrating the Sabbath
By Dr. Ron Wolfson 7 x 9, 320 pp, Illus., Quality PB, 978-1-58023-164-0 **$19.99**

Hanukkah, 2nd Edition: The Family Guide to Spiritual Celebration
By Dr. Ron Wolfson 7 x 9, 240 pp, Illus., Quality PB, 978-1-58023-122-0 **$18.95**

Passover

My People's Passover Haggadah
Traditional Texts, Modern Commentaries
Edited by Rabbi Lawrence A. Hoffman, PhD, and David Arnow, PhD
A diverse and exciting collection of commentaries on the traditional Passover Haggadah—in two volumes!
Vol. 1: 7 x 10, 304 pp, HC, 978-1-58023-354-5 **$24.99**
Vol. 2: 7 x 10, 320 pp, HC, 978-1-58023-346-0 **$24.99**

Freedom Journeys: The Tale of Exodus and Wilderness across Millennia
By Rabbi Arthur O. Waskow and Rabbi Phyllis O. Berman
Explores how the story of Exodus echoes in our own time, calling us to relearn and rethink the Passover story through social-justice, ecological, feminist and interfaith perspectives. 6 x 9, 288 pp, HC, 978-1-58023-445-0 **$24.99**

Leading the Passover Journey: The Seder's Meaning Revealed, the Haggadah's Story Retold *By Rabbi Nathan Laufer*
Uncovers the hidden meaning of the Seder's rituals and customs.
6 x 9, 224 pp, Quality PB, 978-1-58023-399-6 **$18.99**

Creating Lively Passover Seders, 2nd Edition: A Sourcebook of Engaging Tales, Texts & Activities *By David Arnow, PhD* 7 x 9, 464 pp, Quality PB, 978-1-58023-444-3 **$24.99**

Passover, 2nd Edition: The Family Guide to Spiritual Celebration
By Dr. Ron Wolfson with Joel Lurie Grishaver 7 x 9, 416 pp, Quality PB, 978-1-58023-174-9 **$19.95**

The Women's Passover Companion: Women's Reflections on the Festival of Freedom
Edited by Rabbi Sharon Cohen Anisfeld, Tara Mohr and Catherine Spector; Foreword by Paula E. Hyman
6 x 9, 352 pp, Quality PB, 978-1-58023-231-9 **$19.99**; HC, 978-1-58023-128-2 **$24.95**

The Women's Seder Sourcebook: Rituals & Readings for Use at the Passover Seder
Edited by Rabbi Sharon Cohen Anisfeld, Tara Mohr and Catherine Spector
6 x 9, 384 pp, Quality PB, 978-1-58023-232-6 **$19.99**

Life Cycle

Marriage/Parenting/Family/Aging

The New Jewish Baby Album: Creating and Celebrating the Beginning of a Spiritual Life—A Jewish Lights Companion
By the Editors at Jewish Lights; Foreword by Anita Diamant; Preface by Rabbi Sandy Eisenberg Sasso
A spiritual keepsake that will be treasured for generations. More than just a memory book, *shows you how—and why it's important*—to create a Jewish home and a Jewish life. 8 x 10, 64 pp, Deluxe Padded HC, Full-color illus., 978-1-58023-138-1 **$19.95**

The Jewish Pregnancy Book: A Resource for the Soul, Body & Mind during Pregnancy, Birth & the First Three Months *By Sandy Falk, MD, and Rabbi Daniel Judson, with Steven A. Rapp* Medical information, prayers and rituals for each stage of pregnancy. 7 x 10, 208 pp, b/w photos, Quality PB, 978-1-58023-178-7 **$16.95**

Celebrating Your New Jewish Daughter: Creating Jewish Ways to Welcome Baby Girls into the Covenant—New and Traditional Ceremonies *By Debra Nussbaum Cohen; Foreword by Rabbi Sandy Eisenberg Sasso* 6 x 9, 272 pp, Quality PB, 978-1-58023-090-2 **$18.95**

The New Jewish Baby Book, 2nd Edition: Names, Ceremonies & Customs—A Guide for Today's Families *By Anita Diamant* 6 x 9, 320 pp, Quality PB, 978-1-58023-251-7 **$19.99**

Parenting as a Spiritual Journey: Deepening Ordinary and Extraordinary Events into Sacred Occasions *By Rabbi Nancy Fuchs-Kreimer, PhD*
6 x 9, 224 pp, Quality PB, 978-1-58023-016-2 **$17.99**

Parenting Jewish Teens: A Guide for the Perplexed
By Joanne Doades Explores the questions and issues that shape the world in which today's Jewish teenagers live and offers constructive advice to parents.
6 x 9, 176 pp, Quality PB, 978-1-58023-305-7 **$16.99**

Judaism for Two: A Spiritual Guide for Strengthening and Celebrating Your Loving Relationship *By Rabbi Nancy Fuchs-Kreimer, PhD, and Rabbi Nancy H. Wiener, DMin; Foreword by Rabbi Elliot N. Dorff, PhD*
Addresses the ways Jewish teachings can enhance and strengthen committed relationships. 6 x 9, 224 pp, Quality PB, 978-1-58023-254-8 **$16.99**

The Creative Jewish Wedding Book, 2nd Edition: A Hands-On Guide to New & Old Traditions, Ceremonies & Celebrations *By Gabrielle Kaplan-Mayer*
9 x 9, 288 pp, b/w photos, Quality PB, 978-1-58023-398-9 **$19.99**

Divorce Is a Mitzvah: A Practical Guide to Finding Wholeness and Holiness When Your Marriage Dies *By Rabbi Perry Netter; Afterword by Rabbi Laura Geller*
6 x 9, 224 pp, Quality PB, 978-1-58023-172-5 **$16.95**

Embracing the Covenant: Converts to Judaism Talk About Why & How
By Rabbi Allan Berkowitz and Patti Moskovitz 6 x 9, 192 pp, Quality PB, 978-1-879045-50-7 **$16.95**

The Guide to Jewish Interfaith Family Life: An InterfaithFamily.com Handbook
Edited by Ronnie Friedland and Edmund Case
6 x 9, 384 pp, Quality PB, 978-1-58023-153-4 **$18.95**

A Heart of Wisdom: Making the Jewish Journey from Midlife through the Elder Years
Edited by Susan Berrin; Foreword by Rabbi Harold Kushner
6 x 9, 384 pp, Quality PB, 978-1-58023-051-3 **$18.95**

Introducing My Faith and My Community: The Jewish Outreach Institute Guide for the Christian in a Jewish Interfaith Relationship
By Rabbi Kerry M. Olitzky 6 x 9, 176 pp, Quality PB, 978-1-58023-192-3 **$16.99**

Making a Successful Jewish Interfaith Marriage: The Jewish Outreach Institute Guide to Opportunities, Challenges and Resources *By Rabbi Kerry M. Olitzky with Joan Peterson Littman*
6 x 9, 176 pp, Quality PB, 978-1-58023-170-1 **$16.95**

A Man's Responsibility: A Jewish Guide to Being a Son, a Partner in Marriage, a Father and a Community Leader *By Rabbi Joseph B. Meszler*
6 x 9, 192 pp, Quality PB, 978-1-58023-435-1 **$16.99**; HC, 978-1-58023-362-0 **$21.99**

So That Your Values Live On: Ethical Wills and How to Prepare Them
Edited by Rabbi Jack Riemer and Rabbi Nathaniel Stampfer
6 x 9, 272 pp, Quality PB, 978-1-879045-34-7 **$18.99**

Meditation

Jewish Meditation Practices for Everyday Life
Awakening Your Heart, Connecting with God
By Rabbi Jeff Roth
Offers a fresh take on meditation that draws on life experience and living life with greater clarity as opposed to the traditional method of rigorous study.
6 x 9, 224 pp, Quality PB, 978-1-58023-397-2 **$18.99**

The Handbook of Jewish Meditation Practices
A Guide for Enriching the Sabbath and Other Days of Your Life
By Rabbi David A. Cooper Easy-to-learn meditation techniques.
6 x 9, 208 pp, Quality PB, 978-1-58023-102-2 **$16.95**

Discovering Jewish Meditation, 2nd Edition
Instruction & Guidance for Learning an Ancient Spiritual Practice
By Nan Fink Gefen, PhD 6 x 9, 208 pp, Quality PB, 978-1-58023-462-7 **$16.99**

Meditation from the Heart of Judaism
Today's Teachers Share Their Practices, Techniques, and Faith
Edited by Avram Davis 6 x 9, 256 pp, Quality PB, 978-1-58023-049-0 **$16.95**

Ritual/Sacred Practices

The Jewish Dream Book: The Key to Opening the Inner Meaning of Your Dreams *By Vanessa L. Ochs, PhD, with Elizabeth Ochs; Illus. by Kristina Swarner*
Instructions for how modern people can perform ancient Jewish dream practices and dream interpretations drawn from the Jewish wisdom tradition.
8 x 8, 128 pp, Full-color illus., Deluxe PB w/ flaps, 978-1-58023-132-9 **$16.95**

God in Your Body: Kabbalah, Mindfulness and Embodied Spiritual Practice
By Jay Michaelson
The first comprehensive treatment of the body in Jewish spiritual practice and an essential guide to the sacred.
6 x 9, 272 pp, Quality PB, 978-1-58023-304-0 **$18.99**

The Book of Jewish Sacred Practices: CLAL's Guide to Everyday & Holiday Rituals & Blessings *Edited by Rabbi Irwin Kula and Vanessa L. Ochs, PhD*
6 x 9, 368 pp, Quality PB, 978-1-58023-152-7 **$18.95**

Jewish Ritual: A Brief Introduction for Christians
By Rabbi Kerry M. Olitzky and Rabbi Daniel Judson
5½ x 8½, 144 pp, Quality PB, 978-1-58023-210-4 **$14.99**

The Rituals & Practices of a Jewish Life: A Handbook for Personal Spiritual Renewal *Edited by Rabbi Kerry M. Olitzky and Rabbi Daniel Judson*
6 x 9, 272 pp, Illus., Quality PB, 978-1-58023-169-5 **$18.95**

The Sacred Art of Lovingkindness: Preparing to Practice
By Rabbi Rami Shapiro 5½ x 8½, 176 pp, Quality PB, 978-1-59473-151-8 **$16.99**
(A book from SkyLight Paths, Jewish Lights' sister imprint)

Science Fiction/Mystery & Detective Fiction

Criminal Kabbalah: An Intriguing Anthology of Jewish Mystery & Detective Fiction *Edited by Lawrence W. Raphael; Foreword by Laurie R. King*
All-new stories from twelve of today's masters of mystery and detective fiction—sure to delight mystery buffs of all faith traditions.
6 x 9, 256 pp, Quality PB, 978-1-58023-109-1 **$16.95**

Mystery Midrash: An Anthology of Jewish Mystery & Detective Fiction
Edited by Lawrence W. Raphael; Preface by Joel Siegel
6 x 9, 304 pp, Quality PB, 978-1-58023-055-1 **$16.95**

Wandering Stars: An Anthology of Jewish Fantasy & Science Fiction
Edited by Jack Dann; Introduction by Isaac Asimov
6 x 9, 272 pp, Quality PB, 978-1-58023-005-6 **$18.99**

More Wandering Stars: An Anthology of Outstanding Stories of Jewish Fantasy and Science Fiction *Edited by Jack Dann; Introduction by Isaac Asimov*
6 x 9, 192 pp, Quality PB, 978-1-58023-063-6 **$16.95**

Spirituality/Crafts

Jewish Threads: A Hands-On Guide to Stitching Spiritual Intention into Jewish Fabric Crafts *By Diana Drew with Robert Grayson*
Learn how to make your own Jewish fabric crafts with spiritual intention—a journey of creativity, imagination and inspiration. Thirty projects.
7 x 9, 288 pp, 8-page color insert, b/w illus., Quality PB Original, 978-1-58023-442-9 **$19.99**

(from SkyLight Paths, Jewish Lights' sister imprint)

Beading—The Creative Spirit: Finding Your Sacred Center through the Art of Beadwork *By Wendy Ellsworth*
Invites you on a spiritual pilgrimage into the kaleidoscope world of glass and color.
7 x 9, 240 pp, 8-page full-color insert, b/w photos and diagrams, Quality PB, 978-1-59473-267-6 **$18.99**

Contemplative Crochet: A Hands-On Guide for Interlocking Faith and Craft *By Cindy Crandall-Frazier; Foreword by Linda Skolnik*
Will take you on a path deeper into your crocheting and your spiritual awareness.
7 x 9, 208 pp, b/w photos, Quality PB, 978-1-59473-238-6 **$16.99**

The Knitting Way: A Guide to Spiritual Self-Discovery
By Linda Skolnik and Janice MacDaniels
Shows how to use knitting to strengthen your spiritual self.
7 x 9, 240 pp, b/w photos, Quality PB, 978-1-59473-079-5 **$16.99**

The Painting Path: Embodying Spiritual Discovery through Yoga, Brush and Color *By Linda Novick; Foreword by Richard Segalman*
Explores the divine connection you can experience through art.
7 x 9, 208 pp, 8-page full-color insert, b/w photos, Quality PB, 978-1-59473-226-3 **$18.99**

The Quilting Path: A Guide to Spiritual Self-Discovery through Fabric, Thread and Kabbalah *By Louise Silk* Explores how to cultivate personal growth through quilt making. 7 x 9, 192 pp, b/w photos, Quality PB, 978-1-59473-206-5 **$16.99**

The Scrapbooking Journey: A Hands-On Guide to Spiritual Discovery
By Cory Richardson-Lauve; Foreword by Stacy Julian
Reveals how this craft can become a practice used to deepen and shape your life.
7 x 9, 176 pp, 8-page full-color insert, b/w photos, Quality PB, 978-1-59473-216-4 **$18.99**

Travel

Israel—A Spiritual Travel Guide, 2nd Edition: A Companion for the Modern Jewish Pilgrim *By Rabbi Lawrence A. Hoffman, PhD*
Helps today's pilgrim tap into the deep spiritual meaning of the ancient—and modern—sites of the Holy Land.
4¾ x 10, 256 pp, Illus., Quality PB, 978-1-58023-261-6 **$18.99**
Also Available: **The Israel Mission Leader's Guide** 5½ x 8½, 16 pp, PB, 978-1-58023-085-8 **$4.95**

Twelve Steps

Recovery—The Sacred Art: The Twelve Steps as Spiritual Practice
By Rami Shapiro; Foreword by Joan Borysenko, PhD
Draws on insights and practices of different religious traditions to help you move more deeply into the universal spirituality of the Twelve Step system.
5½ x 8½, 240 pp, Quality PB Original, 978-1-59473-259-1 **$16.99**
(A book from SkyLight Paths, Jewish Lights' sister imprint)

100 Blessings Every Day: Daily Twelve Step Recovery Affirmations, Exercises for Personal Growth & Renewal Reflecting Seasons of the Jewish Year *By Rabbi Kerry M. Olitzky; Foreword by Rabbi Neil Gillman, PhD* 4½ x 6½, 432 pp, Quality PB, 978-1-879045-30-9 **$16.99**

Recovery from Codependence: A Jewish Twelve Steps Guide to Healing Your Soul
By Rabbi Kerry M. Olitzky 6 x 9, 160 pp, Quality PB, 978-1-879045-32-3 **$13.95**

Twelve Jewish Steps to Recovery, 2nd Edition: A Personal Guide to Turning from Alcoholism & Other Addictions—Drugs, Food, Gambling, Sex...
By Rabbi Kerry M. Olitzky and Stuart A. Copans, MD; Preface by Abraham J. Twerski, MD
6 x 9, 160 pp, Quality PB, 978-1-58023-409-2 **$16.99**

Social Justice

Where Justice Dwells
A Hands-On Guide to Doing Social Justice in Your Jewish Community
By Rabbi Jill Jacobs; Foreword by Rabbi David Saperstein
Provides ways to envision and act on your own ideals of social justice.
7 x 9, 288 pp, Quality PB Original, 978-1-58023-453-5 **$24.99**

There Shall Be No Needy
Pursuing Social Justice through Jewish Law and Tradition
By Rabbi Jill Jacobs; Foreword by Rabbi Elliot N. Dorff, PhD; Preface by Simon Greer
Confronts the most pressing issues of twenty-first-century America from a deeply Jewish perspective. 6 x 9, 288 pp, Quality PB, 978-1-58023-425-2 **$16.99**

There Shall Be No Needy Teacher's Guide 8½ x 11, 56 pp, PB, 978-1-58023-429-0 **$8.99**

Conscience
The Duty to Obey and the Duty to Disobey
By Rabbi Harold M. Schulweis
Examines the idea of conscience and the role conscience plays in our relationships to government, law, ethics, religion, human nature, God—and to each other.
6 x 9, 160 pp, Quality PB, 978-1-58023-419-1 **$16.99**; HC, 978-1-58023-375-0 **$19.99**

Judaism and Justice
The Jewish Passion to Repair the World
By Rabbi Sidney Schwarz; Foreword by Ruth Messinger
Explores the relationship between Judaism, social justice and the Jewish identity of American Jews. 6 x 9, 352 pp, Quality PB, 978-1-58023-353-8 **$19.99**

Spirituality/Women's Interest

New Jewish Feminism
Probing the Past, Forging the Future
Edited by Rabbi Elyse Goldstein; Foreword by Anita Diamant
Looks at the growth and accomplishments of Jewish feminism and what they mean for Jewish women today and tomorrow.
6 x 9, 480 pp, HC, 978-1-58023-359-0 **$24.99**

The Divine Feminine in Biblical Wisdom Literature
Selections Annotated & Explained
Translation & Annotation by Rabbi Rami Shapiro
5½ x 8½, 240 pp, Quality PB, 978-1-59473-109-9 **$16.99**
(A book from SkyLight Paths, Jewish Lights' sister imprint)

The Quotable Jewish Woman
Wisdom, Inspiration & Humor from the Mind & Heart
Edited by Elaine Bernstein Partnow
6 x 9, 496 pp, Quality PB, 978-1-58023-236-4 **$19.99**

The Women's Haftarah Commentary
New Insights from Women Rabbis on the 54 Weekly Haftarah Portions, the 5 Megillot & Special Shabbatot
Edited by Rabbi Elyse Goldstein
Illuminates the historical significance of female portrayals in the Haftarah and the Five Megillot. 6 x 9, 560 pp, Quality PB, 978-1-58023-371-2 **$19.99**

The Women's Torah Commentary
New Insights from Women Rabbis on the 54 Weekly Torah Portions
Edited by Rabbi Elyse Goldstein
Over fifty women rabbis offer inspiring insights on the Torah, in a week-by-week format.
6 x 9, 496 pp, Quality PB, 978-1-58023-370-5 **$19.99**; HC, 978-1-58023-076-6 **$34.95**

See Passover for *The Women's Passover Companion: Women's Reflections on the Festival of Freedom* and *The Women's Seder Sourcebook: Rituals & Readings for Use at the Passover Seder*.

Theology/Philosophy/The Way Into... Series

The Way Into... series offers an accessible and highly usable "guided tour" of the Jewish faith, people, history and beliefs—in total, an introduction to Judaism that will enable you to understand and interact with the sacred texts of the Jewish tradition. Each volume is written by a leading contemporary scholar and teacher, and explores one key aspect of Judaism. The Way Into... series enables all readers to achieve a real sense of Jewish cultural literacy through guided study.

The Way Into Encountering God in Judaism
By Rabbi Neil Gillman, PhD
For everyone who wants to understand how Jews have encountered God throughout history and today.
6 x 9, 240 pp, Quality PB, 978-1-58023-199-2 **$18.99**; HC, 978-1-58023-025-4 **$21.95**
Also Available: **The Jewish Approach to God:** A Brief Introduction for Christians
By Rabbi Neil Gillman, PhD
5½ x 8½, 192 pp, Quality PB, 978-1-58023-190-9 **$16.95**

The Way Into Jewish Mystical Tradition
By Rabbi Lawrence Kushner
Allows readers to interact directly with the sacred mystical texts of the Jewish tradition. An accessible introduction to the concepts of Jewish mysticism, their religious and spiritual significance, and how they relate to life today.
6 x 9, 224 pp, Quality PB, 978-1-58023-200-5 **$18.99**; HC, 978-1-58023-029-2 **$21.95**

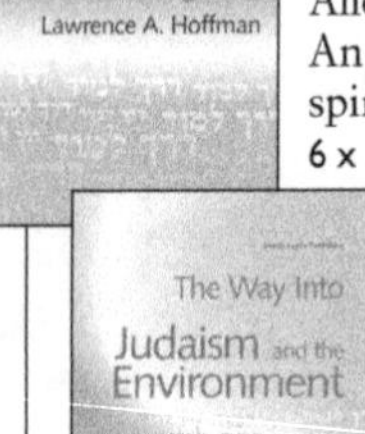

The Way Into Jewish Prayer
By Rabbi Lawrence A. Hoffman, PhD
Opens the door to 3,000 years of Jewish prayer, making anyone feel at home in the Jewish way of communicating with God.
6 x 9, 208 pp, Quality PB, 978-1-58023-201-2 **$18.99**

The Way Into Jewish Prayer Teacher's Guide
By Rabbi Jennifer Ossakow Goldsmith
8½ x 11, 42 pp, PB, 978-1-58023-345-3 **$8.99**
Download a free copy at www.jewishlights.com.

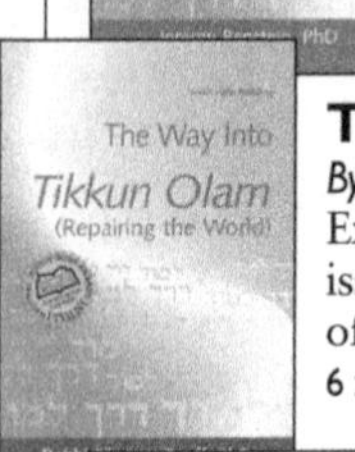

The Way Into Judaism and the Environment
By Jeremy Benstein, PhD
Explores the ways in which Judaism contributes to contemporary social-environmental issues, the extent to which Judaism is part of the problem and how it can be part of the solution.
6 x 9, 288 pp, Quality PB, 978-1-58023-368-2 **$18.99**; HC, 978-1-58023-268-5 **$24.99**

The Way Into *Tikkun Olam* (Repairing the World)
By Rabbi Elliot N. Dorff, PhD
An accessible introduction to the Jewish concept of the individual's responsibility to care for others and repair the world.
6 x 9, 304 pp, Quality PB, 978-1-58023-328-6 **$18.99**

The Way Into Torah
By Rabbi Norman J. Cohen, PhD
Helps guide you in the exploration of the origins and development of Torah, explains why it should be studied and how to do it.
6 x 9, 176 pp, Quality PB, 978-1-58023-198-5 **$16.99**

The Way Into the Varieties of Jewishness
By Sylvia Barack Fishman, PhD
Explores the religious and historical understanding of what it has meant to be Jewish from ancient times to the present controversy over "Who is a Jew?"
6 x 9, 288 pp, Quality PB, 978-1-58023-367-5 **$18.99**; HC, 978-1-58023-030-8 **$24.99**

Theology/Philosophy

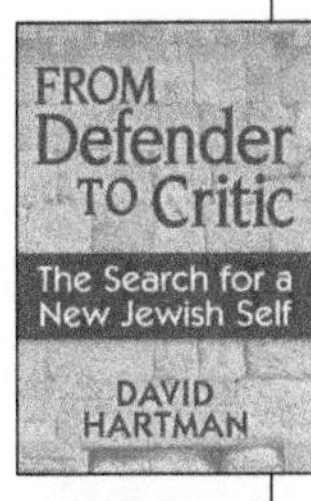

From Defender to Critic: The Search for a New Jewish Self
By Dr. David Hartman
A daring self-examination of Hartman's goals, which were not to strip halakha of its authority but to create a space for questioning and critique that allows for the traditionally religious Jew to act out a moral life in tune with modern experience.
6 x 9, 336 pp, HC, 978-1-58023-515-0 **$35.00**

Our Religious Brains: What Cognitive Science Reveals about Belief, Morality, Community and Our Relationship with God
By Rabbi Ralph D. Mecklenburger; Foreword by Dr. Howard Kelfer; Preface by Dr. Neil Gillman
This is a groundbreaking, accessible look at the implications of cognitive science for religion and theology, intended for laypeople. 6 x 9, 224 pp, HC, 978-1-58023-508-2 **$24.99**

The Other Talmud—*The Yerushalmi*: Unlocking the Secrets of The Talmud of Israel for Judaism Today *By Rabbi Judith Z. Abrams, PhD*
A fascinating—and stimulating—look at "the other Talmud" and the possibilities for Jewish life reflected there. 6 x 9, 256 pp, HC, 978-1-58023-463-4 **$24.99**

The Way of Man: According to Hasidic Teaching
By Martin Buber; New Translation and Introduction by Rabbi Bernard H. Mehlman and Dr. Gabriel E. Padawer; Foreword by Paul Mendes-Flohr
An accessible and engaging new translation of Buber's classic work—available as an e-book only. E-book, 978-1-58023-601-0 Digital List Price **$14.99**

The Death of Death: Resurrection and Immortality in Jewish Thought
By Rabbi Neil Gillman, PhD 6 x 9, 336 pp, Quality PB, 978-1-58023-081-0 **$18.95**

Doing Jewish Theology: God, Torah & Israel in Modern Judaism *By Rabbi Neil Gillman, PhD*
6 x 9, 304 pp, Quality PB, 978-1-58023-439-9 **$18.99**; HC, 978-1-58023-322-4 **$24.99**

A Heart of Many Rooms: Celebrating the Many Voices within Judaism
By Dr. David Hartman 6 x 9, 352 pp, Quality PB, 978-1-58023-156-5 **$19.95**

The God Who Hates Lies: Confronting & Rethinking Jewish Tradition
By Dr. David Hartman with Charlie Buckholtz 6 x 9, 208 pp, HC, 978-1-58023-455-9 **$24.99**

Jewish Theology in Our Time: A New Generation Explores the Foundations and Future of Jewish Belief *Edited by Rabbi Elliot J. Cosgrove, PhD; Foreword by Rabbi David J. Wolpe; Preface by Rabbi Carole B. Balin, PhD* 6 x 9, 240 pp, HC, 978-1-58023-413-9 **$24.99**

Maimonides—Essential Teachings on Jewish Faith & Ethics: The Book of Knowledge & the Thirteen Principles of Faith—Annotated & Explained
Translation and Annotation by Rabbi Marc D. Angel, PhD
5½ x 8½, 224 pp, Quality PB Original, 978-1-59473-311-6 **$18.99***

Maimonides, Spinoza and Us: Toward an Intellectually Vibrant Judaism
By Rabbi Marc D. Angel, PhD 6 x 9, 224 pp, HC, 978-1-58023-411-5 **$24.99**

A Touch of the Sacred: A Theologian's Informal Guide to Jewish Belief
By Dr. Eugene B. Borowitz and Frances W. Schwartz
6 x 9, 256 pp, Quality PB, 978-1-58023-416-0 **$16.99**; HC, 978-1-58023-337-8 **$21.99**

Traces of God: Seeing God in Torah, History and Everyday Life *By Rabbi Neil Gillman, PhD*
6 x 9, 240 pp, Quality PB, 978-1-58023-369-9 **$16.99**

Your Word Is Fire: The Hasidic Masters on Contemplative Prayer
Edited and translated by Rabbi Arthur Green, PhD, and Barry W. Holtz
6 x 9, 160 pp, Quality PB, 978-1-879045-25-5 **$15.95**

I Am Jewish

Personal Reflections Inspired by the Last Words of Daniel Pearl
Almost 150 Jews—both famous and not—from all walks of life, from all around the world, write about many aspects of their Judaism.
Edited by Judea and Ruth Pearl 6 x 9, 304 pp, Deluxe PB w/ flaps, 978-1-58023-259-3 **$18.99**
Download a free copy of the *I Am Jewish Teacher's Guide* at www.jewishlights.com.

Hannah Senesh: Her Life and Diary, The First Complete Edition
By Hannah Senesh; Foreword by Marge Piercy; Preface by Eitan Senesh; Afterword by Roberta Grossman
6 x 9, 368 pp, b/w photos, Quality PB, 978-1-58023-342-2 **$19.99**

**A book from SkyLight Paths, Jewish Lights' sister imprint*

Spirituality

The Jewish Lights Spirituality Handbook: A Guide to Understanding, Exploring & Living a Spiritual Life *Edited by Stuart M. Matlins*
What exactly is "Jewish" about spirituality? How do I make it a part of my life? Fifty of today's foremost spiritual leaders share their ideas and experience with us.
6 x 9, 456 pp, Quality PB, 978-1-58023-093-3 **$19.99**

The Sabbath Soul: Mystical Reflections on the Transformative Power of Holy Time *Selection, Translation and Commentary by Eitan Fishbane, PhD*
Explores the writings of mystical masters of Hasidism. Provides translations and interpretations of a wide range of Hasidic sources previously unavailable in English that reflect the spiritual transformation that takes place on the seventh day.
6 x 9, 208 pp, Quality PB, 978-1-58023-459-7 **$18.99**

Repentance: The Meaning and Practice of *Teshuvah*
By Dr. Louis E. Newman; Foreword by Rabbi Harold M. Schulweis; Preface by Rabbi Karyn D. Kedar
Examines both the practical and philosophical dimensions of *teshuvah*, Judaism's core religious-moral teaching on repentance, and its value for us—Jews and non-Jews alike—today. 6 x 9, 256 pp, HC, 978-1-58023-426-9 **$24.99**

Aleph-Bet Yoga: Embodying the Hebrew Letters for Physical and Spiritual Well-Being
By Steven A. Rapp; Foreword by Tamar Frankiel, PhD, and Judy Greenfeld; Preface by Hart Lazer
7 x 10, 128 pp, b/w photos, Quality PB, Lay-flat binding, 978-1-58023-162-6 **$16.95**

A Book of Life: Embracing Judaism as a Spiritual Practice
By Rabbi Michael Strassfeld 6 x 9, 544 pp, Quality PB, 978-1-58023-247-0 **$19.99**

Bringing the Psalms to Life: How to Understand and Use the Book of Psalms
By Rabbi Daniel F. Polish, PhD 6 x 9, 208 pp, Quality PB, 978-1-58023-157-2 **$16.95**

Does the Soul Survive? A Jewish Journey to Belief in Afterlife, Past Lives & Living with Purpose *By Rabbi Elie Kaplan Spitz; Foreword by Brian L. Weiss, MD*
6 x 9, 288 pp, Quality PB, 978-1-58023-165-7 **$16.99**

Entering the Temple of Dreams: Jewish Prayers, Movements and Meditations for the End of the Day *By Tamar Frankiel, PhD, and Judy Greenfeld*
7 x 10, 192 pp, illus., Quality PB, 978-1-58023-079-7 **$16.95**

First Steps to a New Jewish Spirit: Reb Zalman's Guide to Recapturing the Intimacy & Ecstasy in Your Relationship with God *By Rabbi Zalman M. Schachter-Shalomi with Donald Gropman* 6 x 9, 144 pp, Quality PB, 978-1-58023-182-4 **$16.95**

Foundations of Sephardic Spirituality: The Inner Life of Jews of the Ottoman Empire
By Rabbi Marc D. Angel, PhD 6 x 9, 224 pp, Quality PB, 978-1-58023-341-5 **$18.99**

God & the Big Bang: Discovering Harmony between Science & Spirituality
By Dr. Daniel C. Matt 6 x 9, 216 pp, Quality PB, 978-1-879045-89-7 **$18.99**

God in Our Relationships: Spirituality between People from the Teachings of Martin Buber *By Rabbi Dennis S. Ross* 5½ x 8½, 160 pp, Quality PB, 978-1-58023-147-3 **$16.95**

Judaism, Physics and God: Searching for Sacred Metaphors in a Post-Einstein World
By Rabbi David W. Nelson 6 x 9, 352 pp, Quality PB, inc. reader's discussion guide, 978-1-58023-306-4 **$18.99**; HC, 352 pp, 978-1-58023-252-4 **$24.99**

Meaning & Mitzvah: Daily Practices for Reclaiming Judaism through Prayer, God, Torah, Hebrew, Mitzvot and Peoplehood *By Rabbi Goldie Milgram*
7 x 9, 336 pp, Quality PB, 978-1-58023-256-2 **$19.99**

Minding the Temple of the Soul: Balancing Body, Mind, and Spirit through Traditional Jewish Prayer, Movement, and Meditation *By Tamar Frankiel, PhD, and Judy Greenfeld*
7 x 10, 184 pp, Illus., Quality PB, 978-1-879045-64-4 **$18.99**

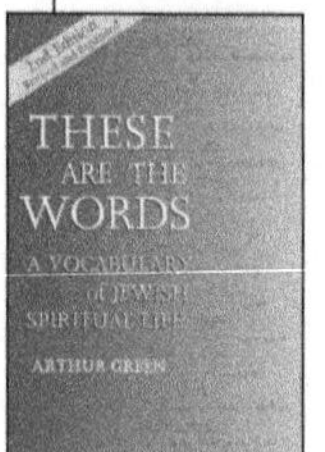

One God Clapping: The Spiritual Path of a Zen Rabbi *By Rabbi Alan Lew with Sherril Jaffe*
5½ x 8½, 336 pp, Quality PB, 978-1-58023-115-2 **$16.95**

The Soul of the Story: Meetings with Remarkable People
By Rabbi David Zeller 6 x 9, 288 pp, HC, 978-1-58023-272-2 **$21.99**

***Tanya*, the Masterpiece of Hasidic Wisdom:** Selections Annotated & Explained
Translation & Annotation by Rabbi Rami Shapiro; Foreword by Rabbi Zalman M. Schachter-Shalomi
5½ x 8½, 240 pp, Quality PB, 978-1-59473-275-1 **$16.99**

These Are the Words, 2nd Edition: A Vocabulary of Jewish Spiritual Life
By Rabbi Arthur Green, PhD 6 x 9, 320 pp, Quality PB, 978-1-58023-494-8 **$19.99**

Spirituality/Prayer

Making Prayer Real: Leading Jewish Spiritual Voices on Why Prayer Is Difficult and What to Do about It *By Rabbi Mike Comins*
A new and different response to the challenges of Jewish prayer, with "best prayer practices" from Jewish spiritual leaders of all denominations.
6 x 9, 320 pp, Quality PB, 978-1-58023-417-7 **$18.99**

Witnesses to the One: The Spiritual History of the *Sh'ma*
By Rabbi Joseph B. Meszler; Foreword by Rabbi Elyse Goldstein
6 x 9, 176 pp, Quality PB, 978-1-58023-400-9 **$16.99**; HC, 978-1-58023-309-5 **$19.99**

My People's Prayer Book Series: Traditional Prayers, Modern Commentaries *Edited by Rabbi Lawrence A. Hoffman, PhD*
Provides diverse and exciting commentary to the traditional liturgy. Will help you find new wisdom in Jewish prayer, and bring liturgy into your life. Each book includes Hebrew text, modern translations and commentaries from all perspectives of the Jewish world.

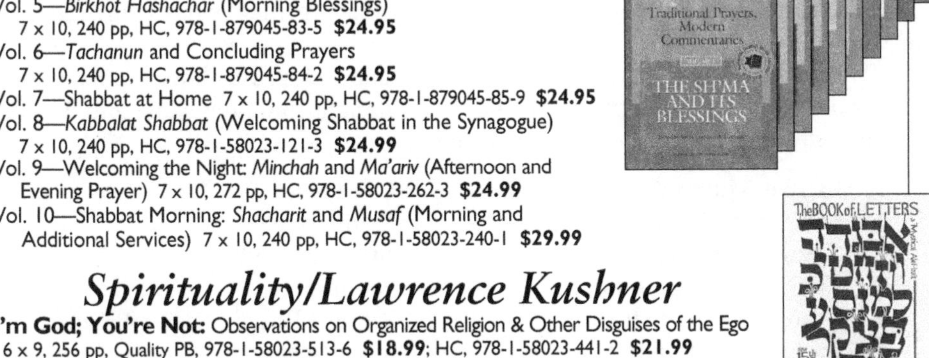

Vol. 1—The *Sh'ma* and Its Blessings
7 x 10, 168 pp, HC, 978-1-879045-79-8 **$29.99**
Vol. 2—The *Amidah* 7 x 10, 240 pp, HC, 978-1-879045-80-4 **$24.95**
Vol. 3—*P'sukei D'zimrah* (Morning Psalms)
7 x 10, 240 pp, HC, 978-1-879045-81-1 **$29.99**
Vol. 4—*Seder K'riat Hatorah* (The Torah Service)
7 x 10, 264 pp, HC, 978-1-879045-82-8 **$29.99**
Vol. 5—*Birkhot Hashachar* (Morning Blessings)
7 x 10, 240 pp, HC, 978-1-879045-83-5 **$24.95**
Vol. 6—*Tachanun* and Concluding Prayers
7 x 10, 240 pp, HC, 978-1-879045-84-2 **$24.95**
Vol. 7—Shabbat at Home 7 x 10, 240 pp, HC, 978-1-879045-85-9 **$24.95**
Vol. 8—*Kabbalat Shabbat* (Welcoming Shabbat in the Synagogue)
7 x 10, 240 pp, HC, 978-1-58023-121-3 **$24.99**
Vol. 9—Welcoming the Night: *Minchah* and *Ma'ariv* (Afternoon and Evening Prayer) 7 x 10, 272 pp, HC, 978-1-58023-262-3 **$24.99**
Vol. 10—Shabbat Morning: *Shacharit* and *Musaf* (Morning and Additional Services) 7 x 10, 240 pp, HC, 978-1-58023-240-1 **$29.99**

Spirituality/Lawrence Kushner

I'm God; You're Not: Observations on Organized Religion & Other Disguises of the Ego
6 x 9, 256 pp, Quality PB, 978-1-58023-513-6 **$18.99**; HC, 978-1-58023-441-2 **$21.99**

The Book of Letters: A Mystical Hebrew Alphabet
Popular HC Edition, 6 x 9, 80 pp, 2-color text, 978-1-879045-00-2 **$24.95**
Collector's Limited Edition, 9 x 12, 80 pp, gold-foil-embossed pages, w/ limited-edition silkscreened print, 978-1-879045-04-0 **$349.00**

The Book of Miracles: A Young Person's Guide to Jewish Spiritual Awareness
6 x 9, 96 pp, 2-color illus., HC, 978-1-879045-78-1 **$16.95** *For ages 9–13*

The Book of Words: Talking Spiritual Life, Living Spiritual Talk
6 x 9, 160 pp, Quality PB, 978-1-58023-020-9 **$18.99**

Eyes Remade for Wonder: A Lawrence Kushner Reader *Introduction by Thomas Moore*
6 x 9, 240 pp, Quality PB, 978-1-58023-042-1 **$18.95**

God Was in This Place & I, i Did Not Know: Finding Self, Spirituality and Ultimate Meaning 6 x 9, 192 pp, Quality PB, 978-1-879045-33-0 **$16.95**

Honey from the Rock: An Introduction to Jewish Mysticism
6 x 9, 176 pp, Quality PB, 978-1-58023-073-5 **$16.95**

Invisible Lines of Connection: Sacred Stories of the Ordinary
5½ x 8½, 160 pp, Quality PB, 978-1-879045-98-9 **$15.95**

Jewish Spirituality: A Brief Introduction for Christians
5½ x 8½, 112 pp, Quality PB, 978-1-58023-150-3 **$12.95**

The River of Light: Jewish Mystical Awareness
6 x 9, 192 pp, Quality PB, 978-1-58023-096-4 **$16.95**

The Way Into Jewish Mystical Tradition
6 x 9, 224 pp, Quality PB, 978-1-58023-200-5 **$18.99**; HC, 978-1-58023-029-2 **$21.95**

Printed in the USA
CPSIA information can be obtained
at www.ICGtesting.com
JSHW022211140824
68134JS00018B/982

9 781683 364788